# Anchored in Hope

# Anchored in Hope

An Awe-Inspiring True Story
Where Blessings & Miracles Confirm
God's Amazing Love & Faithfulness

*A Memoir by*

Sue Rosendahl

Premier Advantage Publishing

# Anchored in Hope

An Awe-Inspiring True Story
Where Blessings & Miracles Confirm
God's Amazing Love & Faithfulness

© 2018 Sue Rosendahl
All rights reserved.

This book or parts thereof may not be reproduced in any form, stored in a retrieval system, or transmitted in any form by any means—electronic, mechanical, photocopy, recording, or otherwise—without prior written permission of the publisher, except as provided by United States of America copyright law.

Unless otherwise indicated, all Scripture quotations are taken from the Holy Bible, New International Version®, NIV® Copyright© 1973, 1978, 1984, 2011 by Biblica, Inc.® Used by permission. All rights reserved worldwide.

Scripture quotations taken from the Amplified® Bible (AMP), Copyright © 2015 by The Lockman Foundation
Used by permission. www.Lockman.org

Scripture quotations are taken from the Holy Bible, New Living Translation, copyright ©1996, 2004, 2007, 2013, 2015 by Tyndale House Foundation. Used by permission of Tyndale House Publishers, Inc., Carol Stream, Illinois 60188. All rights reserved. Author comments or emphasis within Scripture quotations are referenced in endnotes.

International Standard Book Number: 978-0-692-77386-4

*Printed in the United States of America*

To the beloved "man of my dreams" and "perfect mate" Keith Rosendahl, whom God richly blessed me with over ten years ago, thank you for your ongoing love, support, and patience. You are my best friend and there is no one whom I'd rather spend my happily-ever-after with.

To my two beautiful daughters, Jenni and Holly, I love you both so very much and I'm unbelievably proud of the way God has shaped you into the outstanding women you are today. May you always love the Lord with all your heart and with all your soul—model that for your children.

To my wonderful grandchildren—Cheyenne, Aiyanna, Endyra, Allaura, & Greyson, this book was originally written with you in mind so you would never *ever* question God's existence or wonder whether He truly loves you. You are all treasured, valued, and unbelievably loved. Seek the Lord your God with all your heart, because when you do, He promises to reveal Himself.

To my dear, sweet Steve, I am so very sorry for the pain you suffered, yet I thank God for the love, the adventure, the laughs, and the precious memories that will be cherished forever. The girls and I are eternally grateful we will be spending eternity together with you.

*I Can Only Imagine,* MercyMe
Copyright©Simpleville Music (ASCAP)/
(admin at EssentialMusicPublishing.com).
All rights reserved. Used by permission.


*Praise You In This Storm,* Bernie Herms, Mark Hall
Copyright©2005 My Refuge Music (BMI)
(adm. at CapitolCMGPublishing.com) /
Be Essential Songs (BMI) / Dayspring Music (BMI)
All rights reserved. Used by permission.
Copyright©2005 Word Music LLC (ASCAP)
and BANAHAMA TUNES (ASCAP)
All rights on behalf of Word Music LLC and BANAHAMA
TUNES administered by WB Music Corp.
All rights reserved. Used by permission.

# Table of Contents

Preface ............................................................................. 11

Introduction ..................................................................... 13

Chapter 1 .......................................................................... 17
Knowing God—*His Astonishing Reveal*

Chapter 2 .......................................................................... 27
Forget Me Not—*A Stumbling Block*

Chapter 3 .......................................................................... 41
God's Relentless Pursuit—*Chasing After You*

Chapter 4 .......................................................................... 51
Mysterious Maladies—*God's Perfect Timing*

Chapter 5 .......................................................................... 65
Life Turned Upside Down—*Why Worry?*

Chapter 6 .......................................................................... 81
Definite Desert Experience—*Pressing into God*

Chapter 7 .......................................................................... 97
WOW in the Wilderness—*Perceiving God's Voice*

Chapter 8 ........................................................................ 111
The Lord My Provider—*Fully Relying on God*

Chapter 9 ........................................................................ 125
Never Too Far Gone—*God's Incredible Forgiveness*

Chapter 10 ...................................................................... 137
Following the Path to Freedom—*Forgiving Others*

Chapter 11 ...................................................................... 145
Staking Claim to the Truth—*Surrendering to God*
Chapter 12 ...................................................................... 155
Believing for Your Miracle—*Waiting & Walking by Faith*
Chapter 13 ...................................................................... 163
A Twisted Turn—*Perplexing Answer to Prayer*
Chapter 14 ...................................................................... 177
Glimmers of Glory—*Accepting God's Resolve*
Chapter 15 ...................................................................... 187
Hope of a Brighter Tomorrow—*God's Promise*
Chapter 16 ...................................................................... 203
Rainbow After the Storm—*Seeking God's Will*
Chapter 17 ...................................................................... 213
A New Beginning—*Restoration*
Conclusion ..................................................................... 225

## Postscript
God's Ultimate Gift—*Returning Home* ..................... 235
Growing in Godliness—*Christian Living* .................. 247
Eternal Hope of Glory—*End Time Signs* .................. 261

Endnotes ........................................................................ 275

Dedicated to my daughters and my grandchildren—
As this ever-changing world becomes increasingly darker, moving farther away from the Light, may you always seek to know the Lord Jesus Christ—the Light of the world—and may your relationship with Him continue to grow. May the love of God forever shine in your hearts and out from your lives.

There is nothing more important—and no greater joy!

# Preface

The apostle Peter challenges believers to always be prepared to explain our Christian hope to everyone who asks.¹ This book aims to do just that.

According to the Bible, our testimonies have power when they are shared.² Testimonies inspire, encourage, and give evidence or proof to determine reality. *Anchored in Hope* is a compelling "testament for today" that gives witness to the existence of an all-powerful, all-loving, all-knowing, ever-present, faithful God. When God shows up and reveals Himself in ways that only He can, faith flourishes and hope soars.

Some of the greatest stories ever told emerged from eyewitnesses sharing their observations and experiences with others. Those testimonies have influenced millions of people for thousands of years. When word of Jesus' profound teaching, life-giving messages, and incredible miracles spread, raging like wildfire throughout the parched region, it ignited rapid growth of the early church.

Even today, when wondrous acts are witnessed, the typical response mirrors that of a pebble being tossed onto a motionless pond. A ripple effect emanates from the source and creates an uplifting, exuberant buzz of optimism that extends far beyond the individual to impact the hearts and lives of others. Stories of God's love in action are *never* for the sole benefit of the recipient, but are to be used for our greater good and for His glory. For that reason, I refuse to be silent.

One day while thumbing through my tattered journal, tearing up at all the extraordinary ways God made Himself known during the darkest, most difficult decade of my life, I felt compelled to record those WOW moments in an orderly fashion so my grandchildren would never *ever* question God's existence, presence, faithfulness, or amazing love for them. But as soon as the idea sprang to mind God asked, "Why is it only important for *your* grandchildren to hear this message? I love *all* My children." Those words moved me to compose this memoir, an incredible story I believe God wants you to hear.

Despite my dire circumstances, I forced myself to press into God, to walk by faith, and to trust Him through ten years of tribulation and tragedy. And in doing so He revealed Himself to me in a myriad of marvelous and mysterious ways—proving His perpetual presence, demonstrating His extravagant love, and affirming His faithfulness. He strengthened me in my weakness, comforted me in my sorrow, provided peace in my distress, and satisfied my every need—ultimately restoring my life and turning my mourning into dancing. During a time of unmanageable suffering, heartache, and despair, God's full attention and favor seemed to rest entirely on me—forever changing who I am.

I pray that through my testimony the God of our Lord Jesus Christ grants you a spirit of wisdom and revelation into the true knowledge of who He is so you will want to dive into a deeper, more intimate relationship with the Lover of your soul.

God is waiting for opportunities to reveal Himself to you in your life, just as He has in mine...

# Introduction

Trusting God is rarely an issue when life is harmoniously humming along. It's an absolute joy to praise Him when all is going well. But how do you respond when your entire world begins to implode? When you're blindsided by uncontrollable turbulence that violently jolts your reality and threatens the very core of your faith—what then? Do you become angry and turn your back on God or do you remain devoted with the unwavering conviction that God is good and He is faithful?

At the onset of our decade-long ordeal it was easy to believe God could hear my prayers and would intervene to answer them, but as months stretched into years, hope seemed further and further away. I began questioning God—"What was happening to my beloved?" "Why would You allow my husband to be exposed to toxic carcinogens in the workplace only to develop a bizarre, incurable, life-threatening disease no one understood…or believed?" "How could You permit Steve's malady to dictate the direction of our lives—forcing us to sell our business, driving us out of our newly-constructed home near family and friends, then displacing us in the middle of nowhere against our will?"

Like the Israelites, our family of four literally found ourselves stuck in the wilderness for years…just waiting. But unlike God's chosen people, there was no promise of entering a land flowing with milk and honey. With no income, no savings to speak of, and one credit card to pay all the bills, our future was bleak. Isolated in the mountains of southwest New Mexico, Steve's illness escalated and the burden became unbearable. As the thick sludge of our despairing circumstances continued to rise, threatening to consume us, our two young daughters and I desperately cried out to Jesus, clinging tightly onto His promises and pleading for Him to save us.

I had to believe He'd show up. With every fiber of my being I wanted to trust His Word. I needed to know we weren't suffering through this horrible nightmare alone, but that He was with us and that He cared. I was determined to be all in, anchored in hope, and fully secure in what I'd learned over the years about God and His character, but to be honest being that committed was a bit daunting.

It was like standing high upon a colossal cliff staring down at the jagged rocks and whitecaps in the raging water below, then closing my eyes, inhaling deeply, and taking a gigantic leap of faith. I was risking the one thing I valued most in life—my relationship with God. What if He wasn't really with us? What if He didn't hear our cries? What if He didn't answer or intervene to help? What if it was all...a lie? I was truly afraid to find out, yet I owed Him the opportunity to prove Himself faithful.

Walking by faith and not by sight was virtually impossible when my natural eyes contradicted everything I was supposed to believe, everything I wanted to believe. It literally took every ounce of energy I had to put one foot in front of the other to move forward, to continually seek God's face, to press in and persevere. But you know what? God showed up every time I called—and many times when I didn't—repeatedly proving His love, demonstrating His faithfulness, and answering my prayers. Even though I didn't always agree with His response, He fulfilled His role as Loving Savior, Wonderful Counselor, Prince of Peace, and Faithful Friend.

Life is a journey of trials—they are inevitable. Trials come in all shapes and sizes, some are easier to manage than others, but how you respond in turbulent times is extremely important to God. Scripture references and biblical principles on topics such as worry, waiting, expectancy, forgiveness, prayer, perseverance, and disappointment are entwined throughout this memoir to empower, comfort, and encourage you through life's storms while instilling a renewed sense of hope.

*Never* during our season of tragic turmoil would I have ever imagined thanking God for the experience. But now, ten years later, I can honestly say I am truly grateful for His phenomenal gift of faith, Steve's salvation, and this powerful testimony that will draw others into a joyful and abundant life-changing relationship with their Heavenly Father. Our family has been set free and our lives have been completely transformed. I praise God for the privilege of having been rescued from the pit, redeemed and restored to a place high upon a mountain peak where I can shout out to the world how incredibly AWESOME our God truly is!

Wherever you are on your faith walk—whether you're a sincere seeker, a dubious doubter, or a blessed believer—if you're ready to be inspired and enlightened, then dive in and immerse yourself in the splendor of God's extravagant love as it bursts forth in exhilarating and glorious new ways. Faith will flourish and hope will soar as you experience God's grace and goodness through my eyes…

Chapter 1

# Knowing God

*'Be still and know that I am God.'* [3]

Being one of over 7.6 billion people in the world today makes me unbelievably insignificant, yet God has consistently shown me that is not true. According to Him, I matter. And my life matters. You matter. And your life matters. God never shows partiality nor excludes anyone from His blessings.[4] He loves and accepts everyone unconditionally just as they are, right where they are, without exception—that includes *you*![5]

God has planted within each one of us a heart to *know* Him.[6] One of the central themes resonating throughout the Bible is God's longing for His creation to *know* Him. Not only does He want us to be keenly aware of His existence, He wants us to become acquainted with His character in such a way that we would be drawn to Him and desire to enter into a close, personal relationship. He has no interest in simply being acknowledged from afar. His aspiration is, and always has been, to walk with us as He walked with Adam and Eve in the Garden of Eden. He wants us to grow into a deeper, more intimate understanding of who He is and experience a bond that supersedes anything we could ever hope for or imagine.

To get noticed and make Himself *known* God often demonstrates His awesome power in extraordinary ways. And what worked for Him in the past, still works for Him today. This proven attention-grabbing technique is what He used to make Himself *known* to me in the unlikeliest of places...

It was late September, the onset of my college sophomore year, when a friend and I decided to drive across town to a party. The crescent moon was shining and stars were twinkling brightly in the clear onyx sky. Upon our arrival we were engulfed by the frigid night air and greeted with rock 'n' roll music blasting from an old, decrepit two-story building on the opposite side of the street. On the sidewalk below small groups of people were mingling and smoking cigarettes with drinks in hand.

We ripped off our jackets, threw 'em in the back seat, sprinted across the road, and entered the aging wooden structure, following its steep, narrow staircase to the top. The music was deafening, vibrating the floor and making it difficult to communicate. A large crowd spilling out from a room in the back piqued our interest and beckoned us onward. Within seconds we were squeezing our way into the party's nucleus—where all the action was.

The tiny kitchen was jam-packed with college students and young adults congregating around a 30-gallon trash can. "Trash can parties," popular in the late 70s and early 80s, were gatherings where everyone in attendance was supposed to bring a bottle of booze to dump into a new trash can—the punch bowl party guests would drink from. No one ever knew ahead of time what the concoction would consist of or how it would taste, but after a few drinks it really didn't seem to matter.

A quick survey revealed few familiar faces, but one leapt out from the throng of party-goers, it was a face I recognized all too well. I gasped as my eyes caught sight of the thin, scraggly blonde standing in the corner leaning against the wall. It was someone I have come to refer to as "the hell of my life." Although I've forgiven her for years of vicious attacks, her relentless cruelty earned her the title.

Throughout grade school Tammy and I were best friends. We lived a block apart and we were inseparable. It was in seventh grade, year one of middle school, when our friendship took a 180-degree turn. Tammy started chumming around with her older sister who was part of the "popular crowd" in high school and all her so-called new friends were smoking, drinking, and dabbling with drugs. When Tammy was introduced to cigarettes, she immediately took up smoking. To fit in, I followed suit.

By age 12, Tammy was experimenting with drugs—taking handfuls of Midol, sniffing glue, smoking pot, and willing to try just about anything to get high. She was becoming a completely different person...and I didn't like it. Because of the lifestyle choices she was making and the constant pressure I was under to conform, I no longer wanted to spend time with her. Resenting my decision to sever our long-standing relationship, Tammy decided to make "Miss Goody Two Shoes" early teenage years a living hell. And if there were medals to be won, she would have received first prize for persistent bullying.

Almost daily throughout middle school Tammy would slam me up against the lockers; she would follow me home to continue the harassment; and then the threatening phone calls would begin. Numerous attempts were made to terrify me and inflict harm. In the winter she would hurl snowballs through my bedroom window, shattering the glass! And on one occasion she slit all four tires on my mom's car! Believe it or not, that was just the tip of the iceberg!

In high school the chronic badgering finally stopped. New friends were made and I was no longer the focus of her attention or aggression. Praise God! So being at the same party my second year of college wasn't too concerning, but I wanted to slip in under the radar and go unnoticed. With that aim in mind my friend and I swiftly made our way to the trash can, emptied our bottle of rum into the deep green tub, scooped out the purplish liquid with our red plastic Solo cups, and proceeded to the living room.

After a couple swigs of the peculiar substance I ventured off to find the bathroom. On the way I bumped into an acquaintance, shouted "hello" over the music, and set my drink down on a nearby windowsill. Minutes later I returned to retrieve it. The music had been dialed way down and everyone had funneled out into the street to look at one of the partygoer's new ride.

When I picked up my cup to take a swallow, I instantly froze upon hearing a loud, clear, authoritative command that sounded as if it were coming from someone standing right behind me—"Don't drink that drink!" I turned to see who had imparted the warning, but the room was empty, I was standing alone.

The next few moments I stood peering down into the plastic container wondering what was wrong with its contents. *Why shouldn't I drink it?* The liquid didn't look any different than it had before. As I contemplated taking another sip, I heard the strong dominant voice again— "Don't drink that drink. If you want another drink go and get another drink, but don't drink that drink!" Then the reason followed, "There's a hit of acid in it!" While the mysterious source remained anonymous, the warning was too firm and direct to ignore.

Siding with caution, I heeded the command, shrugged my shoulders, and set the drink back down on the ledge. I'd never tried acid, but stories I'd heard about the hallucinogenic drug made me cringe. I wasn't willing to gamble on the reliability of the voice or put my life at risk, so I proceeded to the kitchen, grabbed another cup, and scooped out a second serving of purple potion from the enormous punch bowl. Upon rejoining my friend in the living room, I mused over the strange encounter. *I wasn't drunk. I'd only had two gulps of diluted alcohol. Did someone really drop a hit of acid in my drink?* Hearing the voice was extremely bizarre and the thought of someone doing such a thing was alarming, but was the premonition true?

About 15 minutes later Tammy proudly strutted into the living room with a small entourage. Grinning from ear to ear, she came and stood directly in front of me. "Hey Sue, how ya doin'?" she asked with a devilish smirk. Then raising her hands just inches from my face, she began moving them swiftly—in and out, back and forth while her fingers danced wildly. The mind-altering drug would have caused me to see trails following the erratic movement.

Fully composed, I stared at her in disbelief and firmly stated, "I'm doing fine." She was stunned; that was not the response she and her posse were expecting...or hoping for. Her agitation and confusion confirmed the voice's warning.

"You dropped a hit of acid in my drink!" I charged.

She was enraged! "How the hell did you know? You didn't see me do it!" As Tammy and her onlookers stormed off, her only retort was, "You think you're so damned smart!"

WOW!!! Was I blown away! She was absolutely right, I didn't see her drug my drink—but God did! I should have left when I saw her, but after seven years I would have never suspected she would still be so vindictive.

Jesus tells us to love our enemies.[7] But, I've always told my daughters there are some people you just need to love from afar. Tammy was definitely one of those people.

I am eternally grateful God was with me that night, even though I was unaware of His presence until He spoke and made Himself *known*. Ever since accepting Jesus in the eighth grade my faith sat on a shelf collecting dust like a trivial participation trophy, yet God chose to intervene and protect me, remaining faithful even when I was not.

It's frightening to ponder how differently that night would have been if I hadn't heeded His warning. It's also curious to think that the Holy Spirit would recommend that I "go and get another drink." But that just proves how well God knows us and how willing He is to meet us right where we are—wherever that may be.

*I was found by those who did not seek me;
I revealed myself to those who did not ask for me.*[8]

The incident could neither be denied nor ignored—God successfully got my attention and made His presence *known*. Yet even after that incredible experience of hearing His voice and realizing His prediction was spot on, I continued on my merry way, doing my own thing, giving little thought to my Savior. Instead of pursuing Him the way I should have, I continued living a lifestyle that could only be characterized as outside the will of God.

Before delivering His people (the Israelites) out of bondage in Egypt, God performed numerous miracles to get their attention and make Himself *known*. All who witnessed the wonders had their spiritual eyes opened. As the Egyptian gods were being crushed by the alleged competition, the Israelites experienced a revival of faith with a renewed sense of hope in their God. The constant barrage and succession of plagues, beginning with turning the water of the Nile into blood and ending with the death of every firstborn son in Egypt, not only demanded attention from the slaves, but from the natives and foreigners as well.

Ten plagues totally obliterated all the Egyptian crops, abolished their livestock, and wreaked havoc on their land. The curses adversely impacted the natives' health as well as every other aspect of their lives. Yet to their surprise, none of the plagues affected the Israelites or the land on which they resided. Leaving no question among slave or free as to whether or not the Israelite's God was the one true God. Through His magnificent display of might and clear distinction between races, the Lord made Himself *known* not only to His favored people but to every person in the nation. For that reason, the Israelites weren't the only ones to follow Moses out of Egypt, "a mixed multitude left with them."[9]

When results of the final plague were in and Pharaoh's oldest son was among the dead, the ruler ordered Moses to "Leave my people, you and the Israelites! Go worship the LORD as you have requested."[10] Then taking into account all that had transpired, Pharaoh too acknowledged Moses' God as being the God above all other gods. In the same breath Pharaoh commanded Moses to "Go," he made a very uncharacteristic appeal, "And also bless me."[11]

God continued to make Himself *known* as He led the Israelites out of slavery toward their Promised Land. He parted the Red Sea to protect them and seal their freedom. When there was nothing to eat in the desert, He provided manna. When they complained of having no meat, He made it rain quail. When there was nothing to drink, God made water flow out from a rock. He led the Israelites through the desert as a pillar of cloud by day protecting them from the blazing sun and as a pillar of fire by night providing warmth and light. God was ever-present with His people and they *knew* Him.

Throughout the ages people of faith have been loved and cared for by God in various ways. Although times have changed tremendously, God hasn't. He is the same today as He was thousands of years ago. He still longs for you to *know* Him and still desires to have a relationship with you. But with so many present-day distractions vying for your time and attention, getting to know God, and developing a relationship with Him requires deliberate dedication and determination.

The Lord made Himself *known* to the Israelites and He made Himself *known* to me, yet regrettably, my response wasn't much different than theirs. Even after God delivered His people, split the sea, provided for and protected them, Moses had the monotonous task of having to remind them of the divine occurrences.

> Has anything so great as this ever happened, or has anything like it ever been heard of? Has any other people heard the voice of God speaking out of fire, as you have, and lived? Has any god ever tried to take for himself one nation out of another nation, by testings, by signs and wonders, by war, by a mighty hand and an outstretched arm, or by great and awesome deeds, like all the things the LORD your God did for you in Egypt before your very eyes? You were shown these things so that you might *know* that the LORD is God; besides him there is no other.[12]

The LORD declared through His prophet Jeremiah, "Let him who boasts boast about this: that he understands and *knows* me..."[13] Because there is nothing God wants more than for us to *know* Him, He is still willing to do whatever it takes to make Himself *known*. There is no greater joy than *knowing* the Lord personally and having an intimate relationship with Him.

As you venture through this unfolding story, my appeal echoes Paul's prayer for the Ephesians. "I keep asking that the God of our Lord Jesus Christ, the glorious Father, may give you the Spirit of wisdom and revelation, so that you may know him better. I pray that the eyes of your heart may be enlightened in order that you may know the hope to which he has called you, the riches of his glorious inheritance in his holy people, and his incomparably great power for us who believe."[14]

Chapter 2

# Forget Me Not

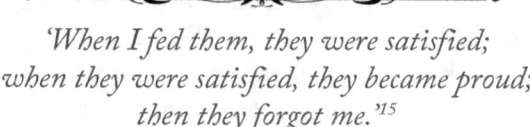

*'When I fed them, they were satisfied;
when they were satisfied, they became proud;
then they forgot me.'*[15]

On a bustling autumn afternoon filled with an air of excitement my teenage mother gave birth to a beautiful baby girl. Although I'm a bit biased, I humbly admit all the hoopla was not due to my entering the world, it was the result of my being born on Halloween—a night for ghouls, goblins, and trick-or-treaters to be mischievous. With my parents at the hospital, instead of home passing out candy, their dark dwelling became a prime target for dozens of raw eggs and multiple rolls of toilet paper trim.

But it's not my birthdate that makes me special. The only thing that makes me extraordinary is that I am a child of the Most High God—just like you! I'm not perfect by a long shot, but like you I've been wonderfully made.[16] Chosen by the King before the world began, set apart, and created for His glory.[17] My only righteousness comes through faith in Jesus Christ. If the experiences shared throughout this memoir don't seem like something God would do for you, you're wrong! Just as He is, and has always been there for me, He is ever-present with you.

I am blessed, yet undeserving of the grace God has bestowed on me. Conceived out of wedlock by parents who eventually got married, then divorced by the time I was six, my younger sister Jane and I were raised in a broken home by a mother in her early 20s. In addition to working a full-time day job, she waitressed nights and weekends, and took on accounting jobs in her spare time. Needless to say, we didn't get to see her as often as we would have liked. Every day after school we came home to an empty house, an empty refrigerator, and empty cupboards. On her nights off we frequented fast food restaurants. By eliminating the time-consuming tasks of grocery shopping, food preparation, and clean up, the three of us could enjoy more time together.

Two elderly neighbors took a real interest in Jane and me. Whether they were paid sitters or not, both were God-sent blessings in our young, impressionable lives. Mrs. Young was a retired schoolteacher who helped with our schoolwork and aimed to improve our reading and writing skills. Mrs. Bockheim was a lovely, large Catholic woman who always wore dresses adorned with a full-front apron. Whenever she sat with us at night before tucking us in, she'd have us kneel at the bedside, and together we'd recite the Lord's Prayer. Both women provided us with a sense of security and love.

Without a Christian upbringing, I never learned about Jesus. And even though I had a close relationship with my grandmother who was a church-going, Bible-studying believer, she wasn't the person who introduced me to Jesus—Mrs. Bockheim was. In grade school my mother dated a Catholic man and for a while we attended Saturday night mass, but that stopped as soon as their relationship ended. Then my junior high school choir director Mr. Sterd, who was deeply spiritual, always chose songs that exalted the name of Jesus. Unfortunately, the time would come when that would no longer be tolerated in the public school system.

In eighth grade, at age 13, a classmate invited me to go to an Awana Club program at his church. Unbeknownst to me, it was a youth and children's Christian ministry.

"Come on," he urged. "It's a cool place to hang out." Then he sweetened the pot by adding, "We have lots of fun singing songs and playing games."

In the 70s, as you may recall, there was no Internet. There were no personal computers, video games, or cell phones to keep kids like me entertained. There were no VHS tapes or DVDs to watch on the TV screen and only a few television channels even existed. How could I, a music-loving extrovert, resist the invitation for fun, friends, games, *and* song?

The following Wednesday evening, peering out into the dark from our living room window, I eagerly waited for a ride to the social event across town. When a yellow-orange school bus marked "North Park Baptist Church" stopped in front of the house, I rushed out and climbed aboard. The Awana Club was everything I hoped it would be. It was so much fun I attended every week for months.

We played games, sang Bible songs, and earned prizes for memorizing Scripture, but most importantly, I learned of God's amazing love for me. I was like a dry, thirsty little seed aching to be watered and hungering to satisfy a deep emptiness only God could fill. So when one of the leaders asked if I wanted to give my life to Jesus and receive His free gift of salvation, I enthusiastically leapt at the chance. Bubbling over with excitement, I couldn't wait to get home and share the news with my best friend, my mother.

On the ride home, with a grin stretching from ear to ear, I envisioned her response. She'd hug me and together we'd celebrate the wonderful decision and the positive impact it would have on my life. As soon as the bus halted in front of our house, I bolted out across the yard, jumped up onto the porch, and threw open the front door hollering, "Hey mom! Come here!" Alarmed by the outcry, she raced into the living room.

"Mom, do you believe in Jesus?" I impatiently queried. She seemed taken off-guard by the question, so I quickly followed up with another. "Do you believe Jesus is the Son of God?" She wasn't answering. She just stood there blankly staring at me, unsure how to respond. I was baffled by her delay. *Why wasn't she responding the way I envisioned?*

After thoughtful hesitation she replied, "I don't know." Then she turned and walked away. My heart sank. It felt as though the spark within me had been doused by a tub of icy cold water.

From the onset of my spiritual journey I was left to fumble through on my own, and although I continued to believe Jesus was who He said He was—the Son of God—I was an "at risk" teen with limited supervision living in a world of reckless adolescence.

Thanks to the expectations of my mother and grandmother, I graduated from college with a Bachelor of Arts degree and at age 22 I married a wonderful man whom I was passionately in love with. Is a matter of fact, I picked Steve up at a popular dance club/drinking hole for young adults. While that may sound like an unscrupulous endeavor, it resulted from one of the strangest experiences I've ever had. It was Wednesday, Oldies Night, 1981. After getting a couple Blue Motorcycles, the alcoholic special of the night, my girlfriend and I sat down at a table right alongside the recessed dance floor.

The lights dimmed as the band commenced their second set of the night with the Monkee's #1 hit *I'm a Believer*. My friend excused herself to go chat with someone at another table, while I contently engaged in one of my favorite public pastimes: people-watching.

As my eyes leisurely gazed down onto the dance floor, sweeping across it, and up over to the other side, the most bizarre thing happened—suddenly everything in sight became blurry, everything that is, except for this one fellow exiting the men's room. There was nothing outstanding about him, but because he was the only thing I could see with any clarity, he had my full attention. The imparity, illusion, or whatever it was, lasted only seconds, but made a terrific impression. Nothing like that had ever happened before and nothing like it has ever happened since.

Mesmerized by the peculiar incident, I stood up and began following the mysterious, dark-haired man from the opposite side of the club. My eyes were transfixed on the moving figure. It felt as though I'd been cast in a dramatic sci-fi episode of Rod Serling's *The Twilight Zone*. It was beyond weird. I curiously pursued him until he joined another young man at a high top table near the bar. Positioning myself within earshot, I listened and observed.

Within minutes his friend stood up, said, "Goodbye Steve," and left.

That was my in. Upon hearing his name I boldly approached the stranger with a broad smile and a cheerful greeting, "Hi Steve!"

Confused, yet intrigued, he searched my face for clues. He was stumped. "Do I know you?"

Dodging the question I swiftly asked, "Would you like to dance?"

"No," he stated flatly, still staring at me, aiming to solve the identity puzzle.

I continued to probe, wanting to understand why I had the inexplicable aberration and why he was singled out from the crowd. "Are you leaving?" I asked.

"No," he answered.

So I did what any assertive woman would have done—I took the beer from his hand, set it down on the table, gently gripped his hand in mine, and dragged him down two flights of stairs informing him, "Then you're dancing with me!"

Within two years that mystery man and I were married! At the altar Steve promised to "almost always" love me after being instructed to repeat the words: "I will always love you." Although his nerves got the best of him, during our 24-year marriage we frequently joked about the mishap. He promised to "almost always" love me and he almost always did!

The day after our wedding we left Michigan and headed toward California's Silicon Valley. Truth be told without a GPS (Global Positioning System), help from the Internet (both non-existent at the time), or name of a nearby city, we were clueless as to the exact location of our destination. But the two of us were determined to seize the adventure and conquer the world.

On our westward journey we stopped at the Grand Canyon; we explored the Painted Desert and Petrified Forest; we celebrated a night in Las Vegas; and after waving good-bye to the Hoover Dam, we ventured toward Los Angeles. Since most of California was north of L.A., we figured there was a good chance we'd find the Silicon Valley if we started there and headed north. We were right! In the big city we learned that San Jose, the hub of Silicon Valley, was about 350 miles north.

Our reason for relocating was so Steve could find employment. Before discrimination laws were in effect, employers could refuse anyone a job for any reason. After graduating from ITT Technical School with a 4.0 GPA, my husband received multiple job offers from some of the most prestigious companies in Michigan, with one stipulation—he had to pass a physical exam. What was a non-issue for most college grads entering the work force, ended up being a huge issue for Steve.

In high school he ran track, and during one of the racing events at a state conference, his right foot landed in a hole and he somehow blew out his knee. After the first of several surgeries, it was discovered that the surgeon had operated on the wrong side of the joint! Consequently, the prescribed physical therapy caused further damage to the initial injury. Because of his knee, Steve couldn't pass the mandatory test and was repeatedly denied employment. The man was crushed and his self-esteem was shot.

As his job-hunting frustration grew, we posed our dilemma to anyone willing to listen, hoping to find answers. We were repeatedly told of a growing demand for skilled technicians in California's Silicon Valley. Again, without the Internet, there was little research that could be done. However at that time, in the early 80s, droves of people were migrating from Michigan to find work. Unfortunately, we too were being forced to flock elsewhere. In two weeks time, I quit my job, sold my car, we said our vows, and were on our way. Within days of our arrival, my bright, handsome husband landed a great job—and all he needed was an eye exam!

The honeymoon years were blissful. We were very much in love and optimistic about our future. It was easy to make friends, because everyone was a transplant from somewhere else. We fit right in. The influx of people to California was so massive that every other car with a state license plate had a bumper sticker that read: "Welcome to California. Now Go Home!" At the same time, Michigan vehicles displayed bumper stickers that read: "Last One in Michigan Turn Out the Lights!"

The world has changed so much since then, especially when it comes to technology. Today you can simply touch a screen to see, hear, watch, or learn about anything. Life is moving faster than it ever has before, billions of people are caught up in the World Wide Web, and it's easy to become distracted, forgetting about the things that matter most. Due to our electronic fixation, quality time with family, friends, and even God is frequently interrupted or ignored. If we're not careful, this preoccupation could pose a huge stumbling block—that not only distances us from others, but from God.

Your Heavenly Father longs to have a deep, meaningful relationship with you, and as it should be with any friend (whom He's referred to *you* as), spending quality time together and engaging in open dialogue (talking, praying, and listening) is imperative.[18] Retaining memories is also a crucial aspect of enduring relationships, particularly with God. Remembering His goodness, recounting His blessings, pondering His promises, securing His Word in your heart, and preserving precious memories all form the fundamental core of your faith. Coveting these treasures is critical to maintaining a close, ongoing relationship with God.

Because of the potent and persuasive qualities memories possess, they pose a serious threat to the Enemy. While God forewarns against forgetting these important things, Satan relishes in the fact that you may be too preoccupied to cherish or hold onto this vital information. As you become increasingly distant from God, the Adversary will slowly infect your unguarded soul and erase vital memories that keep God alive in your heart. This tactful scheme simultaneously gives way to self-sufficiency, arrogance, and the egocentric belief that you don't need God.

In Deuteronomy, God warns His people against falling into this perilous trap:

> When you have eaten and are satisfied, praise the LORD your God for the good land He has given you. Be careful that you do not forget the LORD your God. Otherwise, when you eat and are satisfied, when you build fine houses and settle down, and when your herds and flocks grow large and your silver and gold increase and all you have is multiplied, then your heart will become proud and you will forget the LORD your God, who brought you out of Egypt, out of the land of slavery. He led you through the vast and dreadful wilderness, that thirsty and waterless land, with its venomous snakes and scorpions. He brought you water out of hard rock. He gave you manna to eat in the wilderness, something your ancestors had never known, to humble and test you so that in the end it might go well with you. You may say to yourself, 'My power and the strength of my hands have produced this wealth for me.' But remember the LORD your God, for it is He who gives you the ability to produce wealth.[19]

God saved the Israelites from the hand of the Egyptians to make His mighty power known.[20] They believed His promises and sang His praises, but *they soon forgot* what He had done. They refused to remember and gave into their sin.[21]

In the desert Moses warned the Israelites: "Be careful and watch yourselves closely so that you *do not forget* the things your eyes have seen or let them fade from your heart as long as you live. Teach them to your children and to their children after them."²²

After leading the Israelites safely out of Egypt to Mount Horeb (Sinai), Moses retreated to where the LORD had spoken to him through a burning bush, instructing him to return to Egypt and deliver His people. During that short 40-day period the Israelites grew anxious and impatient. Instead of waiting to see if their leader would return, they rebelled against God.

Shockingly, the entire nation united, gathering around Moses' brother Aaron and saying, "Come, make us gods who will go before us. As for this fellow Moses who brought us up out of Egypt, we don't know what has happened to him." Then melting all of their gold, the Israelites created a calf idol to be worshipped as their new god. All the people proclaimed, "These are your gods, O Israel, which brought you up out of Egypt!" ²³

In little over a month, the Israelites had not only given up on Moses, they had given up on God. The God who revealed Himself and demonstrated His magnificent power in a way no other god could, was completely dismissed. I find that mind-blowing! How could their memories have failed them so soon? Not only had "all the people" agreed to construct a replacement for the Almighty, they "all" agreed to invent another memory that completely removed God from having any part of the Exodus. They established the golden calf as their deliverer!

Remembering people, places, and events with any accuracy over time is problematic. For this reason, the LORD had the Israelites perform various tasks to help them retain vital memories so present and future generations would remain cognizant and reminiscent of God's ongoing presence, providence, and goodness. He instructed them to place the stone tablets of the covenant law (Ten Commandments), the gold jar of manna, and Aaron's staff that had budded inside the Ark of the Covenant.[24] The Israelites were also directed to build altars and memorials in numerous places where they met with God, experienced His presence, or witnessed His power, in order to commemorate the historical event.

After miraculously crossing the Jordan River at flood stage, God instructed His servant Joshua to, "Choose twelve men from among the people, one from each tribe, and tell them to take up twelve stones [boulders] from the middle of the Jordan from right where the priests stood [with the Ark of the Covenant] and to carry them over with you and put them down at the place where you stay tonight."[25] Joshua set up the twelve stones at Gilgal "to be a memorial to the people of Israel forever" and to "serve as a sign among you."

God gave these directions so, "In the future when your children ask you, 'What do these stones mean?' Tell them that the LORD your God did to the Jordan what He had done to the Red Sea when He dried it up before us until we had crossed over. He did this so that all the peoples of the earth might know [remember and never forget] that the hand of the LORD is powerful and so that you might always fear the LORD your God."[26]

Jesus faced similar challenges when it came to His disciples remembering important events. After feeding 5,000 people (only men were counted in those days so the number could easily reached 10-15,000) with just five loaves of bread and two fish,[27] then feeding another 4,000 followers with seven loaves of bread and a few small fish,[28] the Lord heard

His disciples agonizing over how to feed another large crowd. "Why are you talking about having no bread? Do you still not see or understand? Are your hearts hardened? Do you have eyes but fail to see, and ears but fail to hear? And *don't you remember?*" [29]

Isn't it absurd that Jesus had to remind His disciples of the miracles He had just performed? How could they have forgotten in such a short period of time? Not only did they witness Jesus feeding well over twenty thousand men, women, and children with a couple loaves of bread and a few fish, they were with Him when He foretold the future, healed the sick, drove demons out of the possessed, walked on water, and brought the dead to life! Yet they were still unable to grasp, let alone remember, God's magnificent demonstration of power!

Making it priority to retain the knowledge of who God is, what He is able to do, and what He has already done is key to sustaining unshakable faith. Personal and biblical memories empower us to boldly move forward into the future with confident hope in our God. If we become too passive, allowing precious memories to fade, we won't have any building blocks of faith to pass down to our children or grandchildren, to enlighten them with firsthand knowledge of our awesome Creator. Would our negligence to remember make us any different than the Israelites or the apostles?

Our past defines who we are as a people, a nation, a culture, and as individuals. Failing to remember the lessons we've learned, ignoring the difficulties we've struggled through, forgetting the goals we've achieved, and neglecting to reminisce about departed loved ones, diminishes their impression, their power, and their worth. Memories are vital. That's why we make such an effort to keep them alive by taking pictures, recording video, collecting souvenirs, posting on social media, blogging, journaling, etc. The same effort should be made to keep God alive in our lives, in the lives of our children, and into the lives of future generations.

Years ago I began documenting prayers, then answers to those prayers, recording times when God spoke to me, gave me a vision, or did something else amazing. That log is the basis for this memoir. For almost three decades those memories have enabled and empowered me to stay focused on trusting God, especially during our family's time of greatest need. Our Heavenly Father wants us to walk backward into the future with our hearts and our hope steadfastly anchored in Him, remembering everything He's done in the past, so we can move forward with confident assurance that He will continue to be ever-present and forever faithful.

*Sing to the LORD, for he has done glorious things; let this be known to all the world.*[30]

The Lord never changes—He is the same yesterday, today, and always.[31] Having done great and glorious things in the past is a promise that He will continue to do great and glorious things today and on into the future.

Chapter 3

# God's Relentless Pursuit

*You will guard him and keep him in perfect and constant peace whose mind [both its inclination and its character] is stayed on you, because he commits himself to you, leans on you, and hopes confidently in you.* [32]

Because of His great love and mercy, God will never give up on you. He will never stop pursuing you. He is always creating opportunities for you to turn around and get right with Him. A long-lasting, intimate relationship with you is what He desires. As long as you are breathing He wants to be Lord of your life.

It wasn't until 1985, two years into our marriage that I re-dedicated my life to Christ. A friend invited me to a Mario Murillo Crusade. Steve, who wasn't yet sold on the fact that Jesus was the Son of God, accompanied me to the event. It was a powerful message followed by an altar call.

Eager for the opportunity to get right with God and step into abundant living, I immediately jumped up out of my seat and proceeded forward to ask God to forgive me of my sin and be Lord of my life. I was completely unaware that my other half was right alongside, making his own decision to step out in faith. From that point on, my enthusiastic flame for the Lord burned bright. Steve's flame however did not.

When you sincerely give your life to Christ the Bible says you become "a new creation: the old has gone, the new is here!"[33] At the time of conversion you are forgiven of all past sins, the Holy Spirit takes up residence inside you, and God begins transforming you into the likeness of His Son.

This process, known as sanctification, changes the way you think, feel, and behave. If you've already invited Jesus into your life you know what I'm talking about. If you haven't yet made that decision, it's difficult to describe the inner workings of the Spirit's transformational power and the impact it has on you and your daily life. But since that day, my life has never been the same.

Six months after the crusade on the evening of June 24, we were blessed with a beautiful baby girl. Jennifer Sue, our pride and joy, was a delightful child and Steve was a fantastic father. Not only did he adore snuggling with his daughter, he got immense pleasure out of making her squeal, tickling her tummy, giving her raspberries, and playing peek-a-boo. He was always willing to change a diaper and take the late night shift whenever our little bundle had trouble sleeping.

San José was extremely congested and the traffic was atrocious; it was not where we wanted to live or raise our daughter. After experiencing a 6.4 earthquake and its aftershocks, those feelings intensified. I began praying for God to move us somewhere out of the San Francisco Bay area—and within a few months, Steve was offered a promotion along with an chance to relocate to Folsom, California near Sacramento. The move to the gorgeous foothills of the Sierra Nevada Mountains was everything I wanted—and more.

In the tranquil town of Cameron Park, my relationship with the Lord blossomed. God led me to a small, non-denominational community church where He surrounded me with Christ-loving people. He also set me up to meet another young mother in the apartment complex who was strong in her Christian faith. Every day, her and I would get together with our infant children and study the Bible. My desire to know and grow closer to the Lord was insatiable. Regrettably, my unbelieving husband didn't share the same passion. As my excitement gained momentum, it became an escalating irritant to him, one he could barely stomach. Steve's intolerance increased right alongside side my fervent dedication. The antagonistic incompatibility radically rocked our marriage for months.

As a result of sanctification, believers develop an increased sensitivity to the Holy Spirit, acting in ways that aim to please God—loving others more deeply, exhibiting greater patience, forgiving freely, cleaning up filthy language, disengaging from gossip, choosing like-minded friends, watching non-offensive television programs or movies, and avoiding certain websites. While breaking away from former thought patterns, habits, and behaviors is liberating, it tends to make those around you (non-believers and believers who aren't following Christ) uncomfortable, even agitated.

Second Corinthians 2:14-16 explains "God uses us (believers) to spread the aroma of the knowledge of Him everywhere. We are to God the pleasing aroma of Christ among those who are being saved and those who are perishing. To the one we are an aroma that brings life; to the other, an aroma that brings death."

As I fought to curtail my enthusiasm for the Lord and suppress my "new self" in Steve's presence, our relationship returned to its blissful state.

Prior to the arrival of Holly, our second little bundle of joy born Easter Sunday morning, we purchased our first home. "The little blue house," as we fondly referred to the modest 900 sq. ft. dwelling, was at a much higher elevation in the Sierra Nevada Mountains—just 45 minutes downhill from South Lake Tahoe. The realtor who sold us the property said we were on the snowline, yet there was over five feet of snow in our front yard that first Christmas!

Once we were settled, I invited a dear Christian friend of mine from Michigan to fly out for a visit. Kathy had never been to northern California and I was excited to share our little piece of paradise with her. A day after her arrival we took the picturesque drive up the mountain.

It was a gorgeous late October afternoon; refreshingly cool with a mix of sun and clouds. On the way we stopped for lunch at a quaint little restaurant tucked off the highway. While sitting outside at a bistro-style table chatting and laughing about life, love, and memories, we indulged in a light bite we dubbed "weeds (salad) & wine."

After seeing the sights of South Lake Tahoe's main drag, browsing through a half dozen souvenir shops, exploring a couple casinos, then pausing along the beach to watch the sun sparkle on the deep blue lake nestled in the tall pines and snow-capped mountains, it was time to return home.

Since it was early evening, there was plenty of time to take an alternate downhill route. Although I was less familiar with the drive, the splendor of God's magnificence resting on the peaks and hidden lakes of the adjacent mountainside, was too breathtaking to ignore.

It was dusk when we entered the heavily wooded area of the Eldorado National Forest to cross back over to Highway 50 and follow it home. I popped in the cassette tape Kathy brought for us to listen to. It was an interesting sermon on fasting. We were so caught up in the message and discussing its relevance, time just flew by.

After driving close to two hours without seeing any directional signs indicating where we were or where we were going was a clear indication we were lost. We should have already been out of the forest and half way home. Looking down at the gas gauge I gasped, it was well below E, much lower than I'd *ever* seen it!

The sun had set and the forest was now pitch black. There were no streetlights. In fact, there was no light at all. The moonlight was unable to penetrate the dense foliage, and worse yet, since entering the forest we hadn't seen any other vehicles. I ejected the tape and slowly pulled off to the side of the road. As soon as I shut off the car, I turned to my friend to assess our predicament. The consensus was we were in trouble and in desperate need of help. I grabbed my cell phone to try calling Steve, but there was no reception.

With the car engine and heater off we began to contemplate our next move. Kathy and I stared at each other in disbelief as the wind whistled through the trees. It was shocking how much the temperature had plummeted. A gentle wave of goose bumps swept over our arms, then the icy chill began to creep in, threatening to steal our warmth and engulf our bodies. With no jackets, blankets, or anything else to help us maintain our body temperature, it became painstakingly apparent that if we remained here all night, we'd most certainly freeze.

I tried phoning home again and again, hoping for a connection, but my repeated efforts were of no avail. There was virtually nothing either one of us could do. We were like sitting ducks awaiting our fate. Getting out and walking wasn't even an option because we couldn't see our hands in front of our face, not to mention the peril of wild animals that would kill and devour us if they were hungry.

Fully cognizant of our vulnerable situation—no gas, no heat, no light, and no help in the deep, dense forest, we did what any believing Christians would have done—we prayed. Crying out to the Lord for divine intervention, trusting that

He would protect us and provide for us. We needed gas, we needed directions on how to escape the forest, and we needed to return home safely. We both believed for a miracle—our lives depended on it.

It was as if our prayer set off an alarm, alerting heaven that we were in trouble. After saying "Amen" we lifted our heads and opened our eyes to see headlights coming toward us. At the same time, truck lights beamed from behind. Praising God for His impeccable timing, I hastily jumped out of the four-door sedan and darted into the road to flag down the car. When the driver stopped and rolled down her window, I asked for directions to the nearest gas station. Likewise, the truck driver paused when he saw me waving my arms. He confirmed the car driver's instructions. Those were the only two vehicles we saw the entire time we were in the forest. My friend and I were thoroughly convinced they were angels appointed to come to our rescue!

Upon starting the car and cranking the heat to high, I once again glanced back down at the gas gauge. It hadn't moved. There was no way we were going to make it out of the forest to the nearest gas station on a tank that was well below empty. Then something truly amazing happened! Right before my eyes I watched in wonder as the needle gradually moved from where it had been resting up to an eighth of a tank!

Kathy and I were overawed by God's instant response to our frantic plea. He promises to be present with His children. He promises to love, protect, and provide. He was given the opportunity to validate those claims and He took it! He provided more than enough fuel to get us out of the woods, literally and metaphorically, and to the gas station. Then the Lord went one step further to exaggerate His role in this blessed escapade, eliminating any shred of doubt as to whether or not this actually was a miracle.

Right when we pulled into the gas station I sprinted inside to empty *my* tank, while Kathy filled the car's tank. The young man behind the counter appeared bored, picking his nails, and paying little attention to me as I ran in. "Where's the bathroom?" I impatiently inquired.

Without any eye contact, he slid a key across the counter and waved his hand toward the back of the building. Upon returning the key I verbalized my appreciation.

"You know," he started with his eyes intently fixed on mine, "I was supposed to close this joint over twenty minutes ago." He paused. I could almost detect the wheels turning in his head as he wrestled with how to make sense of the message he was aiming to deliver. "I never *ever* stay open late," he divulged looking very perplexed. "It's strange, but for some unknown reason, I felt compelled to stay open late tonight."

I stared at him in disbelief, flabbergasted by his confession! Then it became crystal clear that the Lord not only wanted to make Himself known to us that night, He wanted to use the incident to make Himself known to the service station attendant...and to you. Just then Kathy walked in, and together we enthusiastically began sharing the details of our earlier plight...and how God rescued us.

"He protected us from the freezing cold by sending not one, but two divinely-ordained individuals to furnish us with directions; He provided us with the means to make it here by inexplicably adding fuel to our gas tank; He even subliminally influenced you to remain open for two reasons: one, so we could fill our gas tank to make it home and two, so you could hear this wonderful message of hope." The fella's mouth dropped open after realizing his crucial role in this remarkable chain of events.

"By seeing how God came through for us, you can fully trust that He would do the same for you!" I cheerfully added.

"Thanks so much for your unintentional obedience!" Kathy and I gleefully laughed, dancing our way out the door like a couple high-spirited teenyboppers.

"Happy to oblige," the attendant smiled, grabbing the keys to lock up the station.

*'Because he loves me,' says the LORD, 'I will rescue him;
I will protect him, for he acknowledges my name.
He will call on me, and I will answer him;
I will be with him in trouble, I will deliver him and honor him.
With long life I will satisfy him and show him my salvation.'* [34]

There were few things Steve and I enjoyed more than spending time with our girls. The four of us got along magnificently. Whatever we did was fun and enjoyable, because we were doing it together. Jennifer was now eleven; Holly was seven; and our two large-breed black dogs, Jazz and Bear, were no longer puppies. Needless to say, our little blue house was shrinking…rapidly. Since Steve had just received another promotion, it was an opportune time to begin searching for a larger, more accommodating place to live.

Within a few short months we found a perfect three-bedroom, two-bath ranch in a neighboring county located on five acres of horse property with a fenced-in backyard, a tree house, and a distant mountain view from the kitchen window. Since a Sacramento couple had already made an offer on the property, contingent on the sale of their city home, no other conditional offers were being accepted. If we wanted the place we had to agree to buy it regardless of whether or not we could sell our little blue house. It was taking a big risk, but we were confident that if priced right, we'd be able to sell it in the next 30 days.

We were overjoyed when our offer was accepted and we hustled to get our little blue house on the market. After one week of inactivity we dropped the price. Then we dropped the price again...and again. God didn't seem to be answering our prayers for a quick sale. Less than a week before closing on the new ranch, we found ourselves in a problematic pickle.

Our eagerness to step up into something bigger, better, and more accommodating had gotten the best of us. *Had Steve and I acted too impulsively?* Prior to making the offer we knew we were in no position to make dual house payments, but we were certain the little blue house would sell—we were wrong!

With limited options, we reluctantly made the decision to rent out the smaller home and move into the larger. In our area there was a growing need for rental property and on short notice renters were far easier to find. Days before the closing, we had signed a lease agreement with a young couple who proved to be good tenants.

Although the new place was only a few miles away, the girls had to attend new schools and make new friends. They both got involved in basketball, softball, and 4-H. The four of us even started taking karate classes together. We were acclimating well in our new surroundings. We loved our new house, our new friends, and our new lives. Life was good in the calm before the storm.

Chapter 4

## Mysterious Maladies

*Dear friends, do not be surprised at the painful trial you are suffering, as though something strange were happening to you.*[35]

Living 2,200 miles from family had its pros and cons. Without social media, the chief con was being absent from each other's lives and not truly knowing one another. On the flip side, the four of us got to enjoy oodles of uninterrupted time together, growing closer, and doing things we loved to do—tent camping in the Eldorado National Forest, hiking the mountains, panning for gold, frequenting nearby parks and playgrounds, picnicking, pulling the girls behind our canoe on inner tubes, playing softball, frolicking in the snow, building snowmen, snowwomen, snow forts, and sledding.

Our Thanksgiving and Christmas tradition was to stay home and spend the day playing Monopoly. The board game always commenced early in the afternoon and extended late into the evening. We had a blast accumulating properties, negotiating deals, throwing one another in jail, and making each other squirm with outrageous rent payments. We thoroughly enjoyed the simple pleasure of just being together, and we were very happy. Our home was filled with merriment and laughter...but that was all about to change.

It was a brisk spring morning, the opening day of softball season. The sun was shining and a gentle breeze was blowing. Both girls had games to play in the all-day sporting event. Their presence was required at the 9:00 a.m. flag-raising ceremony. Steve wasn't feeling well and thought he'd benefit from a bit more sleep, so he encouraged us to leave without him, promising to catch up with us at the field before Holly's game since her team was first to play.

When our eight-year-old daughter got up to bat there was no sign of her dad anywhere. From home plate, she shot me a puzzling look of concern. *Where was he?* He had never, and I mean *never ever*, missed an important occasion in either one of the girls' lives. He attended every game, talent show, dance recital, father-daughter event, and even every parent/teacher conference! I too was feeling a bit apprehensive but kept brushing it off, telling myself he simply overslept.

Our anxiety grew when Jenni (12) stepped up to the plate almost two hours later. Her dad was still nowhere to be found and his absence was unsettling. Steve hadn't been feeling well for weeks and was spending extended time in bed, suffering from severe headaches and extreme nausea with sporadic bouts of vomiting. I had no way to call him and I couldn't leave. We were over 30 miles from home, beside that, I agreed to keep an eye on one of Holly's teammates and drive her home at the end of the tournament.

The softball games concluded at twilight, and since Steve never showed up, I was deeply troubled and extremely eager to get home. I hurried the girls to the car, loaded their gear, and sped down the curvy mountain road. Silent tension filled the vehicle. No one said a word. The girls and I suspected something was seriously wrong. No—we were certain of it.

Dave and Cindy, parents of Holly's teammate were close friends of ours, so rather than dropping their daughter off at home and leaving, I raced inside to use the phone. My apprehension escalated when there was no answer at the other end. The constant ringing echoed in my head. *He just had to be there. I knew he was.* I called again, thinking I may have dialed the wrong number. With trembling fingers, I deliberately pressed each of the numbers one by one to make sure they were in the right sequence and there was no mistake—still no answer. With sweaty palms I hung up the phone. My heart was racing, my legs were weak, and I felt sick to my stomach. This was *not* good.

I expressed my concern to the couple, "Steve never showed up to the playing field after promising to be there."

They began consoling me with excuses, "Maybe he needed some alone time." "He could have gone fishing." "Maybe he went out for a hike."

"No," I replied, adamantly shaking my head and protesting their weak efforts to calm my nerves. I wasn't buying it. For Steve, nothing had ever taken precedence over being there for any one of us for any reason. Dave and Cindy continued to downplay my fear, but I knew my husband and this was *not* his normal behavior. After denying my initial request for an escort home because he'd had a couple beers and didn't feel it necessary, my persistent plea prompted Dave to follow us back to the house.

It was late and the darkness only served to accentuate my mounting anxiety. Although I wanted to race home to discover what was wrong, I was dreading what we might find. But with the prayers my daughters and I were imploring as we drove to the house, along with my friend's headlights reflecting in the car's rearview mirror, God gave me the strength and courage I needed to proceed.

An eerie feeling swept over me as soon as we turned off the road and headed up our long gravel driveway. The house was completely engulfed in darkness. Not a single light was on inside or outside of the dwelling. My entire body was trembling with fear. Before I could turn off the car, Jenni sprang out and stormed into the house ahead of Holly, Dave, and me. I chased after her with the others on my tail.

Flipping on the lights gave us all clear visibility down the hall and into the master bedroom. Steve was there, lying in bed. *Had he been there all day?* I slowly approached his lifeless body and gently touched his arm. Nothing. Instinctively, I slowly began rubbing it. "Steve?" I whispered, pausing and waiting for a response. "Are you okay?" Silence. In a normal tone, I repeated questioning, "Steve?" "Steve?" With each attempt to try and elicit some sort of response, the volume and urgency of my appeals grew louder and more intense, but to no avail.

He was completely unresponsive, yet his body was warm to the touch and he had a pulse. Instead of leaving his side to call for an ambulance, which I should have done in hindsight, my unyielding pursuit for some sort of movement or acknowledgment led me to bouncing, then jumping on the bed. I wasn't hysterical, just distressed, and impatiently persistent in wanting to generate *any* type of reaction that would assure me he was okay—although it was painstakingly obvious he wasn't.

Finally a slight whisper escaped his lips. "Stop."

"Do you want me to call for help?" His refusal was barely audible, yet understood.

Late into the night I sat on the edge of our bed crying and in shock, rubbing his back, and trying to rouse him into a cognitive state of consciousness. It wasn't until the following morning that he came to. He got up, went to the bathroom, and returned to bed for the remainder of the day.

That was the turning point. From that moment on, everything in our lives changed. When I say everything, I mean *everything*! Like a surprise attack from an unprovoked enemy, we were given no forewarning of the decade-long storm we were heading into. Life as we knew it would never be the same again.

Unbeknownst to us, Steve was suffering from the early stages of an extremely rare and deadly disease. What commenced as chronic nausea, frequent vomiting bouts, and debilitating headaches, progressed with intensity into something much worse, something that took years to diagnose.

Seeing our loved one in so much pain was extremely difficult. Without relief, he was no longer able to participate in any of the family activities we once enjoyed. Six weeks earlier Steve had promised Holly he'd take the day off work to help chaperone her fourth-grade field trip. She was so excited! But days before the Gold Rush Adventure she expressively excused him from the role of chaperone. "Dad, you don't have to come with me on my field trip. I don't want you puking in front of my friends!"

Even while the possibility of having her father throw up in front of her friends was a genuine and justifiable concern, having Holly point out the heart-breaking reality of his painful predicament was a devastating blow. It wasn't as if he was unaware of it, but her exposing comment made it agonizingly clear that his affliction was starting to have an adverse impact on all of our lives. There wasn't *anything* he wouldn't have done to change that.

Weeks stretched into months and whenever Steve wasn't at work, he was home in bed—miserably sick, enduring insufferable migraines, hugging the toilet bowl, nauseated, and exhausted. I was doing everything I could to get him proper medical care, but multiple visits to his primary care physician, neurologist referrals, and other specialists all led to dead ends. None of the medical professionals could identify the problem or pinpoint the cause. Prescription drugs to relieve the various symptoms were dispensed, but none worked. Our persistent efforts to determine the source of his ailments and find a remedy were futile, not to mention physically and emotionally exhausting.

Every Sunday the girls and I attended church. It was my fueling station for the week. Without God's encouraging Word I had little strength to make it through to the next day, let alone another six. At the end of each service it was extremely difficult to get up and leave my place of inspirational refreshing, so I would remain seated in the pew, immobile and unmotivated to move. Returning to reality was too painful. There, immersed in God's presence, I felt secure, comforted, and at peace.

Outside the confines of the sanctuary walls is where our young family and each one of our lives was crumbling apart, where we were overwhelmed by a situation we couldn't control, and mourning the loss of joy we once shared. Sunday after Sunday, before picking the girls up from their Bible classes, I'd remain in a pew near the back, alone and glued to my spot, tears streaming down my face. Sitting there in brokenness while the congregation was exiting, passing right on by, pouring out of the building chatting, laughing, and discussing where they were going for lunch. It was as if I didn't exist. *Was I invisible?*

I was confused by their apathy. *Didn't they all just hear the same message of love that I had heard? Or were they hearing without perceiving?* Over the course of several months I could count on one hand the number of people who actually took the time to come over, ask how I was doing, or offer to pray with me. I was desperate for someone to care, to express a bit of concern, and extend a little compassion. With no immediate family around and friends who distanced themselves because they didn't know how to be supportive or chose not to be, I wasn't only miserable, but painfully alone. And the thought of losing my best friend intensified those feelings. I sincerely believed God could intervene and turn everything around, but would He? And if so, when?

It wasn't long before Steve began missing extended periods of work. Days swiftly turned into weeks, and after using all his sick leave and vacation time, no compensation was left for the intervals he remained bedridden. With no known cause or label to pin on his peculiar array of abnormalities, my ailing husband was not entitled to receive workers' compensation insurance. And since my income wasn't nearly enough to cover the mortgage and pay our bills, I began searching for a better-paying job and put my newer model Honda Civic EX up for sale.

As the screws tightened, Steve and I realized we would no longer be able to stay in the house we'd been living in for less than two years. Although none of us wanted to move, we had little choice. The unforeseen turn of events was crushing for Steve; he was beating himself up for not being the provider he wanted to be, for being the cause of our distress, and for letting us down.

In an effort to avoid causing him further heartache, I refrained from calling the realtor who sold us the house until Steve was at work. Picking up the phone was like lifting a 16-pound bowling ball. Its sheer weight took me back to my youth, a time when friends would dare me to call a boy I liked, not sure if the boy liked me and not knowing how he'd respond to hearing my voice. I was genuinely nervous and mentally unprepared to hear the answers to the questions that had been keeping me up at night.

Our property was in a very remote location, above the snowline in the Sierra Nevada Mountains, where the demand for housing was almost non-existent. People preferred living closer to town and out of the snow. And because houses in our region were only accessible by treacherous, zigzagging thoroughfares, they remained on the market for months.

When the realtor answered, I identified myself and explained our situation. "We really love this area and our house, but Steve's not doing well. He's very sick and has been missing a lot of work."

"I'm sorry to hear that," she responded empathetically.

"It's put us in a tough financial bind. If his condition doesn't improve soon, we're not going to be able to make the mortgage payments. We'll be forced to sell." I hesitated, tensely biting my lower lip. "How's the local housing market?" I queried.

"Slow," she answered. I wasn't surprised.

"Well in this market, how much do you think our house could sell for? And how long do you think it would take to sell?" I unloaded my questions praying for positive answers. We wouldn't be able to keep our heads above water if the property sat on the market for too long and we certainly couldn't afford to take a huge financial hit. I anxiously awaited her reply.

But instead of reeling out numbers and time frames, what she said was shocking. "Funny you should call," she started, "the Sacramento couple who made the contingent offer on your house before you bought it phoned me just yesterday. They finally sold their house and are looking again for horse property in *this* area!"

I couldn't believe what I was hearing! Grabbing my full attention, I instantly rose from the chair I'd been sitting in and stood up. "Really? No way!" I exclaimed both doubtful, yet extremely hopeful.

"It's true," she convincingly confirmed.

It felt as though I'd hit the jackpot when I was down to my last cent. Discouragement fled the room and my face lit up like the midday sun. I was thrilled! "That's great news!"

After hanging up the phone, I let out a huge sigh of relief, smiled, and immediately started praising God. *What is the likelihood of that?* The timing couldn't have been more perfect! As soon as Steve returned home, I shared the amazing news. With the improbable opportunity before us, we had to spring into action. There was no time to delay. The realtor came out to the house that evening and we listed the property.

The big city couple was overjoyed to hear that the house they had lost months earlier was back on the market. They couldn't wait to get in and see it. With a matched sense of urgency, they asked to come through on Easter Sunday, then again two days later. They were our only prospects. No one else ever came to look at the house. We gratefully accepted their offer of $20,000 more than what we paid!

God's incredible provision—that's what it was! No coincidences, no luck, simply provision in a believer's time of need. We gave our tenants a 30-day notice and moved back into the little blue house. I thought about how much I petitioned and prayed for that place to sell, I can only thank God that He doesn't answer "yes" to all our prayers. Can I get an Amen to that? He is the only One who can see into our future and help us avoid unnecessary pain and hardship. Even though it's extremely difficult at times, we need to trust that He always knows and does what's best.

If our little blue house had sold, there would have been no place else for us to go. Even with nearly perfect credit, our inconsistent income would have prohibited us from buying or renting elsewhere. Considering the circumstances, the prompt sale, the additional cash, along with the ability to move back into our former residence, was the best-case scenario. The familiar place was affordable and offered a sense of solace. The girls returned to their former school and reunited with old friends. We settled in to what would become our "new normal."

Being absent from work for days on end led Steve's employer to begin scheduling appointments with workers' compensation doctors. Their mission was to establish liability, doing everything necessary to identify the source of his problem and ascertain a diagnosis. Neck strain was the first of many analyses. Since the majority of his workday was spent looking down into a microscope, the verdict made sense. Steve was given a neck brace and paid time off. Weeks passed and all that helped were the insurance payments.

By March 1999, Steve no longer had a job because he had missed so much work. At the termination of his disability leave, he was still suffering miserably. Although he would have rather returned to work, leaving all his pain and frustration behind, that wasn't going to happen.

We were hoping his condition would improve, but his symptoms not only intensified, they multiplied—and none seemed to be related. The incongruity stumped all Steve's physicians and neurologists. One by one, as they run out of ideas, recommendations, and referrals, they abandoned his case and gave up trying to help. Without establishing liability or being able to properly diagnose his condition, workers' compensation refused to continue paying.

This enormous kick in the gut knocked the last lingering whisper of wind out of our sails. *What were we going to do now?* My partner and I were physically and emotionally whipped. We had no fight left in us. We didn't even have the strength to wave our white flag of surrender. The healthcare fiasco was grueling. And with it came a deep longing to be back home with my mom, surrounded by family who would willingly offer their love and support.

The day after our wedding we left for California, promising our parents we would return. The idea seldom crossed my mind, but the need for emotional support was mounting, more so for me than Steve or the girls. It was a daily challenge dealing with a husband who was in chronic pain. I quickly learned that a very fine line exists between pain and anger. They are so close there is little distinction between the two. Usually unbeknownst to the one struggling to cope, pain is frequently expressed as anger and is unleashed on the one who is closest to them. In this case, that person just happened to be me.

With Steve unable to work, there was no longer any reason for us to stay in California. I desperately needed emotional support and the girls wanted to get acquainted with their extended family. As an incentive to return, Steve's parents had repeatedly dangled a carrot in front of us—a gift of five acres on the back of their ten-acre wooded parcel where my husband spent his childhood. It was a sweet and tempting offer.

The location was perfect; it was in a highly desirable school district and the property bordered a large nature preserve with trails and a lake. We never seriously considered taking them up on the offer until now. It had been 16 years since we left Michigan, and although I was more than ready to move back, my other half had reservations...so I made a proposition.

"Instead of hiring a realtor, let's overprice this little blue house, run a single line ad one time in the free local classified paper, and see what happens." Steve was intrigued. "That would leave the entire decision-making process to God. If it's His will for us to return to Michigan, He could make that one little line ad work."

"But the house is old and has so many things wrong with it," he protested.

"Okay, then let's agree not to budge at all on price, and if *any* repairs need to be done, they will be the buyer's responsibility." I recapped the game plan, "A full price offer from a single ad means we sell the house and move back to the Great Lakes State." Steve contemplated the odds, and since they were stacked in his favor (against moving), he reluctantly agreed to roll the dice.

This was a life-changing decision that would affect the entire family, so Steve and I set the sale price high enough to make it worth our while. The girls and I prayed for God's will to be done and eagerly waited to see what He was going to do.

The ad generated three showings, and although every prospective buyer thought the house was cute, the prevailing comment was that the ceilings were too low. When the mountain dwelling was constructed in the early 1900s the ceilings were only as high as the carpenter could reach—just a hair over six feet. When the final prospects came through, they loved the house despite the ceilings, and returned the following day with a full price offer! We were stunned! We weren't prepared for such an unlikely and immediate answer. The last time we tried selling the little blue house for thousands less, there was zero interest. After accepting their offer we started deliberating, seriously weighing out the pros and cons of moving.

Our future was hanging in the balance. It could go either way. A thorough inspection still had to be done, but we were halfway home. Although Steve had restored much of the 100-year old structure and we weren't aware of any problems, we were certain the inspector would find something. The girls and I continued to seek God's will, trusting He would do what was in our best interest.

As anticipated, the inspection uncovered a few minor issues, but also a major one. The septic system was fully functional, but completely outdated. The cost of bringing it up to code and in compliance with regulatory standards was $5,000! The house could not change hands without the septic system being modernized.

Since Steve and I had agreed to an all-or-nothing deal, if the buyers wanted to renegotiate the sale price after being informed of the findings, we wouldn't have to follow through with the transaction. We'd have our answer. But if God wanted us back with family, He was going to have to pull some strings because paying for repairs was not part of the agreement.

When the buyers were presented with the inspector's report, instead of asking us to reduce the price in order to compensate for the expensive repair like anyone else would have done, they responded by saying, "That's okay, we'll take care of it!"

*What? You've got to be kidding! No going back to the negotiating table?* That is absurd! Absolutely unheard of in any real estate deal! They wanted the house, were willing to pay full price, and they even agreed to do all the necessary repairs at their expense! It was a done deal. Divine intervention. We had our answer. From that point on we commenced packing our bags, setting our navigational course northeast toward the mitten, optimistic about the future.

Chapter 5

# Life Turned Upside Down

*Therefore I tell you, do not worry about your life,
what you will eat or drink;
or about your body, what you will wear.
Is not life more important than food, and the body more
important than clothes?
Look at the birds of the air;
they do not sow or reap or store away in barns,
and yet your heavenly Father feeds them.
Are you not much more valuable than they?
Who of you by worrying can add a single hour to your life?*[36]

While the girls and I were trusting God's direction, Steve remained unconvinced that the right decision was being made. Nonetheless, he, Holly, and Bear boarded the heavily weighed down 17-foot U-Haul with car in tow while Jenni, Jazz, and I followed in our red Pontiac Sunbird. It was a long trip back east. For five days we tolerated traveling in the slow lane of I-80 at a reduced speeds, our two restless dogs, fast food joints, and budget motels. We even withstood a passing tornado at a Nebraska truck stop. It was an adventure that we hoped would lead to a promising future.

In the Sermon on the Mount Jesus warned against

something we all tend to do in times of transition or uncertainty—worry. Worry insinuates a lack of faith because it focuses on self and limitations rather than on God and possibilities. It also causes stress, and if allowed to linger, can elicit fear and hopelessness. There is danger in allowing worry to take root. That's why Jesus gave us an effective strategy for overcoming it—deliberately shift your focus away from the source of anxiety and onto the only One who can calm your distress with perpetual peace.

Jesus told His followers, "Do not worry or be anxious with troubles and cares concerning your life."[37] "Do not be afraid."[38] Your Father knows what you need, even before you ask, He will provide.[39]

Instead of dwelling on difficulties and dilemmas, the Bible teaches us to, "Cast all your anxieties on him (God) because he cares for you."[40] Divert your apprehensive energy toward seeking God—His kingdom and His righteousness.[41] Tranquility will follow.

Having relinquished our anxieties to God and readjusting our focus, we proceeded with confidence. Reconnecting with family and old friends was wonderful, but the greatest joy was sharing our beautiful daughters with their grandparents. Despite our best efforts, the long distance relationships were difficult to maintain. Phone calls, letters, birthday cards, Christmas gifts, and periodic visits just didn't equate to being physically involved in each other's lives. Finally the girls had an opportunity to get to know their extended family…and I was excited!

As promised, we acquired the back five acres of my in-laws' property, and after finding a contractor, we designed a Cape Cod style house that would be custom-built to our specifications. The spacious three-bedroom, two-bath home would have a full basement, two-stall garage, and eight-foot ceilings. It was a mansion compared to our little blue house, but it took twelve long months to complete. For six months, the four of us somehow managed to function in Steve's parent's musty Michigan basement with just a couch, a television, a refrigerator, and a computer desk. Upstairs we shared a bedroom with two full-size beds. When a family friend asked if we wanted to housesit over the winter, dust clouds formed behind our feet, we couldn't vacate the premises fast enough!

Before leaving California, Steve's father and my mother expressed serious concern regarding impending employment. "What are you going to do for work?" they'd ask. They were both advising me to get a "real" job so I could become the primary breadwinner.

While I understood their anxiety, my entrepreneurial spirit did not. Before Steve became ill, I successfully owned, operated, and profited from the sale of both a small retail store and a direct mail coupon book. I also had several years of direct sales and marketing experience in advertising and home party sales. I was willing to work hard, but I recognized the need for a flexible schedule to care for Steve and be available for the girls.

After selling the retail store we purchased the *Mountain Money Saver* coupon book. It was a joint enterprise—I sold advertising and Steve helped lay out ads in the evening after work. Since the two of us ran a lucrative direct mail coupon book business for a couple years in the Golden State, we were convinced we could launch a similar enterprise in Grand Rapids, Michigan and be successful. Weeks of preliminary research revealed that almost every town across the U.S. had a free "buy & sell" paper, full of nothing but classified and display advertising, but to our surprise, metropolitan Grand Rapids did not!

I began exploring the prospect of taking on such an endeavor as soon as the little blue house went under contract. And Steve was on board. It appeared as though God opened the door wide for us to step right in and grab hold of the opportunity. By the time we left California, over 50 grocery stores, restaurants, and gas stations had committed to being distribution points for our free pick up paper. That was an encouraging start.

As soon as the U-Haul was unpacked, it was time to get to work. I spent hours making phone calls, scheduling appointments, and meeting local business owners. My sales job was two-fold—I not only had to solicit advertising, I had to sell prospects on the concept and effectiveness of advertising in the unfamiliar media source.

Together, Steve and I worked into the wee hours of the night designing and laying out ads to get the paper ready for publication. When pallets of newsprint were dropped on our doorstep, we stuffed them into the car, and spent the next four days delivering them to various locations in a 30-mile radius throughout Kent County. *The Hometown Shopper* was a success!

For three years we worked hard at improving the monthly publication. Even while Steve continued to struggle with chronic headaches and persistent nausea, spending an ample part of his day in bed, he devoted the majority of his wake time to the business. But as the months progressed, so did his mysterious disease. On top of his existing ailments, he was battling fatigue, insomnia, ringing in the ears, anxiety, concentration difficulties, confusion, and depression. Test after test revealed nothing. Prescription drugs offered little relief.

One advantage to being in a new area was the hope of finding a specialist who could examine Steve's case afresh and advance his care in a positive direction. However, after following a long string of referrals, there was still no progress. When his latest neurologist hit the wall, advising us to look elsewhere for answers, our hearts sank.

Few words were spoken on the drive home from these final visits. Like a sailboat without wind, we found ourselves numbly bobbing up and down in the water with no direction and no power to propel forward. For years we'd been searching for a cause, a cure, or some form of treatment that would be helpful. Our efforts were not only exhausting, they were incredibly exasperating, and Steve looked as though he'd aged considerably. The daily struggle of trying to cope was beating him down. He had little fight left in him to continue the pursuit, but I was unwilling to lie down and accept defeat.

This time the neurologist wasn't the only one who had reached the end of his rope; the coals inside me burned red hot. Walking out to the car after that appointment, I didn't utter a word. *Unbelievable! Here we were again.* Shaking my head in disbelief, I wondered: *How is it that not one of these medical professionals has been able to figure out Steve's problem?* I slid into the driver's seat and waited for my passenger to close his door before shooting flaming arrows of interrogation his way.

"What's the big secret?" I demanded. "Tell me everything about your past profession." Angry eyes honed in on my target, "What *exactly* did you do? What *exactly* were you exposed to? What is it you're not allowed to tell anyone? What is destroying your life—our lives?" I was pleading for him to break his vow of silence. "Please? We have to get to the bottom of this in order to get you some *real* help."

Steve's 16-year occupation required security clearance and was considered "classified," which meant he was sworn to secrecy about anything having to do with it, and up 'til now he had never disclosed a thing. When he accepted the position he had to sign papers and take a vow of silence; I was told never to ask about his job, and I never did. But this fiasco had gone on far too long; my patience had reached its limit. I was no longer willing to play by the rules. Game over. I pressed for answers. Like a naughty child avoiding his mother's stare while being scolded, Steve gazed out the passenger's side window and slowly began to open up, fully disclosing what he'd spent years working on and the hazardous materials he'd been exposed to. Most of the terms he was spewing out, I'd never even heard of.

He informed me that his symptoms emerged shortly after he began building and testing high-powered microwave amplifiers for cell tower base stations. He was spending as much as 50 hours a week peering through a microscope with close-range exposure to non-ionizing radiofrequency microwave (RF/MW) radiation—the same power that's used to transmit wireless communication signals. Although I was ignorant of the energy, the word "radiation" gave rise to concern.

Upon sharing this information with a young neurologist some time later, he suggested a strong correlation might exist between the unusual disorder and Steve's extreme, long-term occupational exposure. Based on all the research I was finding online, that was a very definite probability. The scientific data supported similar adverse health effects resulting from non-ionizing RF/MW radiation exposure.[42] As a matter of fact, medical experts from around the globe were recognizing, diagnosing, and treating an epidemic the Russians labeled "Microwave Sickness." However, western physicians either remain ignorant of the disease or were refusing to acknowledge it.

I wasn't completely sold on the premise that Steve was suffering from Microwave Sickness, but there was strong evidence to uphold the theory. For example, one day when our computer crashed, my partner described in detail what was wrong with the device and how it needed to be fixed. We drove across town to Best Buy to bring our PC in for repair. We waited in line to speak with a tech, and when it was our turn, we approached the counter. "What seems to be the problem?" the technician asked.

I turned to Steve and waited for him to give his explanation, but instead of answering the question, he stood there staring blankly at the young man. "Tell him what's wrong with the computer," I urged.

He looked at me but remained mute as a statue. The man was becoming a bit agitated as the line behind us grew. "Steve?" I patiently and inquisitively paused, "Just tell him what you told me back at the house." The technician and I exchanged glances anticipating some sort of response, but we never got one.

"Is he okay?" The question didn't have to be asked or answered. It was apparent by my stunned expression and my husband's empty, unresponsive state that he was *not* okay.

I left the computer and gently took hold of Steve's arm, guiding him out to the car, and helping him inside. Since entering the store, his skin had become inflamed, turning a bright fire-engine red. It was as if his entire body had gotten horribly sunburn while in the store. After closing his door I stood in the parking lot, looking around for any clue that would make sense of the inexplicable phenomenon. Then across the street I spotted one of the largest, most elaborate cell towers I had ever seen. The sheer number of relay panels signified its immense power. That had to be the answer—Steve's long-term exposure must have heightened his sensitivity to the high levels of non-ionizing RF/MW being emitted from the structure. The radiation also must have caused his skin to burn and his entire neurological system to shut down.

This was the first of many exposure-related episodes that totally incapacitated my dear husband and kept him bedridden for days, temporarily disabling his neurological system, along with his cognitive and communication skills. Everyone to whom I divulged the unusual connection with disputed it. "Certainly, if wireless signals were dangerous, we'd know about it…"

Shortly after becoming aware of the trigger that was setting Steve off, we received a phone call from his primary care physician's office. The practice had been sold. You can't even begin to imagine my overzealous reaction when I was informed that the doctor who bought the practice studied in Russia. I was absolutely sure God put him in that position to answer our prayers; especially after learning he was familiar with Microwave Sickness. An appointment couldn't be scheduled soon enough.

When we finally met the new MD, I asked him to educate us on the disease and tell us everything he knew about it. He was more than happy to oblige, demonstrating his level of expertise in the area and elaborating on every query I threw at him. After more than 15 minutes of back and forth Q&A, I was confident we had found a doctor who could identify Steve's quandary and steer us in the right direction for treatment. "We need your help," I declared.

Suddenly, as if flipping a switch with that one statement, the smile that had lit up his face vanished; the enthusiasm with which he expressed himself and conveyed his in-depth knowledge of the disease came to a screeching halt. His eyes grew wide, his eyebrows rose, and his entire demeanor changed. Inhaling deeply, he looked at us as if we were two predatory animals honing in our prey, backing him into a corner. He was unmistakably frightened—No terrified!

His reaction was mind-blowing! We didn't understand it; it seemed completely irrational and unjustified. Feeling overtly threatened, his fight-or-flight response instinctively kicked in and he resorted to a defensive, self-preservation mode. Lifting his hands to his chest, he furiously began pushing the idea away as if we were coming at him with a knife. Backing his way toward the exit to escape, he intensely and very adamantly refused our petition for help. "No! No! I cannot help you. No! Not here in the United States. No! No!" The resounding reverberation of his refusals followed as he swiftly slipped out the door, shutting it tightly behind.

Steve and I were dumbfounded. Extremely taken back, confused, and discouraged. He was supposed to be our answer to prayer. *What was he so afraid of?* I became infuriated, appalled that this medical doctor who had validated the existence of the peculiar disease, had all the answers we'd spent years searching for, and had even taken a vow to help people in need, flat out refused to provide Steve with the medical attention he so desperately needed and rightfully deserved. Just because we live in a country where the adverse health effects of non-ionizing RF/MW radiation (wireless signals) on the human body are concealed, doesn't erase the fact they exist.

A growing deficit in Steve's cognitive abilities was becoming evident. He was having difficulty concentrating, retaining pertinent information, and was easily confused. These developments caused him to make an increasing number of mistakes on the paper. Within a relatively short period of time, it escalated to the point where he would enter our home office, sit down at his desk, and stare blankly at the computer screen, oblivious to what he was supposed to do or how he was supposed to do it. His incompetence forced us to sell the business we had worked so hard to build.

I can't even begin to tally the countless hours Steve and I

would sit in our office chairs knee-to-knee, hand-in-hand, sobbing, feeling so painstakingly helpless and wishing something could be done to improve his incapacitating condition. The girls and I continued crying out to the Lord, praying for improvement, and pleading for a speedy recovery, but nothing seemed to be happening.

Steve's mother, who was in the early stages of dementia, made it her daily routine to walk over to the house. Since her son was usually in bed, she'd ask why. All previous conversations concerning his health seemed to be a blur. In an effort to jog her memory, I'd recap the situation. Each time she'd get upset at the devastating news as if hearing it for the first time, and we'd both end up crying. The vicious cycle was exhausting. And to make matters worse, as soon as she left, Brian, Steve's younger brother born with cerebral palsy, would wander back to the house. Trying to explain what was happening to his best friend was equally challenging.

For months a continuous stream of tears flowed from my eyes. They were persistently bloodshot, swollen, and burning with pain. Living such a nightmare was devastating. The mournful sobbing bouts were all consuming; not only did they invade my everyday life, they overtook my prayer time. On my knees, broken before God, there was little else I could do but weep.

My heart was breaking, our lives were shattering, and it was painstakingly obvious we weren't the only ones being affected by the distressing chain of events. Steve's affliction was also taking a hefty toll on the girls. They were both grieving the absence of their father's involvement in their lives and struggling to cope with the emotional trauma of losing him to some elusive malady. In less than five years time, their lives had been completely uprooted and turned upside down.

As a new driver, Jenni was coping by staying away from home as much as possible, busying herself with school, work, and friends. The only time she returned was to sleep. I really missed her, but totally understood her need to escape the desolate situation.

Holly's mode of survival was barely that. She was becoming extremely withdrawn and depressed, spending every day after school in her room with the shades drawn and the lights out—suffering miserably. Unbeknownst to me, she was cutting herself with sharp objects to physically mask the deep emotional torment she had no control over.

Individual and family counseling offered little support. Steve's illness was progressing, and unless he got suitable medical attention to put him on the road to recovery or God healed him, I didn't see how our predicament was going to improve. Since we were grieving the loss of someone who rarely got out of bed and was as good as dead, I searched for grief counseling support groups, but they only seemed to exist for cancer patients and their loved ones.

Here we were, sitting in another physician's office anxiously waiting for the results of yet another test. It'd been weeks since making the appointment. Steve and I were fighting to be optimistic because this specialist had expert training in the area of hazardous exposures and their impact on the human body. Maybe he held the key that would unlock this ongoing enigma. When the stocky, red-haired man in the white lab coat stepped into the room, we intuitively reached for each other's hand. *This was going to be our answer. We just knew it.*

Pulling up a chair from across the room, the doctor sat down in front of us. A taunting smile swept across his face as he opened his mouth. "I have good news!" My husband and I squeezed hands, leaning forward to absorb all the data the test results disclosed. With a cutting grin, he mockingly announced, "There's absolutely nothing wrong with you!"

In that instant, the cork that contained years of pent-up anger and frustration popped. Steve lunged forward. I hastily flew in between the two men, keeping my ordinarily mild-mannered husband from seizing the physician's throat. "What do you mean there's nothing wrong with me? *Everything's* wrong with me!" Steve lashed out.

"That just can't be right! There's got to be some mistake!" I exclaimed. I attempted to explain all we'd been through—Steve's myriad of symptoms, how many medical professionals he'd seen, our extreme level of irritation and escalating impatience—so he'd understand Steve's aggressive outburst. But he had no empathy.

In his blistering aggravation and with the increasing severity of his condition, Steve openly expressed thoughts of suicide.

"I'm sorry, there's nothing I can do." The all-too-familiar words trailed the doctor right out the door.

To our surprise, within 24 hours of that visit, a sheriff cruiser pulled up into our driveway. The official got out, approached the house, handcuffed Steve, and hurled him into the back seat of the squad car as if he was a felonious criminal. He was taken to a psychiatric ward against his will where he was locked up in a padded cell.

I wasn't home at the time, but as soon as I returned, the girls told me what had happened. I quickly grabbed my father-in-law and rushed to the facility where Steve was being held. The staff members adamantly refused to release him! Instead, they kept him imprisoned for one full week—the week before Christmas. Every day I visited and pleaded for his discharge, but my numerous appeals were repeatedly denied. His freedom was finally granted Christmas Eve day.

That was the worst Christmas ever. Steve didn't want anyone coming over and he didn't go anywhere. He was overly paranoid of everyone and everything for weeks after the traumatic incident.

Like a rat trapped in a maze looking for cheese, I was desperately running around searching for answers, hitting the wall at every turn. After prayerfully starting a new online search, I began conversing with a woman who'd spent years researching the field of electromagnetic radiation. She recommended that Steve see a toxic exposure specialist in Los Angeles, California. While finances were tight, she promised it would be well worth the trip.

I thank God for His leading, because we finally got the only diagnosis that ever made sense—toxic encephalopathy, a neurological disorder caused by exposure to neurotoxic organic solvents, and progressive frontal lobe brain damage, resulting from Steve's long-term, close-range exposure to non-ionizing radiofrequency microwave radiation. The prognosis? A brain tumor or brain cancer.

Since nothing could be done to repair, reverse, or aid his condition, the only benefit to having an actual, evidence-based diagnosis was that it was a necessary requirement to apply for Social Security Disability. To date, Steve had never received an all-encompassing diagnosis for his peculiar array of symptoms. Although he had undergone extensive testing, no one had ever been able to pinpoint his exact disorder. Jumping through hoops to qualify for the insurance Steve had paid into since he first started working was not an easy process. Without proper medical equipment to duplicate the findings, there was no way for the Social Security doctors to validate his condition. For that reason alone, he was denied benefits the first two times he applied. Along with his health, his self-esteem was diminishing.

Now it was up to me to figure out how to make ends meet. Since I wasn't interested in a traditional 8-5 job, I used the money from the sale of our publication to enroll in a real estate class to become a licensed realtor. Selling real estate is no get-rich-quick scheme; it's a career that takes years to build. We were in a tough predicament, but I believed God would come through for us—and He did!

In less than a year, without a familiar name, without being associated with a well-known broker or real estate company, without any experience, or clientele, God blessed me with three closings—all with random strangers! Isn't that incredible? Those three commission checks paid our bills for months!

During that time, I was introduced to a mortgage broker/realtor who was recruiting real estate agents to originate mortgages. Recognizing the value of offering this additional service, I invited Keith over to show me how to process and submit my first mortgage application. He spent two-and-a-half hours walking me through the step-by-step process.

Keith was kind, attractive, patient, and professional. While escorting him to the front door, thanking him for his time and the opportunity, a very unusual thought crossed my mind—*If I weren't married, I'd go out with him!*

Like everyone else, I thought Steve's extreme sensitivity to the invisible waves and intense power emanating from cell towers was extremely bizarre, but to convince me of his implausible ability to detect the signals, we'd play a game of sorts. While I drove down the highway, he'd drop his head, close his eyes, and point in the direction of every cell tower we passed! In addition to other oddities such as painful MRIs and burning sensations from airport screening detectors, I became a believer.

Beginning with the Best Buy incident, Steve's reaction to close-range cell tower exposure remained consistent—within minutes his entire body would be covered with a bright red rash and his neurological system would shut down, producing such debilitating consequences he'd be bedridden for days! For that reason, he rarely left the house or went into town.

Realizing the extent of this perilous problem, you can begin to imagine my fury when the postal carrier informed me that our neighbor had signed a contract with AT&T to erect a cell tower on his adjoining property!

In tears of rage, panic, and disbelief, I frantically sped over to the township hall where the zoning administrator confirmed the news and attempted to calm my fears by assuring me the residents would never approve of a tower being placed in that location. But I had done enough research to know better. There was absolutely nothing she or anyone else could do to prohibit the placement of a cell tower once a signed agreement exists between a landowner and a wireless carrier. The only public decision is tower style, not whether or not the tower can be erected.

To add fuel to the fire, according to The 1996 Telecommunications Act, a law established by the cell phone industry, it is illegal to refute placement of a cell tower for health reasons! There was no way to fight the inevitable—the tower was going up.

This was yet another devastating blow in a long line of discouraging disappointments dictating the direction of our lives! Hysterical and unbelievably sick to my stomach, I stormed out of the township building and drove like a bat out of hell to regurgitate the news to my father-in-law who'd graciously given us the back half his property. We'd been in our newly constructed home for little less than three years—

and now this!

My heart plummeted. I didn't want to move, the girls wouldn't want to move, and Steve would be devastated, having already caused his family an over abundance of pain and anguish. We didn't need more stress; we were barely hanging on as it was. But we had no choice—we couldn't stay! What were we going to do? Where were we going to go?

Chapter 6

# Definite Desert Experience

*Be merciful to me, L*ORD*, for I am in distress;*
*my eyes grow weak with sorrow, my soul and body with grief.*
*My life is consumed by anguish and my years by groaning;*
*my strength fails because of my affliction,*
*and my bones grow weak.*[43]

"Dear friends, do not be surprised at the painful trial you are suffering, as though something strange were happening to you."[44] "In the world you will have tribulation *and* distress *and* suffering, but be courageous; I have overcome the world."[45] These words from the apostle Peter and Jesus tell us we should expect tough times. Life isn't always going to be easy, but through Him who loves us, we are victorious in every situation and over all our troubles.[46] "And if God is for us, who can be against us?"[47] Be courageous, confident, and full of joy because the Lord has already won every battle you will ever face.

Caught in crisis, overwhelmed by circumstances we weren't prepared to face, reminded me of the amazing story of King Jehoshaphat. Israel was being invaded; they were greatly outnumbered and powerless against the mighty army coming against them. The king prayed to the Lord, "We do not know what to do, but our eyes are on you."⁴⁸

Prior to marching toward the frontline, the nation received a message from God. "Do not be afraid; do not be discouraged because of this vast army. Go out to face them tomorrow, and the Lord will be with you."⁴⁹

Jehoshaphat rallied his troops by advising them to, "Have faith in the Lord your God and you will be upheld."⁵⁰ Then he appointed men to go out ahead of the army, worshippers to sing praises to the Lord. As they headed into battle, the Lord set up ambushes against the nation's aggressors. "When the men of Judah came to the place that overlooks the desert and looked toward the vast army, they saw only dead bodies lying on the ground; no one escaped."⁵¹

A newfound hope surged within me. Without the strength or desire to proceed, I recited the king's prayer—"We do not know what to do, but our eyes are on you." Trusting the Lord, I chose to relinquish my fear and discouragement. I knew He was with us. We would be upheld. He would direct our path and help us find a safe haven. We had to believe the outcome would be good.

Grabbing an encyclopedia off the shelf, I began flipping through pages to find the state with the least amount of people per square mile. I reasoned fewer people meant fewer cell towers. I also advocated that if we had to live in some remote place of refuge for Steve, the girls and I deserved to be somewhere sunny and warm. New Mexico topped the list.

Knowing absolutely nothing about New Mexico, I turned to the state map. It looked nothing like Michigan or California. Instead of being green with lakes and rivers of blue, the landscape was predominantly brown. In the upper left corner: Santa Fe. In the upper right corner: Albuquerque.

In the lower right: Sand. But the lower left offered a green splotch of promise—Silver City, located in the Gila (He-la) National Forest.

Pointing to the map, I spoke aloud, "City. City. Sand. Oh, here's a bold word. Silver City." Silver City was a small town of 10,000, nestled in the foothills of the Piños Altos Mountains.

That sounded like the kind of refuge Steve needed. So without hesitation, I went online to check housing prices and view available properties. Then I proceeded to schedule a showing for one of the listings that was very secluded and far from town. Since RF/MW radiation cannot penetrate lead or rock, the mountain barrier between the property and nearby cell towers prominently positioned on the highest peak, would serve as a long-term place of respite and protection. Little else was given as much consideration as Steve's health and wellbeing.

In March of 2004, over the girl's spring break, the four of us took a road trip out west. We weren't sure if Silver City would be a fit, but we had no time to waste. We had to move somewhere—and fast. Once the tower was up, it would be too late.

Time was not on our side. There was a race among wireless carriers to erect as many cell towers as possible in the shortest amount of time to ensure maximum coverage. Verizon was airing millions of commercials with the nerdy guy asking the one question every cell phone user wanted answered with a "yes." "Can you hear me now?" Trying to run from the rapid expansion of towers would be a never-ending nightmare. We needed a permanent solution. And this could be it.

The drive through the Land of Enchantment from Albuquerque to Silver City was uninspiring. For hours the scenery never changed—nothing but dirt and rocks; there were few trees and no color except varying shades of tan. But in contrast, the sky was the most astonishing blue I'd ever seen and the sun shone brilliantly. With miles of barren landscape behind us, we were finally approaching our destination. I was hopeful that green splotch on the map would prove to have some real significance. As we drove over the hill leading to the city, the panoramic scene changed. It was as if we had found the state's hidden treasure, an exquisite flower emerging from a sun-dried cactus. There were mountains, trees, and life! It was stunningly breathtaking!

The realtor I spoke with over the phone led us into the 2.7 million acre Gila National Forest to inspect the property. The house was actually *in* the forest. We'd already been driving fifteen minutes when the road split, sending us down a long, dusty two-track. We snaked our way around rocks and trees with limited visibility. Not being able to see oncoming vehicles made this route tremendously treacherous, so we proceeded with caution.

Half-hour from town the track abruptly stopped. In its place was a creek bed full of massive rocks with water trickling through. I wish I'd given some thought to what that creek might look like after a heavy rain, but that eye-popping experience would be reserved for later. At a turtle's pace, I continued shadowing the four-by-four in front of us. There was no way our Toyota Camry would survive the abuse of driving through what appeared to be the scattered remains of a blown-up mountain on a regular basis.

After the rough, uncomfortable ride over boulders that hammered the underside of our vehicle, I was relieved to turn off onto a fairly smooth dirt driveway. The setting of the ten-acre parcel was magnificent! Mountains closely surrounded its perimeter on two sides. The three-bedroom, two-bath dwelling, near the back of the property, offered amazing mountain views from the sunroom and living room windows. There was a seasonal creek, a large fenced-in garden, a greenhouse, a shed, a two-stall garage converted into living space, plus the landscape was adorned with hundreds of large Pines and Junipers. The place was picturesque—but more importantly, it provided the protection Steve needed.

Together we prayed about it, and with the girls' permission, we made an offer contingent on the sale of our northern home. Within a week, the place we had loved and called home for less than three years was on the market. None of us were looking forward to the move and that consumed Steve with feelings of guilt. He didn't want his girls displaced on account of him. He would have preferred us to stay put, but we all knew full well that a tower less than a hundred yards from the house would have devastating consequences and paralyzing effects. A huge sacrifice had to be made. Moving wasn't an option.

At the end of the month Jenni was graduating from Rockford High School and we were very proud of her. Holly however, would be starting high school in Silver City. She despised the thought. We checked out the facility while we were there. It was nothing like Rockford's state-of-the-art institution, recognized for being one of the nation's top schools in academic achievement. Silver City High School was the exact opposite; the building was significantly older, the grounds were littered with trash, the students were less respectful of their teachers, and on a national scale, New Mexico schools rank near the bottom in academic excellence.

Ten days after listing the house with Keith, the realtor who'd taught me how to process mortgages, we were presented with an offer close to our asking price. It was bittersweet. We, like the wireless service providers, were on a race against time. Once construction on the cell tower commenced, there would be fewer prospects—maybe there wouldn't be any. That was not a risk we could afford to take. Waving the Buy/Sell Agreement in front of my husband's face I asserted, "This is our ticket to ride. We can either take it or haggle and chance losing the deal."

Not wanting to be part of any decision that moved us from where we wanted to stay to somewhere we didn't want to go, Steve looked at me with tear-filled eyes. Together, standing in the garage with the door open, we gazed out over the forest of budding trees on the edge of our property in silence, brooding over our precarious predicament. Steve knew the property like the back of his hand, having spent his entire childhood here. Building our dream home in such beautiful surroundings and being reunited with family and friends had truly been a blessing—now we were being forced to leave it all behind.

Slowly shuffling his feet, he stared down at the ground contemplating our dilemma. Then sadly conceded. "We have to take it."

"You're right. We do." I softly and reluctantly agreed. The buyers were surprised we didn't counter their offer. They expected us to and were willing to pay more, but we chose not to prolong the agony of defeat.

With well wishes from family and friends, along with hope and a prayer, we were back in another U-Haul, dragging our pets and belongings halfway across the country to a modest three-bedroom, two-bath ranch style home in the wilderness. At that time the address couldn't even be found on MapQuest! The property was so remote that in the four years we lived there, two mountain lion kills took place at the end of our driveway and there were multiple bear sightings. Only three sounds could ever be heard—howling wolves, chirping birds, and the blustery breeze. It was serene and beautiful, but it was also the epitome of isolation. I loved the peace and quiet, but sometimes it only served to magnify the essence of our depressing quandary.

Our new habitat was completely different from any of our previous ones. The landscape was different, the people were different, and the culture was different. Holly hated school. She didn't fit in. Students were tough and threatening, disrespectful and rude. She felt particularly unsafe, because the high school girls were not at all tolerant of white female newcomers. After pursuing several educational alternatives, including sending her back to live with my mother and stepfather to attend an equally unknown school in Michigan, she returned to Silver High.

Jenni got hired as a server at a Chinese restaurant and was taking college classes at Western New Mexico University. My job was caring for Steve since it was no longer safe for him to be home alone. Although he still spent the majority of time in bed, when he did get up he was extremely unstable and exceedingly confused. Even so, this proved to be a very good move for him. Aside from his declining physical and mental capacities, he was experiencing tremendous relief from the constant pressure on his brain.

However, the ongoing day-in and day-out drag was weighing heavy on me; it was all-consuming and life-sucking. I couldn't escape it. As Steve's health continued its downward spiral, it felt as though our entire world was imploding, I was deeply concerned about our family and its future. Our lives had been orbiting around Steve and his disease now for almost ten years.

Physicians in the new community had nothing more to offer to improve the man's quality of life. Unlike a battle with cancer where there is a progression of steps that can be taken toward the hope of healing and support groups to encourage one another through a journey of common challenges, we suffered alone. I longed to be surrounded by people who could identify and empathize with Steve's brain damage abnormalities as well as other difficulties our family was facing, but we were on an island of our own, each existing in our own private hell.

You can imagine my gratitude when I was introduced to a man in his early 40s who suffered a traumatic brain injury and shared similar symptoms. Steve finally had someone he could talk to, someone who could relate to his feelings and understand what he was going through. I was just as thankful to learn that Joe had a wife who shared some of my struggles. The two of them were in a support group for traumatic brain injury victims; with so many parallels, they invited us to the upcoming meeting. We were overjoyed!

The group was made up of people who had suffered severe head trauma and their spouses who were finding ways to deal with their unusual quirks. While unfortunate for all in attendance, it was comforting to be part of an empathetic group who warmly accepted us into the fold. That was until the meeting's end when the group leader pulled us aside to point out that Steve's brain damage was cumulative, not instantaneous like theirs, therefore we didn't fit in and weren't welcome back!

Although we kept in touch with Joe and his wife, it still felt as though we were suffering alone. The burden of our wretched lives was becoming far too great for me to bear. I can't count the number of times I'd sit on the edge of our bed weeping, watching the man I love sleep, attempting to evade the world he no longer felt part of.

While the Enemy worked diligently to convince me I was powerless against the invisible antagonist that was threatening to destroy our family, the Lord gave me strength to step out onto the spiritual battleground to fight through the pain with the only weapons I possessed—prayer and praise. Despite my lack of energy, I refused to quit praising God and trusting Him for a healing victory.

Every day I *chose* to fight the strong currents pushing against me, treading water and clinging to God's promises to keep from being swept under. The daily exercise was so taxing that on multiple occasions Steve's psychiatrist offered to write me a prescription for anti-depressants. While the thought of a pain-numbing drug was tempting, I knew it would do nothing to improve the situation.

In its place, I decided to take another stab at family counseling, but it only served to aggravate my frustration when the counselor insisted on seeing weekly progress and improvement. *Well yeah, we all would have liked to see that!* After weeks with no measurable success, we were involuntarily dropped from the program.

Moments of clarity were becoming less and less frequent. My spouse's brain damage was accelerating to the point where he could no longer communicate in any depth. He was unable to follow threads of conversation and was more easily confused. As long as we spoke to him as a young child, he could comprehend and correspond. If he happened to stumble out of bed to watch television, during the commercials I'd ask what program we were watching, he never had a clue. He even confessed that sometimes he didn't know who I was! So after 24 years of marriage, I dug out our wedding photos and placed them around the house to help ease his anxiety.

Every morning Steve would get up for an hour or two only to retreat to the bedroom for the remainder of the day. I'd head out to the sunroom and talk to the only One who truly able to understood my agony and heartache. I'd spend hours sitting in my powder blue Adirondack chair talking to my Best Friend, reading His Word, and enjoying the breathtaking mountain view He so graciously blessed me with. It was my time to press in, pour out, question, and contemplate. But moreover, accept the fact that I may never understand the purpose of our pain or the reason for our suffering. My role was to simply trust God—no matter what. His desire is that we "live by faith and not by sight,"[52] believing His Word and acknowledging that His ways are higher than our ways, and His thoughts are higher than our thoughts.[53]

God's message of encouragement is as prevalent today as when it was spoken through His prophet Isaiah:

> I have chosen you from the ends of the earth and have not rejected you. So do not fear for I am with you; do not be dismayed (discouraged or disheartened thinking what you're going through is hopeless; and do not look around in terror), for I am with you. I will strengthen you and help you (and harden you to difficulties); I will hold you up and retain you with my righteous right hand (a hand of power and salvation).[54] I am the LORD your God, who takes hold of your right hand and says to you, Do not fear; I will help you.[55]

I continued trusting God would come through for us and fought to believe His timing would be perfect, but why was He taking sooooooooo long? Evenings were especially difficult. The girls were usually working, out with friends, or hiding in their rooms with the doors closed in an effort to avoid the extreme darkness that filled the house. Just as before, they were distancing themselves from the problem in order to cope.

In an effort to alleviate some of my pain I turned to alcohol. I know it wasn't the best choice, but it served as a temporary coping mechanism in the evenings. Better than anti-depressant drugs, I reasoned. Months later, I began to feel as though I was consuming an unhealthy amount of booze. I prayed God would remove my desire and keep me from drinking.

That night sitting in front of the TV, depressed and alone, I thoughtlessly got up and made my way to the refrigerator. I reached in, pulled out an unopened bottle of wine, grabbed the corkscrew, and began twisting it into the cork. When I pressed the levers down to pull the cork up and out of the bottle, the cork wouldn't budge. I tried and tried to get it to move, but it wouldn't.

Then I remembered my prayer from earlier in the day, I smiled, and in agreement with God, I took the corkscrew out of the cork and returned the bottle to the fridge. In all my years of serving wine as a waitress and the bottles I've uncorked for myself, there was never a time when I had a problem getting the cork out of a bottle—until God intervened to answer my plea for help!

*I remember my affliction and my wandering (misery), the bitterness and the gall. I well remember them, and my soul is downcast within me. Yet this I call to mind and therefore I have hope: Because of the LORD's great love we are not consumed, for his compassions never fail. They are new every morning; great is your faithfulness. I say to myself, 'The LORD is my portion; I will wait (hope) for him.' The LORD is good to those whose hope is in him, to the one who seeks him. His loving kindness begins afresh each and every day.[56]*

Up to this point, my prayers had always been for Steve and the girls, seldom were they ever for me. Others prayed for me and with me, but the only prayer I ever remember praying for myself was, "Return already! Come get me (us) out of this mess!" The thought of facing another day like the one before was simply too much to bear. I just wanted the merry-go-round to stop so I could get off.

Since I didn't dare leave Steve unattended for extended periods of time, and we lived so far from town, I rarely left the house. Sunday was my only day out. I went to church with the girls, went grocery shopping, and hurried home. Sometimes, we'd go out to lunch, but it was a somber existence. My once jovial life had slowly been slipping away and was now completely gone. It disappeared without a trace and it was getting increasingly difficult to hang onto any recollection of "good times."

But here it was another bright, beautiful sunny morning. The girls were at school; Steve remained in his place of solitude; and I was out in the sunroom, back in my chair, crying out to the Lord through tears of anguish—just like the day before and the day before that—grieving the loss of joy we once shared, deeply saddened by Steve's suffering, and distressed over my inability to help.

While praying with my eyes closed, I had my first vision. I was forcibly being dragged, then yanked down into a deep, black abysmal chasm filled with thick, foul-smelling sludge. I was totally submerged, swallowed up, and imprisoned. Like wet cement, I could feel myself suffocating under the incredible weight that was enveloping me—completely engulfed, unable to move, powerless to escape. Years of pain and affliction landed me in this dreadful place.

Instantly my eyes shot open, while gulping in air and trying to shake the petrified feeling, they were drawn to a ragged white washcloth that must have been used to mop up a spill. It was in the corner of the room, waded up, and completely dried out by the sun. I sat staring at the piece of fabric for minutes. It captivated me. *What was it about the washrag that had me so entranced? Why couldn't I turn away?*

Then God opened my eyes to see—it was a mirror image of me! I burst into tears. Steve's incurable, irreversible malady had sucked the life right out of me. There was nothing left. That ratty, old worn-out dehydrated piece of material was useless in the shape it was in...and so was I. The Lord made it clear I could no longer exist in my present condition, I needed to move forward, but I couldn't do it on my own—He assured me that I wouldn't have to.

That morning I prayed for myself in a way I never had. Suffocating in the black abyss and finding my identity in that dried up, dirty old dishrag was not the way I wanted to live. And it wasn't the way God wanted me to live. His desire is for us to live a life of victory and abundance—not a life of want and defeat.

Jesus told His followers, "The Thief comes only to steal and kill and destroy; I have come that they [believers] may have *and* enjoy life, and have it in abundance [to the full, till it overflows]."[57] Fully confident His Word is true, knowing He is close to the brokenhearted,[58] and carries us through our troubled times,[59] I prayed for help to discover *that* abundant life...and I asked for friends.

Sometimes God makes you wait for an answer to prayer. Other times He doesn't. The next day I had a few errands to run and I needed to get out of the house. One of my stops was the library and it just so happened that on the way out I bumped into a gal I'd walked with a couple times on the high school track after dropping Holly off. Cindy and I sat on the wall outside the library talking for almost two hours. Then she invited me to a women's Bible study that met weekly at her friend's house.

"They're a great bunch," she promised.

Tuesday morning couldn't come soon enough. I was eagerly looking forward to getting out of the house and making some friends. Unsure of what to wear for the occasion, I dressed business casual. When I rang the doorbell, Rebecca the hostess convinced I was a Jehovah Witness, opened her front entry with uncertainty. "Can I help you?" she asked.

"Am I at the right house for the Bible study?"

With a friendly smile and a sigh of relief she opened the door and invited me in. I was the first of eleven women to show up that morning. Before diving into the Word, they were all curious to know who I was, where I was from, what I did for a living, and how on earth our family ended up in Silver City, New Mexico.

While I walked through the door a strong, confident woman on the outside, I was anything but that on the inside. As I opened up in response to their questions, I fell apart. Through waves of tears I opened up and poured out how God moved our family from California to Michigan, how we were driven from our new home in Michigan to find Steve a safe haven, and how his long-term disease had adversely affected our family.

In my vulnerable, broken state this small group of women I had never met listened intently. They empathized with me, cried with me, prayed over me, prayed with me, hugged me, and loved me just as you suppose Jesus would have. Over the next four years, these women and their passion for God were my saving grace. I love them all and tear up every time I think about how things might have been different if God hadn't answered my prayer that day in a way that only He could.

That wasn't God's only answer to prayer. Every morning as I continued praying for myself, I became increasingly aware that my deep sense of distress was being lifted and replaced with an unimaginable sense of peace. It was as if Jesus miraculously calmed the raging sea within me. Nothing about our situation had changed, yet everything internally had. It was perplexing.

The only way I can describe the amazing transformation is by using Paul's words to the Philippians—"Do not fret *or* have any anxiety about anything, but in every circumstance *and* in everything, by prayer and petition (definite requests), with thanksgiving, *continue* to make your wants known to God. And God's peace [shall be yours, that tranquil state of a soul assured of its salvation through Christ, and so fearing nothing from God and being content with its earthly lot of whatever sort that is, that peace] which transcends all understanding shall garrison *and* mount guard over your hearts and minds in Christ Jesus."[60]

"The LORD gives strength to his people; the LORD blesses his people with peace."[61] Even though your problems linger and you continue to fight through the cesspool of sludge surrounding your circumstances, God's inconceivable peace not only surpasses understanding, it is readily available and abundant. So, "Let us strip off every weight that slows us down, especially the sin that so easily trips us up. And let us run with endurance the race God has set before us. We do this by keeping our eyes on Jesus, the champion who initiates and perfects our faith."[62]

Whatever challenges you may be facing today, know this—"The LORD longs to be gracious to you; he rises to show you compassion. The LORD still waits for you to come to him so he can show you his love and his mercy. The LORD is a faithful God. Blessed are all who wait for him. How gracious he will be when you cry for help! As soon as he hears, he will answer you."⁶³

"The LORD heard my cry. He drew me up out of a horrible pit [a pit of tumult and of destruction], out of the miry clay, and set my feet upon a rock and gave me a firm place to stand. And he has put a new song in my mouth, a song of praise to our God."⁶⁴

Chapter 7

# WOW in the Wilderness

*There is a God in heaven who reveals mysteries.* [65]

"I was sure by now, God You would have reached down and wiped our tears away, stepped in and saved the day. But once again, I say 'Amen,' and it's still raining—As the thunder rolls I barely hear Your whisper through the rain 'I'm with you.' And as Your mercy falls I raise my hands and praise the God who gives and takes away."

"I'll praise You in this storm. And I will lift my hands. For You are who You are, no matter where I am. And every tear I've cried, You hold in Your hand. You never left my side and though my heart is torn, I will praise You in this storm."

These lyrics from the Casting Crowns song "Praise You in this Storm" exemplify the tenacity it takes to praise God during turbulent times. To fight past your feelings and everything your natural eyes are seeing, to force yourself to view your struggles through eyes of faith, trusting God is with you and orchestrating all the pieces of your muddled mess to come together in a way that will lift you up and advance His kingdom.

Over and over I played that song, sobbing through the verses, fighting through the pain, determined to flood my head, my heart, and my oppressive reality with hope—doing what my spirit wanted and my natural self opposed—praise God. The girls and I were suffering, mourning the loss of our loved one who was still breathing. Our lives felt as though they were swirling down the toilet like a dead goldfish being flushed. We had to force ourselves to press in to God and remain optimistic while being patiently expectant for our miracle. We were sure God would heal our beloved if we continued to ask, believing that He would and knowing that He could.

Part of walking by faith and pressing in to God was taking advantage of every opportunity to advance our relationship. I had a deep longing to saturate my soul with truth and a craving for God's outpouring of goodness. So when the ladies from my Bible study group signed up for a three-day prophetic workshop, I jumped at the chance to join them. I'd never been to anything like it before and didn't know what to expect, but it was there God revealed His glory to me and through me in a very unique and tangible way.

One of Jesus' last promises to His apostles before ascending into heaven was, "You will receive power when the Holy Spirit comes on you."[66] This power, the incarnation of God's Holy Spirit living inside Jesus' physical body, is what launched His ministry. God's embodiment empowered Jesus with wisdom and spiritual discernment along with the ability to hear from His Father, to heal, to perform miracles, and to see into the future. At the time of conversion *all* Christ followers receive the gift of God's Holy Spirit, a seal identifying them as His possession, an indwelling that endows believers with Jesus' same God-given abilities.[67]

Because of this divine power, Jesus told His disciples, "Whoever believes in me *will* do the works I have been doing, and they will do even *greater things* than these, because I am going to the Father."⁶⁸ "He will give you another Helper (Comforter, Advocate, Intercessor, Counselor, Strengthener, Standby), to be with you forever—the Spirit of truth, whom the world cannot receive because it does not see him or know him, *but* you know him because he (the Holy Spirit) remains with you *continually* and will be in you."⁶⁹

The apostle Paul wrote about these God-given abilities in his first letter to the Corinthians, referring to them as "spiritual gifts." He stated, "Now about spiritual gifts, brothers, I do not want you to be ignorant."⁷⁰

> To every believer the manifestation of the Spirit is given *for the common good* of the body of believers. To one there is given through the Spirit the message of wisdom, to another a word of knowledge *and* understanding, to another wonder-working faith, to another gifts of healing, to another miraculous powers, to another prophecy [foretelling the future, speaking a new message from God to the people], to another discerning between spirits, to another speaking in *various* kinds of [unknown] tongues, and to still another the interpretation of tongues. All these are the work of one and the same Spirit, and God distributes them just as He determines. ⁷¹

> On the Day of Pentecost the apostles were all together in one place. Suddenly a sound like the blowing of a violent wind came from heaven and filled the whole house where they were sitting. They saw what seemed to be

tongues of fire that separated and came to rest on each one of them. All of them were filled with the Holy Spirit and began to speak in different and foreign languages (tongues) as the Spirit enabled them.[72]

Later in the book of Acts another similar incident transpired. Cornelius, a God-fearing military commander, and the disciple Peter both had a vision from God who ordained a divine meeting. The Roman soldier, who was expecting Peter to come to his house, invited a large gathering of people to hear the disciple's message. Peter spoke to the crowd, informing them of how God anointed Jesus with the Holy Spirit, empowering Him to perform miracles. While Peter was speaking, the Holy Spirit came on all who heard the message. They too began speaking in tongues and praising God.[73]

Speaking in tongues is one of several manifestations of the third member of the Holy Trinity. While some Christians reject the Holy Spirit's gift of speaking in tongues, the New Testament clearly implies this divine gift is one of significant value that continues to promote spiritual growth in the lives of believers today.[74] Speaking in tongues is a self-edifying prayer language, an indiscernible spoken utterance between God and His Spirit that bypasses the mind of the praying believer.[75]

Speaking in tongues has numerous advantages. "The Spirit helps us in our weakness. We do not know what prayer to offer *or* how to offer it as we should, but the Spirit himself [knows our need and at the right time] intercedes on our behalf with sighs *and* groanings too deep for words. And he who searches the hearts knows what the mind of the Spirit is, because the Spirit intercedes [before God] on behalf of God's people in accordance with God's will."[76]

"The Spirit also speaks mysteries [secret truths, hidden

things] and enlightens believers with the wisdom of God."[77] God's people are advised to, "Build yourselves up on [the foundation of] your most holy faith [continually progress, rise like an edifice higher and higher] and pray in the Holy Spirit on all occasions."[78]

Paul goes on to say, "The one who speaks in tongues edifies himself, but the one who prophesies edifies the church (the body of believers) [promoting growth in spiritual wisdom, devotion, holiness, and joy] and [speaks words of] encouragement [to uphold and advise them concerning the matters of God] and [speaks words of] consolation [to compassionately comfort them]."[79]

He told the people of Corinth, "I would like every one of you to speak in tongues, but I would rather have you prophesy. The one who prophesies is greater than the one who speaks in tongues, unless someone interprets, so that the church may be edified."[80] "Be eager to prophesy, and do not forbid speaking in tongues."[81]

Because speaking in tongues, foreseeing into the future, and having visions seem particularly peculiar to many of today's Christians, these gifts of divine favor are not always accepted. Even so, the reality is the Holy Spirit empowers *all* God's children with one or more of these amazing gifts. And whether they're acknowledged or not, approved of, or ever put to use, their purpose and power are indisputable. Despite where you are on your faith walk, you can probably concur there are things in the spiritual realm we don't fully understand.

"Since ancient times no eye has seen, no ear has heard, and no mind has imagined all that God has prepared for those who love him [who hold him in affectionate reverence, promptly obeying him and gratefully recognizing the benefits he has bestowed]."[82]

Every day the kingdom of God is actively at work here on

earth. This workshop was definite confirmation of that fact. My spiritual eyes were opened as the assembly of Christ followers tapped into the Holy Spirit's distinctively divine power. The conference began with a lengthy introduction of all the spiritual gifts. Biblical references gave insight to support the role each gift played in the past and how it continues to function in the present.

With that fundamental understanding we were instructed to do our first activation exercise. I was paired up with an older man, someone I'd never met. The objective was to invite God to provide a prophetic word (a vision or predictive message) for your partner. We were to begin by speaking in tongues, praying to God through the Holy Spirit, then we were coached to focus in on what God was trying to show or say to us.

Standing face-to-face with my assigned partner I deliberated. *There is no way I can do this. I know nothing about this man. Maybe I don't possess this gift.* The lead instructor reminded us we were not relying on ourselves, but God. Without Him this was just a foolish exercise that could never be executed.

Relieved the task wasn't dependent on me, I enthusiastically relinquished it to God. Glancing one final time at the man standing in front of me I closed my eyes. On cue, everyone in the church sanctuary began speaking in tongues hoping God would provide a prophetic revelation for them to share with their partner.

We stopped and waited, focusing in on what God might be revealing to us. Something was coming to me. It was a scene of someone on a ranch painting a wide-rail fence white. That was it. Shaking my head in disappointment I slowly opened my eyes to the balding, middle-aged fellow standing in front of me. His expectant expression left me feeling defeated. I slowly and halfheartedly shared the snapshot of what I believed God had given me.

"God is showing me someone in a ranch-like setting painting a wide-rail fence white." I paused. He was anticipating more. "That's it. That's all I got," I concluded shrugging my shoulders.

His blank stare confirmed that I'd totally missed the mark and failed the task. *Apparently I hadn't heard from God.* Then to my surprise a smile began to form on his lips. "All week long I have been painting a fence just like that," he encouraged. "White!"

"Get out o' here," I exclaimed with a chuckle of disbelief. "Really?"

He affirmatively nodded. I was blown away. I didn't get it. It made no worldly sense. All I did was invite the Holy Spirit to work through me...and He did! *That* was exciting!

The following morning the conference resumed and we engaged in more activation exercises. They were all inspiring. One of the most amazing was when half the class was led to the front of the sanctuary and the other half was instructed to stand back-to-back with the person of their choice. I was standing in front and had no idea who was behind me. The objective was to give that person a prophetic message from the Lord.

Again, the exercise commenced with speaking in tongues, then inviting the Holy Spirit's presence in and focusing on what He wanted to say or reveal to the person in back of us. This time the vision God gave me was longer, clearer, and more descriptive than ever before. It was like an eight-second video clip.

Without turning around or opening my eyes I pressed in to what God was showing me, then slowly articulated the revelation. "I see a blue, yellow, and red striped hot air balloon in a sky scattered with dark gray clouds. It's a very blustery day and the strong winds are threatening to take the balloon for a wild ride. But the basket is firmly being held by the Lord's hand. Instead of allowing the balloon to flail around out of control, He is holding it safely and securely in place." I paused. "The Lord wants you to know that He's got this. He is in control."

By way of His message, it was evident the person behind me was facing turbulent times. I heard sniffling as I spoke God's consoling words. When I turned around the pastor's wife impulsively wrapped her arms around me and gave me a huge hug. "You have no idea how much those words mean to me," she said fighting to hold back her tears.

"My mother was just diagnosed with Alzheimer's Disease," she told me. "A couple weeks ago she moved in with us. It's been a real struggle. I've been feeling as though my entire life is spinning out of control." Then she smiled and said, "Those words of reassurance really meant a lot."

"It truly is incredible to have our eyes opened to see into the spiritual realm and experience God in this exciting new way, isn't it?" I asked.

"That's for sure!" she enthusiastically agreed.

Prophetic words, like these from the Lord, are spiritual gifts to be used by believers to enlighten and encourage each other, to bring hope, comfort, joy, healing, and faith-building confidence in God.

*Do not quench [subdue, or be unresponsive to the working and guidance of] the [Holy] Spirit. Do not scorn or reject gifts of prophecy or prophecies [spoken revelations—words of instruction or exhortation or warning]. But test all things carefully [so you can recognize what is good]. Hold firmly to that which is good.*[83]

Everyone at the conference witnessed signs of God's magnificent power and glory. It was truly a privilege to be involved in such an enlightening and amazing event. On the last day a small group of prophetically-gifted individuals was invited to come in and use their gifting to give each attendee a personal revelation. No one had ever met these people and they knew absolutely nothing about any of us.

In groups of three they stood before each class member with cassette tape recorder in hand. I listened intently to each prophetic message as they moved from one participant to the next. All their words were uplifting, promising, and encouraging. I couldn't wait for them to get to me. I desperately needed to hear some of those same life-giving words. At the end of each recipient's turn they sat down, elated and satisfied with their personalized message from above.

It was finally my turn. The trio came over, stood directly in front of me, looked at my nametag, smiled, and closed their eyes. After tapping into God's power via speaking in tongues, they opened their eyes, stared deeply into mine, and clicked on the recorder. The smiles left their faces, their body language changed, and their demeanor was entirely different than when approaching anyone else. "Sue," the first prophet somberly started, "You have been weighed down, pushed down, spat upon. There has been a hole dug for you and *they* want to put you in it!"

I was shocked! The accuracy of their revelation hit me hard, like a boxer being knocked out in the first round with a surprise punch. Gasping to catch my breath, I burst into tears. *There was already a hole dug for me and they want to put me in it!* I shuddered to think who *they* were and what power *they* had over me. The prophetic word God had given to the first prophet was spot on. It confirmed everything I'd been feeling for years, but validation of the fact did nothing to encourage or boost my spirit.

*To you, LORD, I called; to the Lord I cried for mercy: 'What is gained if I am silenced, if I go down to the pit? Will the dust praise you? Will it proclaim your faithfulness? Hear, LORD, and be merciful to me; LORD, be my help.*[84]

Glory to God, that wasn't the end of the message. The second prophet jumped in to save me from the aforementioned words, to ease my pain, and to shine some light into my distressed soul. "*But the Lord* is saying, 'There *is* a call on your life. I want to breathe new breath into you. Breathe life into you. You can't do it on your own. You need to breathe My breath.' Invite God in. He *is* going to answer what you've been crying out for." She paused. "God is taking you into a season of renewal. He says, 'You will fly like an eagle. Stay close to Me. Wait on Me. I will pour Myself out on you. There *will* be a healing of the heart.'"

The third prophet chimed in. "I hear the Lord saying, 'I want you to know I love you. Share that [truth] with others.'"

Throughout the three-day event God revealed Himself to me in astonishing ways—re-confirming His close, ongoing presence in my life, affirming that He understood my inmost thoughts and deepest feelings, and proving to me that He was fully aware of all I was going through—not only was He willing to meet me right where I was, He was unwilling to leave me there alone. His compassionate, prophetic words offered hope and encouragement for a better tomorrow as I waited and continued to press in. The beauty of these words is they're directly from the Bible, as all prophetic messages should be, therefore this promise isn't just for me—it's for you too!

While I was persistently seeking God, our girls were on a spiritual journey of their own. For years they'd been striving to grasp why this atomic bomb had exploded on *our* family. After wrestling through the vast range of emotions, which are normal when adversity strikes, there comes a point where you either move closer to God or fall farther away. There is no in between. If you're not advancing toward Him, you're distancing yourself from Him.

I am eternally grateful Jenni and Holly both made the decision and the effort to move closer. Together we were united in faith, prayer warriors trusting God to miraculously restore their father's health. After all, according to my prophetic word, "He is going to answer what you've been crying out for!"

For nine and a half years our lives had been revolving around Steve's disease, yet the girls' faith escalated dramatically, right alongside mine. Amid the storm, God was revealing Himself to them in a mighty way and they too witnessed His presence alive and active in their lives. He was working on their hearts, exhibiting compassion, and molding them into the likeness of His Son. So when the opportunity arose, they both leapt at the chance to get baptized—to rededicate their lives and allegiance to Christ. They were so excited to move forward and take the next step in their faith walk. What an excellent illustration of God making beauty out of ashes!

Because of his frailty and the amount of effort it required for him to move, it took some persuasion to motivate Steve to attend the baptism. It wasn't that he didn't want to join us and support the girls in their decision, but getting out of bed, getting ready, and going into town where he'd be exposed to debilitating cell tower radiation would take a great deal of energy. Even so, he understood how important it was for the girls to have him present.

It was a cool Sunday afternoon when I slowly escorted my feeble husband to a poolside chair at the Super 8 Hotel where the baptism was set to take place. The sun's heat was penetrating through the large plate glass panels that surrounded the pool area. Its warm, humid climate was inviting.

Others being baptized were also sitting along the pool's edge. A total of 14 people, ranging from ages 8 to 58, were scheduled to take the plunge. Excitement filled the air on this joyous occasion. Everyone eagerly waited as Pastor Monte and one of the church elders, we lovingly call Papa Clayton, took their place in the water. One by one those waiting were invited into the pool to make their proclamation of faith.

"I baptize you in the name of the Father, Son, and Holy Spirit." The men of God declared as they slowly submerged each believer back into the water. A roar of applause followed as each individual arose from the water—a "new creation" in Christ.

Jenni and Holly climbed down the steps and entered the water together. Just as before when they were much younger, they wanted to be baptized together and share the wonderful experience. "Yay," I shouted. Noisily clapping my hands when they jointly popped up out of the pool arm in arm.

After the remaining believers were baptized and the men of God were still in the pool, I turned to Steve and asked, "Do you want to profess your faith and get baptized too?"

His answer was weak, but firm. "No."

I wasn't willing to give up so easily. "Maybe you'd experience a miraculous healing if you gave your life to Christ." Instead of verbally responding, he gave me an irritated look of disgust.

I wanted so much for Steve to be saved. I know it sounds merciless, but if pushing him into the pool were a way for him to receive healing, forgiveness, redemption, enter into a personal relationship with the Lord, and acquire the gift of eternal life, I wouldn't have given it a second thought! Maybe after coming up out of the water he too would be a changed man. But that's not how it works. Accepting Jesus is a decision everyone has to make on his own. No one else can make that decision for you—no matter how much they want to.

Even so, there is no greater joy than knowing my children are walking in the truth!

During the Israelites 70-year enslavement in Babylon, the prophet Isaiah offered God's people hope, proclaiming the year of the Lord's favor (when salvation would be realized). Jesus fulfilled this biblical prophecy using the same words given to Isaiah.[85] These words resonate in my spirit when I think about the revelation of His glory during our most troublesome times.

> The Spirit of the Sovereign LORD is on me, because the LORD has anointed me to proclaim good news to the poor. He has sent me to bind up the brokenhearted, to proclaim freedom for the captives and release from darkness for the prisoners, to proclaim the year of the LORD'S favor and the day of vengeance of our God, to comfort all who mourn, and provide for those who grieve in Zion - to bestow on them a crown of beauty instead of ashes, the oil of joy instead

of mourning, and a garment of praise instead of a spirit of despair. They will be called oaks of righteousness, a planting of the LORD for the display of his splendor.[86]

Chapter 8

# The Lord My Provider

*God will meet all your needs
according to the riches of his glory in Christ Jesus.*[87]

As the girls and I chose to put our unwavering trust in the Lord our faith was growing, but our finances were not. They were dwindling—rapidly. In the past two years Steve had been denied Social Security Disability (SSDI) twice. Not only that, it had been almost six years since he left his job and we were still waiting for his Workers' Compensation claim to be settled. It was absolutely preposterous! We never imagined we'd be waiting so long to receive restitution for his work-related injury. Like a rubber band, our money had been stretched as far as it could go, and the elastic was about to snap. Without an income, we had to find other means to get by.

So collectively, we scavenged around the house and the garage looking for anything of monetary value. We had to sell whatever possessions we could to help pay the few bills we had. The obvious and most difficult concession Steve had to make was letting go of his Harley Davidson Road King. Although he'd been unable to ride his dream bike for years, let alone manage its massive weight, the grim reality of realizing his "hog days" were over was particularly painful...and depressing. He was not only turning over his bike, he was sacrificing a lifestyle and the fond memories that were tied to it.

Money from the motorcycle and a few other belongings brought short-term relief, but it wasn't long before we were right back to square one. Bills don't stop just because you run out of money. We needed an alternative solution to keep our ship afloat. Plan B was turning to the one credit card we maintained for emergencies. Not a strategy I'd recommend, but one I hoped would carry us through.

The VISA card was used to pay all of our expenses—including the house payment! While taking care of our obligations the best I could, I quickly learned the only payment that can't be made with a credit card was the credit card bill. Funds for that had to be withdrawn as a cash advance from the credit card and paid with a money order. We were digging a hole I was hopeful we'd soon find our way out of.

In a relatively short period of time as I continued to dig, the credit card was reaching its limit. Using it as our sole source of financial sustenance was no longer going to be an option. Until one of the lifelines—SSDI or Workers' Compensation—was thrown out to rescue us, we needed assistance well beyond our means. That meant it was time for Plan C, a plan that was never meant to be, a plan I never wanted to execute.

Humbled by our deteriorating circumstances, I resigned to Plan C—seeking eligibility for government aid. On my way to the Department of Social Services I was reminiscing about happier times, they seemed so long ago. Like most young couples we didn't have a whole lot of disposable income, but we were rich in so many other ways before Steve became ill. Now, because of his former employer's negligence and unreasonable procrastination in righting the wrong that had been done, I was going to ascertain whether or not our family would qualify for food stamps. The action felt unjustifiable, but I was left with no other option.

A bright yellow sign near the entrance of the large, newly constructed building advised me to take a number. The room was full of adults and small children sitting in long rows of armless chairs waiting for their turn to approach the thick Plexiglas window to state their case. When my number was called, a door opened and a young woman escorted me down a long, narrow hallway. She offered me a seat across from a heavyset woman who was introduced as my caseworker.

Feeling like a defendant at my own trial, the caseworker glared at me from behind the desk and began asking a litany of questions. She had done this so many times she had the routine down pat. She barely made eye contact and her pre-rehearsed conduct seemed callous and accusatory. I didn't want to be sitting in that chair any more than she wanted to help me. However, after being drilled and filling out pages of paperwork, I was relieved and truly grateful to have qualified for what I hoped would be a temporary bridge of support.

Although government assistance helped with food and healthcare, it didn't cover things like gas, electricity, mortgage payments, credit card bills—or toilet paper! Cash was still a necessity. Acknowledging our impoverished predicament for what it was, I put our fate in the hands of the only One truly able to help. I knew the Lord would hear my plea and answer as He had numerous times before. I believed that with everything in me. I trusted, I expected—and He delivered.

I once heard a pastor preach that if you don't bring your requests to the Lord, you deprive Him of the opportunity to reveal Himself in a mighty and marvelous way. Denying Him that opportunity would be foolish. So I faithfully got down on my knees next to the couch, folded my hands, closed my eyes, and bowed my head. For the first time ever I requested a financial bailout. We desperately needed one, but I couldn't begin to imagine how God was going to pull money out of thin air. Thankfully I didn't have to; it was up to Him, all of our human efforts had been exhausted.

Jesus made this promise to His disciples, "Whatever things you ask for in prayer [in accordance with God's will], believe [with confident trust] that you have (already) received them, and they will be *given* to you."[88] Since that's what I was supposed to do, that's exactly what I did.

God knew our quandary long before I ever started praying. He always knows exactly what we need before we even know you we it, and He prepares to fill that need long before we even ask.[89]

Within days we got wind of an ongoing government project that paid people living within the boundaries of the national forest to remove excess trees and scrub brush from their property in an effort to inhibit the spread of wildfires. We were intrigued and called City Hall. An inspector came out to the property and explained what the grant entailed, pointing out everything that would have to be done in order to receive what we believed to be generous compensation. It sounded like a great deal of work and I wasn't sure we were up for the task, but the good news was we didn't have to commit and there was no specified time frame for completion. An official just had to record the "before" condition in order to evaluate the "after" results.

Steve was willing to do whatever it took to keep a roof over our heads, so he adamantly accepted the project as a challenge. Only problem was he'd have to use a chainsaw—that terrified me! This would be an extremely dangerous undertaking. I lacked confidence in both his coordination and his ability. To further complicate matters, his chronic headaches blurred his vision, so much so that when we moved back to the little blue house he cut through his right thumb with a table saw. Vision however, wasn't his only impairment. I questioned whether he'd have the strength to hold, let alone operate a heavy piece of machinery like a chainsaw for any length of time. His inner man emerged and begged to differ.

The endeavor gave Steve a renewed sense of purpose and pride. Once again he felt as though he was contributing to the family. It was a slow, ongoing process, but every morning, when he was at his best, he resolutely headed out with chainsaw in hand to slay some trees. It was Steve against the forest. After an hour or so he'd return on the verge of collapse and crash into bed for the remainder of the day. After six weeks we scheduled a re-inspection to see if his labor paid off.

Steve did a fantastic job cleaning up debris, removing scrub brush, and cutting down trees on six of the ten acres. The property had taken on a whole new look. Its well-manicured, park-like setting was a significant improvement, but the forest ranger said more trees had to come down. Steve was whipped. The project had extracted every ounce of energy from him. He hung up his hat and announced he was done.

Considering Steve's physical, mental, and neurological state, it was not at all surprising that he experienced some real close calls during this laborious season. One day after returning home from a jaunt into town, I found my husband sprawled out on the living room sofa with his tennis shoes on. When I noticed the toe of his shoe had been slashed by what appeared to be a chainsaw, I gasped, waking him up.

"What?" he wearily asked, sitting up.

"What happened to your foot?"

He looked down, surprised by what he saw. Then leaning over, he untied his shoe and took it off. His sock had a clean slit right between his big toe and his second toe. He carefully removed his sock. There was no cut, no scratch, no burn, and no blood! Nothing!!! Knowing Steve was going to be alone for a while, I distinctly remember asking God on my way out to protect him—and this was the result!

Ten days after the inspector's visit we received a check in the mail for $2500. We weren't sure what to think because we had made it perfectly clear that we were done with the project and unwilling to remove any more trees. Since he knew our intentions, we concluded the funds were partial payment for the completed work.

Twenty-five hundred dollars was definitely a gift from God—at least that's how I saw it. Steve reasoned that since the grant money was available to anyone owning forest property, finding out about the project was sheer coincidence. I was hoping he'd see the blessing through my eyes. I prayed for financial aid, then days later someone told us about the program. I don't believe in coincidences—I viewed *that* as an answer to prayer, just like his foot miraculously being unscathed after the chainsaw sliced through his shoe and his sock!

Full time caregiving was a thankless job that didn't pay, and once those quarter-million pennies were maximized to their full extent, we found ourselves right back where we started—with no SSDI and no Workers' Compensation settlement. *Why were they both taking sooo long?* One of them had to come through for us...and fast. I repressed my anxiety and continued to keep my eyes on the Lord, trusting and waiting on Him who never runs out of resources and never falls short of creative ways to answer prayer.

Jesus taught His followers to bring their needs and requests to the Father and be persistent in doing so until their prayer is answered. He advised them to, "Ask *and* keep on asking and it will be given to you; seek *and* keep on seeking and you will find; knock *and* keep on knocking and the door will be opened to you. For everyone who keeps on asking receives, and he who keeps on seeking finds, and to him who keeps on knocking, it will be opened."[90] God promises to give what is good *and* advantageous to those who are persistent and never give up asking!

The heartfelt *and* persistent prayer of a righteous believer has tremendous power.[91] Therefore, whatever your needs are today—ask, seek, and knock, because God is the giver of all good things.[92] Richly blessing all who call on His name.[93] He finds joy in meeting your every need in accordance with His will. When you delight in the Lord, you can expect to be given the desires of your heart.[94] That's a direct promise from your Heavenly Father.

When Moses died, Joshua had some pretty big shoes to fill. The Lord promised Moses' successor, "As I was with Moses, so I will be with you. I will never leave you or forsake you. Be strong and very courageous because you will lead these people (the Israelites) to inherit the land I swore to their forefathers to give them."[95]

To prepare for the great migration, Joshua inspired the nation with this promising message—"Tomorrow the Lord will do amazing things![96] So "consecrate yourselves" today, because by doing so you can expect to experience "great wonders" tomorrow.[97]

The next day, with the Jordan River at flood stage, the priests who were instructed to carry the Ark of the Covenant into the deep, raging waters, stepped in. As soon as their feet touched the river, the water upstream a great distance away stopped flowing and mounted in a heap. The priests stood in the middle of the Jordan, with the Ark of the Covenant, on dry ground as the entire nation of Israel crossed![98]

Oftentimes in the Old Testament God required His people to go through an external cleansing ritual prior to meeting with Him. The outward preparation symbolized the inward consecration (purification).[99] A similar thread is continued throughout Scripture—God frequently wants believers to partake in a spiritual act of faith before He shows up. This act of faith is also known as "sowing a seed." When a seed is planted in fertile soil, you expect something to grow. Likewise when a seed is sown for God, you can expect great things.

In the aforementioned verse Jesus instructs us to, "Ask, seek, and knock." These deliberate, intentional actions require faith and reinforce the biblical principle that when we initiate the first form of action, God responds. Our actions determine His reaction. Under the right "soil" conditions of faith, love, a humble heart, a repentant spirit, and pure motives, you can sow your seed and expect something amazing to happen!

The seed God is asking you to sow may be different from mine. Since God is the only One who knows where you are on your faith journey and what's best for you in your situation, He is the only One who knows what you need to do to enrich your relationship with Him. Every action is personalized for a specific time and purpose.

Maybe God is calling you to repent and to turn away from your past. Maybe you're being led to recognize your need for a Savior and you're being asked to initiate that relationship. Maybe a spiritual cleansing, a confession of your sins and a request for forgiveness will move God into action. Maybe it's forgiving someone, asking someone to forgive you, or letting go of a past offense. Your act of consecration may be as simple and as powerful as a prayer. Whatever act of faith the Holy Spirit places on your heart do it, because obedience leads to increased favor, blessings, and rewards.

After asking, seeking, and knocking, along with initiating spiritual acts of faith and believing with confident trust that I'd already received what I'd been praying for, I waited expectantly for God to come through—*again*. This time I informed Steve of my petition, so when God responded he couldn't simply write it off as coincidence or luck.

Two weeks later on a drizzly gray afternoon while in the kitchen making chocolate chip cookies, I heard a car making its way up the driveway. The girls were home, Steve was in bed, and I was starting to feel a bit uneasy. Being so isolated in the middle of nowhere I never knew what to expect. We never had uninvited guests just stop by. We were miles from town and the ride to the house was long and treacherous. It was extremely rare to hear any motor vehicles, let alone one coming up toward the house unannounced. The abnormal incident demanded my full attention.

The roar of the approaching vehicle put Jazz and Bear on high alert. They began running around and barking wildly, wanting to go outside to see what was happening. Holly and I raced into Jenni's room where she was lying in bed reading. The three of us gathered 'round her bedroom window and secretly peered out.

None of us recognized the newer model Chevy truck that had parked in front of the garage. As we spied, trying to keep the curtain from moving, a smartly dressed middle-age man stepped out of the vehicle and came striding up to the house. When we heard knocking at the front door the girls and I exchanged wide-eyed glances. They chose to stay put while I suspiciously proceeded with the dogs, trying my best to restrain them, yet wanting the security they provided.

Cautiously, I advanced toward the door. *What did this man want? What reason would he have for coming all the way out here?* Through the screen I hesitantly asked, "Can I help you?"

Dave, an out-of-state elk hunter, surprised me with his query. "Do you have any property you'd be interested in selling?"

With great skepticism and extreme perplexity I asked him to repeat the question, "What?" The property wasn't on the market, no ads had been placed, no "for sale" signs were posted, and although we had considered selling 4-acres of our 10-acre parcel to help relieve our financial stress, we figured no one would want to buy a steep mountainside with no flat surfaces on which to build.

He repeated the question just as I thought I'd heard it the first time. "Do you have any property you'd be interested in selling?" He elaborated, explaining his intent. "You see, I'm from Florida and am looking for a piece of land to build a house where I can retire and hunt elk. I love it out here in the forest, but forest property is scarce."

His inquiry really piqued my interest. I wanted to hear more, so I called Jenni to come take the dogs into her room. I invited the Floridian to step inside while I roused the man of the house. Steve wearily followed me out to the sunroom where the prospective land buyer was waiting. After describing the seemingly useless piece of real estate, he was still interested and asked to see it.

Before trudging out in the rain to walk the vertical slope's perimeter, a hike that could easily overwhelm Steve, there were a few questions that had to be answered in order to determine the likelihood of a possible transaction. I turned to Dave. "If interested, are you planning on financing the property?" If so, I knew the land would have to be appraised and priced according to current market value.

"Nope," he said. "I'll be paying cash!" *Good answer.*

"Are you married?"

"Yes, but my wife's in Florida" he replied.

"Won't your wife want to see the property since her name will be on the title along with yours?"

"Nope. We've been married 31 years; she trusts my judgment," he answered with a confident smile.

"Great!" I responded, returning the smile. "Those are all my questions. Have fun!"

After the guys left my head was spinning. I was so excited and hopeful. Jumping up and down in my spirit, I wondered—could this be my answer to prayer? I was sure of it! Money from the sale would be a long-term resolve to our financial crisis and a potential deal would not interfere with our magnificent view. The abundance of trees left on the four acres would hide any building site. I could see no downside. I raced in to share the news with the girls, but they'd been eavesdropping on the entire conversation. They too were optimistic. We held hands and said a quick prayer.

When they returned from walking the property, the men came inside and sat down. Dave had no idea how financially strapped we were and I wasn't about to clue him in. Taking a seat next to Steve, I inquisitively queried the potential buyer, "So, what'd ya think?"

He enthusiastically reported, "I love it! It's *exactly* what we're looking for." I thought he might have wanted to curb his zeal, just as I was masking our desperation, but I was wrong. He didn't conceal his feelings at all. After shooting the breeze for a few minutes, he concluded the conversation by attempting to close the deal. "I'll call later tonight after you've had a chance to talk and establish a price." He stood up, shook our hands, and left.

Steve and I were speechless, staring at one another in utter amazement and disbelief. What just happened was truly incredible! Once we were over the initial shock, we sat down to determine a price. Even though Dave was paying cash, and price wasn't contingent on value, we still wanted to be fair.

I threw out a random number. "Seventy-thousand."

Steve immediately shot it down. "That's ridiculous! Way too high. Nobody would pay that!"

The previous year a relatively flat five-acre forest parcel sold for $50,000. This was a steep four-acre mountainside. Probably not worth nearly as much, but with appreciation, who knew? What we did know was Dave wanted the property, he was paying cash, and he wasn't going to have the property appraised. All we had to do was agree on price.

"Fifty-thousand seems reasonable," I proposed. "We'd probably never get more than that anyway."

Steve nodded in agreement. "Sounds good."

When the phone rang that evening I rushed over to answer it, then stood by letting it ring a few more times so I wouldn't appear overanxious. I was thrilled to hear Dave's voice on the other end. After we said our hellos, he asked the million-dollar question—"How much do you want for the property?"

I began answering the question by explaining how we arrived at the asking price. "I was thinking $70,000," and before I could say, "but Steve thought that was too high…"

He eagerly and impatiently jumped in and cut me off. "Great I'll go down to Grant County Title tomorrow and put $10,000 into escrow." Without taking another breath he asked, "What time can we meet to get the paperwork started?"

My jaw hit the floor! I was stunned! He never even let me finish what I was saying and he didn't try to negotiate! With that money we were able to settle our credit card debt, make some home improvements, pay off the entire mortgage, and deposit the rest in savings! *Savings!*

Dave cut into the rock and built a gorgeous two-story home with a deck overlooking the spectacular mountain terrain. That's where he and his wife plan to spend their golden years.

There you have it—The glory of God revealed! How great is Our God?!!

Chapter 9

# Never Too Far Gone

*Bear with each other and forgive whatever grievances you may have against one another. Forgive as the Lord forgave you.*[100]

God loves you immensely and unconditionally. His amazing love for you cannot be earned—it is already constant, never-ending, and unwavering. Regardless of anything you've ever done, despite every bad, rebellious, and immoral decision you've ever made, God loves you with an everlasting love.[101] His agape love for you is infinite, boundless, and without exception. Even while God remains faithful, our sinful nature has a tendency to infect our lives, to cause us to stumble, and to lead us astray. But because of His great love we are not consumed; His compassion is new every morning.[102]

Every day is a new day. Every morning is a new beginning. Even though it sounds cliché, today really *is* the first day of the rest of your life. How would you like *your* new life to look? What changes would have to be made for you to walk from the black and white state of Kansas through the door leading to the colorful brilliance of Munchkin Land as in the classic tale of *The Wizard of Oz*?

Truth is we've all done things God wouldn't approve of.[103] "We have all sinned and we all fall short of the glory of God."[104] Not one of us is perfect—but God is. So when we confess our sins to Him, "He is faithful and just to forgive us our sins and purify us from all unrighteousness."[105]

If you're ready for a fresh start, free from the heavy chains that have been weighing you down, today is the day to admit your wrongdoing and to "strip off every encumbrance that hinders and the sin that so easily *and* cleverly entangles."[106] Doing this will set you free from your past and your sins will be remembered no more![107] Hallelujah!

Several months after relocating to Silver City we discovered its long-term history of gang violence and spiritual tension. A more thorough investigation of the region prior to moving may have uncovered the corruption and demonic activity, but because of the urgency of our situation we were forced to take immediate action. With rapid cell tower expansion, the impenetrable barrier of the Piños Altos Mountains served as a permanent solution to eradicating future exposure or driving us out of our home ever again. Steve's wellbeing was our primary concern; few other factors were considered. Even so, I believed God planted our family in Silver City for a season and a reason.

It wasn't solely for Steve's protection—it was also to draw us closer to Him. Maybe God's purpose for leading us here was to equip us so He could use us as instruments to play a role in advancing His kingdom. I relished the thought. One thing was certain, it wasn't all about us…

A girl's night out turned into something miraculous when my best friend Sylvia and I met for dinner at a local

Main Street restaurant. A doorman in his mid- to late 20s greeted us and checked our IDs. We were promptly seated at a high-top table right next to the front entrance where the young man, we'll call José, was working.

The lights were dim, chatter and soft jazz filled the newly renovated old building. Before ordering, Sylvia and I leisurely sipped on a couple native microbrews, conversing and watching as a slow, steady stream of people came in through the doorway only to be stopped and carded.

Sylvia discreetly pointed to José. "You see those small dark tattoos on his face?"

I tried to catch a glimpse of the ink marks as the young man checked IDs, but it was difficult to see his face with his back toward us. Then I noticed what she was referring to. They looked like tears falling from the outside of his left eye. I'd seen similar markings on others in town. I nodded in acknowledgment.

"Do you know what they represent?" she asked.

"No," I replied, "I have no idea."

Sylvia had worked as a correctional officer for several years in California's State Penitentiary. She seemed to be familiar with the expressive symbolism. "That's what gang members have tattooed on their face every time they kill a person," she explained.

I didn't believe her. I was sure she was pulling my leg. While shaking my head, doubting her insight, I challenged her statement with an extended, "Unh-uhhhh."

*Why would anyone want to publically and permanently exhibit that they had done such a horrible thing? To boast? To instill fear? Whatever the reason, it made little sense to me.*

She adamantly confirmed that what she was telling me was true. I had to believe her. What the heck did I know?

After we finished our meal the flow of incoming traffic tapered off. José was obviously bored. He was looking around for something to occupy his time. He turned toward us and smiled. We engaged in some light-hearted conversation. He was a pleasant young man who was very easy to talk with. After a few minutes he straddled the rope that separated us and approached our table. We learned that he was a local fire fighter and father of at least one child.

I've never been considered shy, quite the contrary, but I've discovered that a bit of boldness, a psychology background, and a hint of ignorance make a great recipe for drawing information out of the unsuspecting. By being inquisitive and acting naïve, people are often more willing to open up and share. They rarely get defensive or argumentative because they don't feel threatened by non-judgmental queries. This subtle interrogation makes it easy to ask anyone almost anything. Wisdom would suggest that the significance of the tattoos would be a subject to avoid, but I was curious how he would respond. Besides that, what's the worst that could happen in a public restaurant?

While chatting with José it was tough not to stare at his permanent tears, especially after being told what they stood for. When the conversation gave way to a new subject, I asked about the tattoos. "Are the tears symbolic of anything in particular?" I questioned.

Immediately he responded, "One is for my sister who passed away." Then he stopped, dropped his head, and stared at the floor. We watched as a strong wave of emotion swept over him. Without lifting his head, he softly and thoughtfully resumed, "The other tears are for all the bad things I've done. Things I did while I was in a gang—things I'm not proud of."

Feelings of anguish, guilt, and shame consumed him. It appeared as though he had been tied to a massive anchor that was just thrown overboard into a dark abysmal pit. José was transported back to a different time and place, where violence, greed, and power reign. Where escape is not an option. Where grusome memories are birthed, haunting you for the rest of your life. A past that elicits eternal consequences.

We were moved by José's openness and honesty. His excruciating pain was equally matched by profound remorse. It was obvious that if he were given a second chance to relive that part of his life, he'd make different decisions—better decisions.

It was heart-wrenching to see José in such a broken state. With his head down and his eyes still fixed on the floor, I could think of only one thing to say, "Do you know there's a God who loves you and will forgive you for all the evil things you've done, if you just ask?"

He gradually lifted his head and looked up at me with tear-soaked eyes. Then he slowly and sadly shook his head. "No," he replied. "I can't forgive myself for the things I've done. Why would God forgive me?"

There was no time for a rebuttal. The restaurant was closing and José had to get back to work. Sylvia and I slid down from our high chairs and made our way toward the door. My heart ached for the shattered man standing by the exit. Consumed with compassion, I instinctively hugged him on the way out and said good-bye. Without any hesitation he responded in kind.

I embraced my girlfriend and left, hurrying toward my car. On the 30-minute drive home I couldn't stop thinking of José. I thought of the most horrific acts of violence—cold-blooded murder, assault, and rape. Not being a fan of horror movies or violent television programs, the images I was conjuring up probably weren't as graphic as they might have been otherwise. But as I attempted to visualize the worst case scenerios, I knew what the Bible said—there is nothing *so* horrendous that God wouldn't be willing to forgive if the person seeking forgiveness repented and was genuinely remorseful. With that realization, I was overcome with a strong sense of compassion and sincere concern for this man's soul. That night I went to bed praying for José.

My thoughts returned to him the following morning during my time with God. I felt led to look up verses on forgiveness. Using my Bible's concordance I referenced and recorded Scripture verses that seemed most relevant. They appeared to be in sequential order and when I finished writing, I flipped through the pages and realized something extraordinary—The words flowed smoothly like a letter. And there was a total of seven pages—God's number for completeness! It was revealed to me that I had just composed a letter from God to José. But it wasn't just any letter—it was a *love* letter!

Consumed with emotion, my eyes filled with tears. It was then that I began to understand the strange and overwhelming sensation of unconditional love I'd been feeling toward José since the night before. After actually reading the verses as a letter in its entirety, that feeling intensified. However, it wasn't *my* love for José I was sensing—it was God's love for José. It was unlike anything I'd ever experienced. It was as if for an instant I beheld a fraction of heaven that broke through the boundaries of earth. The expression of God's love for this broken, sinful, repentive spirit was so powerful and amazing. Even more incredible is that God has that same indescribable love for me…and for you!

To conclude the letter, I inserted a greeting at the top and a signature at the bottom. A church invitation was also given as a postscript (P.S.). Before sending the document off to its rightful owner I informed Steve of what happened in my prayer time that morning. I'd already shared what took place at the restaurant the night before. Although he had difficulty comprehending, he trusted that I was being obedient to what the Lord was asking me to do.

Since Jenni was working that evening I asked her to drop the sealed envelope off to José. I assumed he'd be working. Both my girls thought a love letter to José from God was awesome. What they thought was weird was their mother had written it. Sylvia agreed. But all three were also cognizant of the fact that God works in mysterious ways and He works in us so He can work through us to accomplish His plans for His purpose.

With envelope in hand, I gave my oldest daughter two simple instructions. "When you give him the letter tell him it's from your mom, Sue, who he met last night." And, "Tell him not to read it until after work." It'd be best for him to focus on what God wants to communicate to him without distractions.

I was overjoyed for José. God was pursuing him and *that* was exciting. I prayed the letter would contain the freeing power he so desperately needed—and wanted. I held onto the promise God spoke through His prophet Isaiah. "My Word will not return to me void; but will accomplish what I desire and achieve the purpose for which I sent it."[108]

The next day as soon as Jenni got up and out of bed, I asked, "How'd the delivery go?"

"It was strange," she admitted. "José was receptive, but extremely curious."

"I can imagine—a mysterious letter from an unknown woman that he wasn't supposed to read until after work? No, that didn't sound peculiar!" I sarcastically teased with a big smile. The two of us snickered.

Sunday morning at church was like every other. It'd been almost a week since meeting José, but once the letter was delivered, thoughts of him began to fade from my mind. It was only while praying that I pondered how God was working on his heart.

Every service ends with an altar call. Today was no different. For me, there is nothing more exciting than seeing the unsaved publically surrender their lives to Christ. They have no idea how dramatically their lives will improve once that one decision is made. With heads bowed and eyes closed, we pray for those wanting to enter into a relationship with Jesus. Then they are invited to approach the altar for prayer. This is always a time of spiritual jubilation.

Did you know the angels in heaven rejoice every time a soul gets saved? It's true—God's Word says, "There is rejoicing in the presence of the angels of God over one sinner who repents."[109] I was still praying at the service's conclusion. I didn't open my eyes until I felt a gentle tap on my shoulder. It was Sylvia's son sent down from the balcony with a message from his mother.

"Isn't that José?" he said pointing to one of the men being prayed for up front.

Gazing over in that direction I couldn't believe my eyes. It *was* José! Even now, my eyes tear up at the depth of God's incredible love for us. "Yes, it is," I whispered pulling him in for a big hug. "Yes, it is!"

A grin from ear to ear froze on my face as I watched the pastors lay hands on and pray for one sinner who wanted to be restored and walk in new life with Jesus Christ. Overwhelmed with immense joy, I followed the young boy up to the balcony where my best friend was sitting. "Why don't you go down and say hello," she enthusiastically encouraged.

"It's not about me," I explained as I sat there looking down in awe, praising God for His generous outpouring of grace and mercy. Several minutes later we got up to leave.

When we reached the bottom of the stairs I felt led to join those who were praying for José. I gently placed my hand on his shoulder. The feeling was electrifying. You could sense the power and presence of the Holy Spirit on this child of God. When the prayers ceased, José turned around without opening his eyes, and with tears streaming down his face, he hugged me, and repeatedly thanked me.

"Sue, you have no idea…" His voice trailed off.

A new, fully restored man stood in front of me. A man free from bondage, guilt, and shame. One who just laid down his entire past and all of his burdens at the foot of the cross. His heavy chains had been broken and his sins were erased. He was so grateful. "It was all God!" I answered.

Standing there alone with José felt a bit awkward. The pastors and elders had left. From a front row seat Sylvia was coaxing me to invite the new convert to lunch. After every service we took the kids to Taco Bell. I wasn't really interested in asking because my involvement was never meant to extend beyond the letter. I understood that. She didn't. But since he appeared to be alone and could overhear what she was saying, I asked. When he declined the invitation, I was relieved.

But while we were enjoying our lunch, José walked into the restaurant. "There's something I need to tell you," he said. I motioned for him to sit down. He smiled, accepting the offer, and seriously fixed his eyes on mine. "It was really bizarre receiving a letter from you. I was intrigued and anxious to read it, but waited to open the envelope until after work as your daughter instructed." He paused and looked away. "It made me cry," he confessed. After re-establishing eye contact he continued, "Even though it was one in the morning I called my ex-girlfriend, the mother of my child, and told her it was urgent that I speak with her. After some convincing she invited me over. I showed her the letter. She read it and her response was the same as mine. We were both deeply moved. Because of that letter we made the decision to forgive ourselves…and each other." With child-like enthusiasm he beamed, "On top of that, she and my son came to church with me today! That letter did so much for me—and for us. God bless you, Sue."

All of us at the table intently listened as José shared how God had orchestrated this beautiful story to come together in a way that would benefit them *and* glorify Him. The entire set-up was to reconcile their broken relationship and to restore the relationship with their Heavenly Father. God's outpouring of mercy, grace, and love on José provided freedom and relief from his past, renewal for the present, and hope for the future.

The end result of following the unusual prompting was awe-inspiring. Our eyes were opened to God's glory in action, His will being executed right here on earth. I was exceedingly moved. José and I locked eyes sharing in an extraordinary moment; the connection was intense, as if the Holy Spirit inside each of us was communicating with the other. No other words were spoken. With tears of joy glistening in our eyes, we simultaneously stood up, and affectionately embraced. Then with a broad smile he turned and walked out the door with a newfound spring in his step. Never to be seen again.

"The LORD is slow to anger, abounding in love and forgiving sin and rebellion."[110] "I take no pleasure in the death of anyone, declares the Sovereign LORD. Repent and live!"[111] "Repent, then, and turn to God, so that your sins may be wiped out, that times of refreshing may come from the Lord."[112] "In His great mercy He has given us new birth into a living hope through the resurrection of Jesus Christ from the dead, and into an inheritance that can never perish, spoil or fade—kept in heaven for you."[113]

Past thoughts, decisions, and behaviors no longer have to dictate who you are. Live free from guilt, shame, condemnation, and acts that lead to death by being fully cleansed by the blood of Christ.[114] If you're ready for change, your life can be different—it *can* be better! We have a great and merciful God who patiently and eagerly waits for you to humble yourself, confess your sinful nature, repent, and recognize your need for a Savior. When you do this, none of the offenses you've ever committed will be remembered or held against you![115]

Chapter 10

# Following the Path to Freedom

*Be kind and compassionate to one another,
forgiving each other, just as Christ forgave you.*[116]

Steve was becoming weaker and increasingly fatigued with each passing day; he was no longer eating or tending to his personal hygiene. Determined to remain anchored in hope, the girls and I perpetually prayed, crying out for a healing miracle. Searching for the hidden key that would unlock the heavens and release God's blessing onto this poor soul. What more did we need to do to get God to respond to our despairing pleas? Or was there something Steve had to do?

The debilitating disease was advancing; not only was it adversely affecting his brain, memory, and cognitive function, it was now impacting his neurological, cardiovascular, and digestive systems. Over time his symptoms had intensified and multiplied exponentially. As his condition progressed, it seemed less and less likely there would be a reversal.

In Mark's Gospel, the disciple Peter pointed to a fig tree Jesus had cursed days earlier. Seemingly surprised he exclaimed, "Rabbi, look! The fig tree you cursed has withered!"[117]

Jesus said to His disciples, "Truly I tell you, if anyone says to this mountain, 'Go, throw yourself into the sea,' and does not doubt in their heart but believes that what they say will happen, it will be done for them. Therefore I tell you, whatever you ask for in prayer, believe that you have received it, and it will be yours."[118]

The girls and I stood firmly and faithfully on those words. We fought to believe that Steve had already been healed, crushing every hint of doubt that reared its ugly head. Night and day our spiritual certainty battled our physical and emotional reality. It was challenging to look through eyes of faith when our natural eyes opposed everything we believed God to do.

To validate and reinforce my faith in the healing power of Jesus Christ before it actually manifested in my beloved, I would lie awake in bed and envision the Lord walking through the streets of Jerusalem. Shouts of exhilaration and shrieks of joy burst forth as men, women, and children raced to see the Messiah, the Miracle Worker, the King of kings, and the Lord of lords. Crowds swarmed around Him, yearning to be close, longing to hear Him speak, craving His touch, and aching to be healed of their infirmities.

I'd visualize the distressed woman who'd been suffering from a bleeding issue for 12 years, an affliction that would have segregated her from society, making her a social outcast. She had tried everything to remedy her problem, but nothing worked, everything was ineffective. All of her hope, any optimism or expectation of wholeness and healing was right there in that moment with Jesus. She was focused on one thing—turning her life around. She believed wholeheartedly that if she could only get close enough to touch His cloak, she would be healed.[119]

Her faith-filled determination gave her the strength she needed to fight through the crowd, to come up from behind, and touch the edge of Jesus' cloak. As soon as she did, the Lord sensed a magnificent magnitude of power leave Him, and He suddenly turned around. Upon seeing her, He compassionately responded, "Take heart, daughter, your faith has healed you."[120]

Sound like a familiar scenario? No one understood the woman's ailment or what she was going through. She had exhausted all remedies and was unable to find help or support. Her abnormality caused her to be isolated from society and dictated her lifestyle. Jesus was her only remaining source of hope. She was desperate for a healing and wasn't going to let anything or anyone get in the way of her receiving it.

The girls and I identified with the woman's desperation. We shared her faith and determination, but since Steve didn't, it was up to us to stand in the gap and believe Jesus for *his* miracle, just as the faith-filled Roman soldier did for his paralyzed servant and the royal official did for his dying son.

Recognizing Jesus' authority, the Roman soldier trusted the Miracle Worker to heal his servant from a distance by simply giving the order—and it was done just as he believed it would be.[121] Likewise, the royal official believed for a healing miracle for his dying son in a neighboring town. Without going to his side, Jesus said, "You may go. Your son will live." Taking Jesus at His word, the man departed and learned that his boy had been healed the exact moment Jesus spoke those words.[122]

The common denominator of these healings, as well as other similar intercessory accounts in Scripture, is that they appear to be a direct result of the believer's faith. Nothing is ever mentioned about the sufferers' convictions. The girls and I longed for a similar outcome to our story. Why wasn't our faith in Jesus' miraculous healing power working for Steve in the same way?

Over the years my prayers for Steve were always changing. If one prayer didn't seem to be working, I'd chuck it and move on to the next, concluding that maybe a different prayer would generate the desired results.

My initial prayer was conditional, "God please heal Steve as long as he gives You the glory." That one I often felt guilty about. There were desperate pleas made on my knees. "Please God, please heal Steve." There was the prayer of surrender. "God I give up. I don't know what to do or how to pray any more. Your will be done." As things progressed, my prayers were focused on spiritual healing, rather than physical healing. "Lord I long to have him know You the way I do. If you need to break him—break him."

This last prayer was by far the most difficult to pray. It was so painstakingly obvious that this once vibrant young man had already been broken. The physical and mental deterioration of mind and body had taken its toll. The last thing I ever wanted was to see my best friend suffer any more. The request to spiritually humble him *always* brought me to tears, but I was convinced if Steve allowed God to change his heart, maybe then he'd have enough faith to believe in a healing miracle for himself. Only time would tell how my "knee mails" would be answered.

On yet another beautiful sunshiny morning in New Mexico the Holy Spirit was prompting me to persuade Steve to devise a list of everyone who'd ever offended him and anyone he held a grudge against. I just love how the Lord pursues the lost and uses His unlimited resources, including people like you and me, to draw them from wherever they are to where He wants them to be—in a relationship with Him. I obediently obliged, but I was sure Steve would be unwilling to participate.

It was then I remembered the contingency Jesus placed on His promise in Mark 11:24. "Therefore I tell you, whatever you ask for in prayer, believe that you have received it, and it will be yours. And when you stand praying, *if* you hold anything against anyone, forgive them, so that your Father in heaven may forgive you your sins."[123] Oftentimes in the Bible when God forgives sins, complete healing and restoration follow.

So with a quick prayer that this exercise would go according to God's plan and produce His desired result, I sprang into action—casting out the idea and hoping Steve would bite the bait. "Maybe a healing is being withheld because there are people you need to forgive."

With a sarcastic nod and a smug smirk he rejected the lure, believing it to be a ridiculous claim. "Yeah right."

Sitting down next to him on the sofa I gently probed for a lead in. "Who in your life do you need to forgive?"

"I don't want to do this," he protested.

Moving ahead I gently wheedled him along by suggesting, "Let's begin with me. I'm sure there's *something* you need to forgive me for." We'd been married 24 years, you know that's a given.

He flashed me a grin, acknowledging that as an accurate statement. "Okay."

Before giving him another chance to dispute the activity, I quickly grabbed a notepad off the end table, opened it up to a blank page, and scribbled S-U-E. He expressed disinterest, but I persisted by suggesting other names. I brought up incidents from his past he'd been unable to let go of.

He'd always been especially tight with his younger brother Brian. Born with cerebral palsy, Brian unfortunately became a target for despicable ridicule. Fellow students, teachers, co-workers, and others abused him physically, verbally, and emotionally. Steve resented those people for their cruel, insensitive behavior. He was still holding onto that bitterness, burdened by what happened decades earlier. When it comes to forgiveness, it's especially difficult to forgive those who have shown no remorse for their actions, but Steve willingly added their names to the list.

People from his childhood also made the list; including a friend's mother who made sexual advances toward him. As each name or incident made its way onto the paper, a brief description of the offense was usually offered. It was apparent this trip down memory lane was a painful one.

Forgiving the undeserving and the unforgivable for words spoken or deeds done is not something people are typically inclined to do on their own. It clashes with our selfish human nature. Our natural tendency is to hold the perpetrator liable until a sincere apology is given or some other form of restitution is made…or pay them back for their wrongdoing.

The only way anyone is truly able to forgive those who don't deserve to be forgiven is if the Lord leads them to do so. God is the only One who initiates the liberating process. The act of forgiving is not to benefit the wrongdoer but to free the forgiver. It doesn't mean you forget the offense, but you release it to the righteous Judge. By forgiving others, God will forgive you, free you from bondage, and draw you into a deeper relationship with Him.

After half an hour of recollecting life's most unpleasant moments, Steve had come up with 32 individuals (and groups) he needed to forgive. While this list may have only scratched the surface, God knew his heart, his intent, and the motive behind his obedient act. With the oppressive exploits exposed and offenders named, I asked if he'd join me in prayer.

He willingly bowed his head. As I began to pray aloud, with the list tightly secure between our locked hands, the Lord told me to have Steve read the name of every person on the list aloud. I raised my head to look at my spouse and relayed the message. "The Lord wants you to read each one of the names out loud."

I pushed the crumpled piece of paper into his hand, he looked down and clutched onto it. His hands were shaking involuntarily as a result of his compromised nervous system. Expressionless, he looked up at me then back down to the paper he was struggling to open. As instructed, he read each name off the list, one by one. Each name carried a different degree of weight and pain. Some names took longer to voice than others. Those, I could tell, were hefty burdens carried throughout this dear man's life. Through tears of anguish and tremendous relief, we concluded our prayer with a "Hallelujah" and an "Amen."

But for him, the process wasn't quite complete. He was fumbling with the piece of paper, tearing it into itty-bitty pieces. Instead of just throwing the list away in the trash, he announced, "I'm going to burn this then flush it down the toilet."

Proud of his accomplishment, I shot him a big smile and encouraged him to do just that! "That sounds like a great idea!"

Off he went with a genuine feeling of satisfaction. I could tell an enormous weight had been lifted. When you let go of past hurts and forgive those who've done you wrong, an unbelievable sense of freedom is experienced. Too many people allow the past to pollute their future. They hold onto grudges, embrace their anger, and even seek revenge; justifying their angst and refusing to release the offense.

The Enemy loves this because it gives him a stronghold in your life—the ability to keep you trapped in bondage. As long as these feelings are allowed to linger, they intensify and can become controlling influences in your life. The only person it hurts is the one who is unwilling to forgive. If you are a follower of Christ, forgiving others is not an option. Whether you want to forgive or not is irrelevant. It is an act of obedience.

In the Lord's Prayer Jesus instructed believers to ask God to, "Forgive us our trespasses as we forgive those who trespass against us."[124] "If you forgive others when they sin against you, your heavenly Father will also forgive you. But if you do not forgive others their sins, your Father will not forgive your sins."[125]

Be advised that while the Adversary wants to deceive you into believing that people are your opposition, the reality is "our struggle is not against flesh and blood, but against the rulers, against the authorities, against the powers of this dark world and against the spiritual forces of evil in the heavenly realms."[126]

Chapter 11

# Staking Claim to the Truth

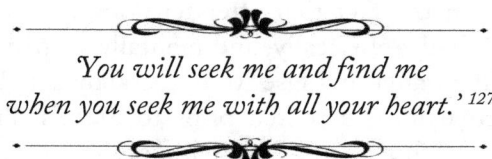

*'You will seek me and find me
when you seek me with all your heart.'* [127]

Weeks passed. It didn't seem as though our prayers were ever going to be answered. Every day became more and more challenging as we watched Steve's physical and mental health progressively deteriorate. His failing memory made it near impossible to converse. Without eating, he was withering away and becoming increasingly feeble. Maintaining his personal hygiene was exceptionally difficult, requiring way too much energy. So instead of getting up to take a shower, change his clothes, or brush his teeth, he remained in bed.

While sitting on the sidelines watching and waiting for God to respond to our ongoing prayer for Steve's healing, the girls and I wished there was something more we could do to help relieve his chronic pain. We wanted to comfort him in some way, to assist in managing his depression, to find him something to eat that would appease his nausea, to stop the ringing in his ears, or to quiet the antagonizing voices in his head. We missed his company, his smile, his spark, and his laughter. We longed to have his presence back in our lives. Because there were no visible signs of improvement, we did the only thing we knew to do—we cried out to God with yet another prayer.

Shortly after arriving in New Mexico—the Land of Enchantment, which the girls renamed "the Land of Entrapment," we settled into a moderately sized Assemblies of God Church. In the four years we were there, I had multiple discussions with the pastoral team about our family's predicament. Most everyone in the congregation knew of our ongoing struggle. They were supportive, prayerful, and empathetic to the fact that after ten long arduous years we were emotionally, physically, and mentally sapped.

More than anything else we desperately sought to return to the normal life we shared prior to Steve's illness, but it didn't look as though that was *ever* going to happen. Jesus had healed so many people, *why wasn't He healing Steve?* I wrestled with my emotions to remain faith-filled, believing that my husband had already received a miraculous healing in response to our prayers, but to be honest my natural eyes were contesting my conviction.

One Sunday morning, long after the service was over, I met with the pastoral staff in the church foyer to pray once again for Steve and our family. Sitting in the center of a long wooden bench with the senior pastor on my right, the associate pastor on my left, and a few elders crowding in around us, I sensed their love and genuine concern for our family's wellbeing. As soon as the senior pastor reached over and put his hand on top of mine, I attempted to update them on Steve's rapid decline.

It was extremely emotional voicing our dire predicament and sharing my inmost thoughts. "Steve is extremely weak and fatigued. He's tired of being tired and he's sick of being sick." My eyes welled up with tears. "His pain has dramatically intensified and his depression has worsened. He hasn't gotten out of bed for days," I sniffled. "He has no strength to shower or even change his clothes. I'm at a loss for what to do or how to help." With tears streaming down my face, I inhaled a slow deep breath and exhaled a long drawn out sigh. "We've tried everything. His physicians have exhausted all means to relieve his symptoms or improve his condition. We've reached another dead end."

Fully aware of our long-term search for medical attention, treatments, and relief for Steve's symptoms, along with our struggling to cope with the impact his disease continued to have on the family, this group of men was very empathetic, supportive, and willing to help any way they could. Then the excruciating reality quietly escaped my lips. "His memory is failing...Sometimes he doesn't even remember who I am...He's no longer eating...He's basically wasting away..."

Earlier in his office, I conferred with the senior pastor about the prayer I'd been intending to pray with him and the elders of the church. It was a prayer unlike any other—a radical prayer that I hoped would be answered quickly and never have to be repeated. Due to the severity of the invocation he gave me a very stern look before commencing and asked, "Are you *sure* you want to do this?"

Sniveling, I slowly and solemnly nodded. *It had to be done.* The seriousness of the moment made it unbelievably intense. Everyone leaning in toward me was forewarned as to what was going to take place when we joined together. We all shared a deep, unwavering conviction in Christ and firmly believed in the incredible power of prayer. Prayer is not something to be taken lightly—God listens and God responds.

The prayer was poignant and direct. It went something like this, "Lord Jesus we need a miracle. Steve has been suffering far too long. We're asking for your divine intervention. Please heal him completely...or take him." This was a black and white prayer. There were no shades of gray. Our plea was for God to either heal him completely or take him. That was it.

For two weeks straight that group of prayer warriors continued to intercede on our behalf with that same prayer. Every one of us, including the man we were praying for, wanted nothing more than to witness a miraculous healing. Yet despite the outcome, Steve, the girls, and I were long overdue for a change. We were more than ready to break free from the heavy chains that had been weighing us down for such a prolonged period of time, but what that would look like, we weren't sure.

It was Sunday, June 10, 2007. Exactly one week before Father's Day. The girls and I were getting ready for church when Steve asked a very uncharacteristic question, "Can I go to church with you?"

"What?" I had to ask him to repeat himself to make sure I heard him correctly.

"I'd like to go to church with you and the girls this morning." He reiterated.

"Absolutely!" I gleefully exclaimed, trying to contain my enthusiasm so I wouldn't scare him into retracting his request. *I'd been praying for this day for years.*

We'd been together for over a quarter century and I considered it a blessing when he chose to accompany us to church on Christmas or on Easter. He never came on Sunday. Although he was always welcome to join us, after multiple invitations were met with recurring rejection, I stopped asking. But for some reason this Sunday was different. God was obviously tugging on his heartstrings, motivating him to take action; maybe today's message was one the ailing man needed to hear. Whatever the reason, I was delighted that my husband was finally going to be sitting by my side in the Lord's house.

Everyone in our church family kept Steve in prayer, not only because of his illness, but also because he didn't yet have a personal relationship with Jesus Christ. Years ago I thought Steve had accepted the gift of salvation at the Mario Murillo crusade, but he later denied the claim, which became painstakingly evident shortly after the event. While he believed in Jesus the man, along with His crucifixion, he wasn't convinced Jesus rose from the dead or that He was truly God in flesh. The fact that he'd been raised in a Christian home seemed to have no influence on his spiritual outlook.

It was so encouraging to see Steve up and out of bed, suppressing his pain, rising above his depression, and moving around getting ready for church like a normal, healthy human being. He'd been wearing the same blue plaid, button-down shirt and jeans for weeks and he hadn't showered, shaved, or brushed his teeth in several days. As he stepped out of the shower to grab a towel, his dark curls were dripping with water; his body was so thin his ribs and hipbones prominently protruded from beneath his skin. Watching my invalid husband make a deliberate effort to prepare for this particular outing was extremely heartwarming, because for him it was a very difficult and time-consuming process.

However, it wasn't Steve who was dragging his feet this morning, it was Jenni. A couple weeks earlier she had her jaw reconstructed and she was having an awful allergic reaction to the surgical tape. Her face was bright red, still slightly swollen, and covered with blotches, bumps, and open sores. And although it was incredibly painful, she admitted that her appearance was much worse than the discomfort and burning sensation she was experiencing. Her beautiful face was repugnant, making her extremely self-conscious and unsure about showing up at church where people would see her in such an objectionable state.

Her dad was having concerns of his own. "I'll have to wear my cap, ya know," he established while sitting on the edge of the bed floundering to get his pants on.

"Yeah, I know." I answered nodding in affirmation, untwisting the lower part of his pant leg so he could pull it on.

Then he apologetically added, "But I really don't want to, because wearing a cap in church is disrespectful—but I *have* to..."

I sympathized with him, fully understanding the moral dilemma he was facing. The only way he'd be able to sit through the service without experiencing extreme pain or having a neurological meltdown from the radiation emanating from nearby cell towers was to wear his black leather Harley Davidson cap lined with special shielding material. Knowing churchgoers would likely frown on anyone wearing a cap into the sanctuary without ever taking it off, Steve began to have serious reservations about following through with his plan. His cap would make him appear downright rude, but without it, the discomfort would be far too great for him to endure.

There was a reason Steve asked to come to church with us this morning and I wasn't going to allow this excuse, however valid, to keep him away. "It's okay if you wear your cap, God understands. He knows your heart," I reassured. I really hoped the churchgoers would be accepting of the man who was taking a giant step just to make his way through the church doors.

While nothing was more important than getting Steve to church, Holly and I had a previous commitment, requiring us to leave the house earlier than usual, but neither one of us wanted to go. Without our coaxing, the two of them had enough excuses to talk each other out of making the trip into town. Staying home would be much easier and less stressful. As my youngest daughter and I were pulling out of the driveway we prayed that we'd see our loved ones at church and the Enemy wouldn't get the best of them.

Ten minutes into the service there was still no sign of our two stragglers. As Holly and I stood singing with the congregation, our eyes shifting from the worship team up front to the side doors behind, we prayerfully and patiently waited for their grand entrance. One reverent song led to another...and another. When we finally saw the two of them walk into the sanctuary, we instinctively grabbed each other's hand and shared a gentle squeeze. We smiled with pride as we watched Jenni with her blotchy, crimson-colored face slowly lead her frail father in his black leather cap across the room toward us where two seats were being saved. I immensely thanked God for their attendance.

Throughout the entire service I was praising my Lord and Savior for getting the feeble man beside me to come to church. For years I sat alone, hoping and praying that one day Steve would sit by my side in a sanctuary where we could worship together. Today I rejoiced in the fact that he was here, sharing in this special part of my life, but the best was yet to come...

As mentioned earlier, our church gives an altar call every week—an open invitation for anyone wanting to enter into a relationship with Christ. The sermon was on "staking your claim" to faith and believing Jesus to be victorious in overcoming the impossibilities in your life. Those ready to receive His wonderful gift of salvation, trusting that He can do exceedingly more than we dare ask, ever hope for, or imagine, were given the opportunity to go forward and accept the tangible token of a nine-inch wooden stake to symbolize their spiritual commitment. Instructions were given to plant the stake in your yard as a sign that God would do whatever you believed Him to do.

Since Steve was physically unable to take that step forward on his own, I asked if he wanted to walk up and stake his claim as described in the sermon. Not sure how much of the message he was able to grasp; I simplified the concept, urging him to surrender his life to Christ and to believe Him for the healing miracle he so desperately needed. Slowly and decisively he shook his head indicating no interest. But instead of being discouraged, I closed my eyes and began to pray.

You know how sometimes experiences happen in slow motion so you remember them more vividly? Well this was one of those times. The swarm of people making their way upfront to the altar to claim their stake, to surrender their life to Christ, and to partake in communion which was simultaneously being served, moved at a snail's pace. Five minutes must have gone by before I turned to my partner and asked a second time if he wanted to take a step forward as an act of faith.

This time his eyes locked on mine and the shifting in his seat seemed to indicate that he was ready to make the best decision of his life. My heart leapt with joy! Holly, who was sitting on the other side of her father, beamed from ear to ear and quickly began helping me lift him up out of his seat. I firmly took hold of Steve's bony upper arm and gently led him, weak and unsteady, to the front of the sanctuary. I couldn't believe it! The feeling was exhilarating—a spiritual high.

The worship team was distributing stakes from up on stage, so in order to seize one you had to reach up and take it out of someone's hand. With a sense of urgency my husband stared at me, wanting me to grab *his* stake from the young man leaning down handing it him, but I refused. Despite how badly I wanted Steve to accept God's amazing gift and His eternal promises, I wasn't going to claim them on his behalf. If he wanted the symbolic token as evidence of his decision to follow Christ and his believing by faith for a divine healing, he'd have to exert the effort to snatch the stake himself.

Standing side-by-side just a couple feet below the stage, I patiently assisted and encouraged my dear, sweet Steve to raise his arm higher in order to obtain the prize. It took a tremendous amount of energy for him to stretch his arm and hold it out far enough to claim his stake. When he triumphed over the physical obstacles that stood between his present state and the spiritual hope of a brighter future, I was overjoyed…and so was he. He embraced the stake, holding it tightly against his chest as if his life depended on it. I helped him over to where communion was being served.

Tears flowed freely as my bubbling exuberance sought to find a viable outlet. Then together, for the first time ever, my beloved and I shared in the sacred act of communion—drinking the grape juice symbolic of Christ's blood shed for us and eating the bread representative of His flesh, remembering the Savior's ultimate sacrifice for us until He returns.

Back at our seats Jenni and Holly were on their feet eagerly waiting with open arms to congratulate their father. Their tear-soaked eyes mirrored mine. The three of us had long been praying and anticipating the day when the most significant man in our lives would make the same spiritual decision we'd each made years earlier. We were thrilled and so very proud of his declaration of faith. Watching Steve sitting quietly in his chair and staring blankly into space, while hugging his wooden token of redemption and promise of hope, was incredibly moving.

While the girls and I exchanged thoughtful glances, pondering what the man sitting in between us might be thinking, we were rejoicing with the angels in heavenly celebration. God's amazing love toward Steve and His generous outpouring of grace was overwhelming. Our petition and prayers had not only been heard, they had finally been answered. We were so grateful our hearts were bursting with thanksgiving. Would Steve's declaration of faith be the key to his healing? We were confidently optimistic.

As my thoughts and feelings reeled, the pastor's niece who was visiting for the day broke into song. "I Can Only Imagine" by MercyMe resonated throughout the building, filling the sanctuary with holy wonder. The chorus sparks the imagination, inviting you to ponder what your heart might feel and what you might do the instant you finally meet Jesus face-to-face—"Will I dance for you Jesus or in awe of you be still? Will I stand in your presence or to my knees will I fall? Will I sing Hallelujah? Will I be able to speak at all? I can only imagine."

Beautifully packaged in a spiritual atmosphere, with the preceding events and a melodious soprano voice singing the award-winning lyrics, made it easy to envision entering the kingdom of heaven and being in the awesome presence of Almighty God for the very first time! What a glorious moment that will be!

It's a promise every believer holds onto so tightly and so dear; there is nothing more precious than knowing we have been chosen to spend all of eternity with our loving Creator. This morning the thought of passing from this life into the next captivated the hearts of most everyone in the congregation. However, I would not fully understand the true meaning and purpose behind that particular song choice until the following Sunday.

Chapter 12

# Believing for Your Miracle

*We wait in hope for the L<small>ORD</small>; he is our help and our shield.
In him our hearts rejoice, for we trust in His holy name.
May your unfailing love rest upon us, O L<small>ORD</small>,
even as we put our hope in you.*[128]

Monday morning, with steamy hot coffee in hand, I headed out to the sunroom and sat down in my Adirondack chair. Taking a sip of the strong brew, I gazed out over the rim at the beautiful mountain view. *What a gift!* It was another glorious day in the southwest. The sun was brightly shining in the infinite blue sky. Relishing the magnificent splendor that surrounded me, I was once again overcome by a deep sense of gratitude. My eyes flooded with tears as I reflected on the commitment Steve made the previous day at church.

On his own, without any prompting from his wife or his daughters, he made the decision of a lifetime—to accept the gift of God that brings spiritual healing, forgiveness, eternal life, and complete restoration—a gift that only comes through faith in Jesus Christ. We'd been praying years for *that* miracle.

While reliving those treasured moments, I once again found myself praising God for drawing Steve closer to Him—for planting within him a desire to attend the church service, for softening his heart to receive the message, for making him receptive to the calling, and for motivating him to take action. During this peaceful spell of adoration and thanksgiving, the Holy Spirit broke through with a question. "Don't you remember the prayer that you prayed?"

Diverting my attention away from joyful reflection, I focused on the sudden, unexpected query. *What prayer?* I closed my eyes to recall past prayers. It wasn't easy to pinpoint any particular one. Over the past ten years I'd prayed hundreds of different prayers for Steve—prayers for salvation, improved health, healing, answers, peace, pain relief, comfort, medical direction...and most recently a final end to his decade-long affliction. As previously mentioned, if one prayer didn't seem to be working I'd move on to the next—hoping for faster, more favorable results.

I was stumped. I had no idea which prayer the Holy Spirit was referencing. So I asked, "What prayer?"

The answer came quick—firm and direct. "You said if I needed to break him, to break him."

Stunned by the Holy Spirit's instantaneous comeback and word-for-word accuracy, I burst into tears. *Yes, I remembered praying that prayer for months.* However, the revelation of its execution *now* was particularly heart wrenching, but God had been waiting patiently for Steve's will to align with His. And in doing so, Steve finally surrendered his life to Christ. He was saved! A new creation! On track for a better life here *and* eternal life with God.

While contemplating the divine interface, I was suddenly struck with a profound spiritual reality—the last time I prayed *that* prayer was over four years ago! *You mean to tell me You were still working on a prayer I prayed more than four years ago?* So many other requests had been made since then. Why did God choose to answer *that* prayer over some of the others? Apparently, *that* prayer request was in accordance to His will (in agreement with His own plan and purpose).[129]

"This is what the LORD says, he who made the earth, the LORD who formed it and established it—the LORD is his name: 'Call to me and I will answer you and tell you great and unsearchable things you do not know.'"[130]

Perhaps that's why the Lord asked, "Don't you remember the prayer that you prayed?" It was important for Him to enlighten me as to which prayer was being answered, so I'd be cognizant of the fact that He'd been working on that same prayer for over four years. And just because there were no visible signs of any changes taking place in the natural realm, did not mean something wasn't happening in the spiritual realm. Things *were* happening!

Changing hearts, modifying behavior, relinquishing addictions, healing relationships, even breaking a defiant spirit aren't typically things that transpire overnight. They take time. While I was moving from one prayer to the next, thinking God wasn't answering, He was being faithfully responsive—I just didn't know it!

In today's world where virtually everything can be done with a click of a button or by a tap of a screen, waiting has become an incredible irritant. Patience is a virtue that seems to be slipping away. If *something* doesn't happen right away we persistently click until something does. That's exactly the way I'd been praying for years. The lack of instant gratification tends to challenge our ability to trust God. But this example establishes that whether we recognize it or not, God always hears and acts on prayers that align with His will long before we ever see any evidence of it.

You've heard it said, "God's timing is perfect." Yet more often than not, His timing is out of sync with ours, because

He usually takes much longer than we anticipate. Four years was a long time for me to wait, but four years was nothing compared to the length of time Abraham had to wait for God to answer his prayer and fulfill His promises.

A number of saints in the Bible understood waiting for God's perfect timing, but none more than Abram (later renamed Abraham). For 25 years Abram faithfully waited for God to answer his prayer and fulfill His promises—"I will make your offspring like the dust of the earth."[131] "All the people on earth will be blessed through you."[132]

There was just one problem—Abram and his wife Sarai had no children, and when God made these promises, Abram was 75 years of age and Sarai was 65.[133] After ten years of waiting to become pregnant, Sarai grew impatient. Since God seemed unable to get the job done in a timely manner, she devised a plan of her own to expedite a family. Since it was common to have multiple wives, Sarai gave her Egyptian maidservant to her husband; they conceived and gave birth to a son.[134]

When the Lord appeared 13 years later to fulfill His promises, He changed their names to Abraham and Sarah. Abraham was 100 years old and Sarah was 90 when she gave birth to their son Isaac![135]

Although Sarah wavered in her faith, Abraham did not. He was empowered by faith, praising and glorifying God for what he had already received long before it ever materialized. Even at the ripe old age of 99, against the odds of his impotent body and Sarah's barren womb, which were both good as dead, Abraham continued to believe that all things were possible with God. By faith Abraham and his offspring received God's promises.[136]

"Faith is being sure of what we hope for and certain of what we do not see."[137] Faith never denies the existence of a problem, but focuses on the Problem-Solver in lieu of the problem. Fixing our eyes not on the visible here and now, but daring to look beyond into the invisible and eternal, is an empowering way to overcome adversity and experience victory in life.[138] With the emphasis on God, there is confident optimism and a hopeful expectation that He is orchestrating all things to work together for good.

The majority of miracles in the Bible were fueled by faith-driven actions—*By faith*, we understand God created the heavens and the earth. *By faith*, before it had ever rained, Noah built an ark to save his family from the coming flood. *By faith*, when God told Abraham to "go," he obeyed without knowing where he was being sent. *By faith*, Moses' mother hid the extraordinary child, unafraid of Pharaoh's edict to kill all Hebrew males at birth. *By faith*, the Israelites passed through the Red Sea on dry land, while the Egyptians following drowned. *By faith*, the walls of Jericho came tumbling down after the trumpet sounded and the people shouted. *By faith*, Shadrach, Meshach, and Abednego refused to worship a golden idol as ordered and were kept from being consumed by the flames of the king's fiery furnace.

People who choose to live *by faith*, relying on God and His ability to do the impossible, have gained incredible favor throughout time—kingdoms have been conquered by armies ill equipped to fight, enemies have been defeated using remarkable tactics, escapes have been made by believers being hunted down or imprisoned, justice has been served in extraordinary ways, typical animal behavior has been altered, and the very course of nature itself has been interrupted in order to accommodate God's people.

The Lord is always looking for opportunities to bless, strengthen, encourage, and move mountains for those fully devoted to Him.[139] He longs to exert His power and reveal Himself to those with resilient faith. To God, there is nothing more precious than faith. Faith is like a red carpet being rolled out, it's an enticing invitation that beckons Him to step into an active, leading role in your life. "Without faith it is impossible to please God, because anyone who comes to him must believe that he exists and that he rewards those who earnestly seek him."[140]

Do you lack faith? If so, do what the apostles did—ask Jesus to increase your faith.[141] Faith will embolden you to rise above every pain, worry, doubt, fear, and obstacle that stands in your way of living a life full of joy and abundance. God's desire is to lavish you with blessings, so feed your faith daily with Scripture, because faith comes from hearing the Word of God.[142]

Perhaps today you find yourself in a difficult situation that's requiring you to wait on the Lord and fully trust Him for what seems to be a real impossibility. How long you'll have to wait for your prayer(s) to be answered is uncertain, but don't lose heart…and refuse to give up. The issues currently demanding your attention, threatening to steal your joy, are only temporary. Every day is overflowing with endless possibilities and renewed hope.

Although waiting is never easy, if we model our lives after those in God's Hall of Faith—remaining faith-filled, trusting, and obedient, knowing full well that God has a plan and purpose for our lives—our prayer(s) will be answered and His promises will materialize.

*'For I know the plans I have for you,' declares the* LORD, *'plans to prosper you and not to harm you, plans to give you hope and a future. Then you will call on me and come and pray to me, and I will listen to you. You will seek me and find me when you seek me with all your heart. I will be found by you.'* [143]

"But those who wait for the LORD [who expect, look for, and hope in Him] will gain new strength *and* renew their power; they will lift up their wings [and rise up close to God] like eagles [rising toward the sun]; they will run and not become weary, they will walk and not grow tired."[144] Blessed are those who wait on the Lord, who seek Him and wait expectantly for Him to respond.[145] Those who hope in the LORD will not be disappointed.[146]

Chapter 13

# A Twisted Turn

*Jesus said to His disciples,
'Peace I leave with you; my peace I give you.
I do not give to you as the world gives.
Do not let your hearts be troubled and do not be afraid.'* [147]

The following Wednesday night around ten o'clock, after watching a little TV, I quietly made my way into the bedroom where Steve was sleeping. Slowly I pulled back the blankets and crawled in next to him, trying to limit my movement so he wouldn't be disturbed. The ailing man had been lying in the same position all day long, but since he was still breathing there seemed to be little cause for concern. That was until my head hit the pillow, I let out a long gentle sigh, and he mumbled, "Take me to the hospital."

Did you say, "Take me to the hospital?" Over the past ten years our perception of those in the medical profession had become less than favorable, so I had to be sure I accurately understood what he was striving to communicate. He strained to repeat the instruction through a vaguely discernible murmur.

With a keen sense of urgency I threw off the covers, leapt to my feet, and scurried over to his side of the bed. Bending down, I wrapped my arms around his chest, and with all my might I tried elevating his body to a sitting position. It took way more effort than expected. He was extremely weak and completely out-of-it, unable to sit up, move, or assist in any way. For someone who was wasting away to nothing, he weighed a ton!

I immediately started hollering across the house for the girls to come and help. In a mode of panic they rushed to my aid. Even with the three of us working together, moving their father was impossible. I ran to the phone, picked it up, and with trembling fingers pressed 9-1-1.

It took close to an hour for the ambulance to make its way down the long, winding one lane dirt road through the forest, into the creek bed, and up the driveway. While anxiously waiting for the medical unit to arrive, two distant neighbors who were paramedics and volunteer firefighters were dispatched to the house. They came in, marched straight to the bed where Steve was now lying unconscious, and began checking his vital signs. When the flashlight was shining directly in his eyes and there was no response, my heart sank.

From across the bed Jenni, Holly, and I locked tear-filled eyes. This was yet another heart-wrenching episode in the saga of our lives. Our thoughts melded together—*Was this the end?* Just two weeks earlier I'd prayed a dangerous prayer with the senior pastor and church elders. We pleaded for an end to this draining, decade-long ordeal, requesting that God either heal Steve or take him. *Was this His answer?* We were sure of it.

As soon as the ambulance arrived, the EMTs raced in and the volunteers began rattling off all the data they had collected. Without any hesitation or effort, they managed to shift Steve's lifeless body from the bed unto a stretcher, which they wheeled out and pushed into the rear opening of the ambulance. The girls and I jumped into our SUV and followed the medical unit as it cautiously crept out of the jet-black forest toward the hospital.

On the way I had Holly phone pastor Monte, Papa Clayton, and my best friend Sylvia. "This is it," she assuredly declared. "Please pray!"

Once Steve was admitted and in an emergency room hospital bed, the girls and I stood over his motionless body, staring down at the man we so dearly adored. His body was there, but he wasn't. I couldn't have asked God for a more loving husband or a more patient, giving, and caring father for the girls. We'd been blessed in so many ways. As a family our priority was always to spend both quantity and quality time together. We enjoyed each other's company immensely; our lives had been full of fun and laughter. And even though a dark shadow loomed over the previous decade, an intentional effort was made to cling tightly to the memories we'd created before our beloved was sick.

In the privacy of Steve's hospital room the only sounds were those of sobbing and sniffling. We were deeply saddened and justifiably angry by the issues that led up to this point. Because of one Fortune 500 Company's negligence in protecting their employees from toxic chemicals and exposure to close-range radiofrequency microwave radiation, we were robbed of our happily-ever-after together.

Within an hour of our arrival the lead physician came into the room to assess the situation. He examined Steve's Ziploc baggie full of prescription drugs and reviewed the available information, then without so much as a greeting, looked at us and reported there was little that could be done to improve his condition. With that, he abruptly turned and walked out.

With that, we concluded it was time to say our final

good-byes. Through tears of great sorrow, one by one we painfully took a turn standing at the head of our loved one's bedside looking down at the vaguely familiar face. It was a haunting sight—his flesh was an odd greyish-tone, his eyes were closed and dark charcoal circles were set deeply below their sockets, his cheekbones protruded as the flesh acutely sank into his skull, his lips were parched and peeling, his breathing was weak and shallow. "I love you" and "I'll miss you" were the heartfelt phrases woven into our last words. Truth was, we'd been missing him for years.

With tear-soaked eyes, Holly rested her hand on her father's arm. "Thanks for being my dad," she whispered.

"You were the best," Jenni murmured. A tear fell from her eye as she gently stroked her father's cheek with the back of her hand.

"In heaven you'll be with Jesus, free from pain and out of misery," I reminded him before kissing his forehead. We all agreed that since Steve had given his life to Christ, eternal life would prove to be a magnificent reward.

After being confined to the sterile cubicle for over two hours, sobbing and waiting for the end to come, the unimaginable happened—spiritually as well as physically. Suddenly, it was as if the bowels of the earth opened up and sadistically regurgitated all of its demons out into that emergency room to invoke terror. In one abrupt movement, Steve lunged forward with ferocious vigor from his lifeless state, and as if being held against his will, he attempted to leap off the bed. With no thought or conscious awareness of where he was or what he was doing, he viciously ripped the IV out of his arm and began tearing off all the monitoring lines that were attached to him. If you've ever seen the Incredible Hulk transition from man to beast then you can begin to imagine the kind of horrifying incident we were witnessing.

Shocked and extremely frightened, the girls and I simultaneously screamed for help! Three male nurses from down the hall dropped what they were doing, rushed to the room, and tore open the privacy curtain to see their previously unresponsive patient raging with energy and fighting for his freedom.

As one of the nurses was hollering for backup, the other two sped over to try and restrain the monster. While fighting to grab hold of his limbs, Steve was aggressively kicking, twisting and turning to loosen their grip, trying his best to flee. Other staff members raced in to assist.

I couldn't believe what I was seeing! *How could this be the same frail man I had to help walk up to the altar just a few days ago?* During the lengthy power struggle one of the nurses was able to inject the patient with a mild sedative and strap him down to the bed.

The girls and I never ever experienced anything like that before. Steve's outrageous behavior was terrifying! We were taken aback by the unexpected turn of events. One minute we're saying good-bye, mourning the loss of love; the next minute we're traumatized, questioning God's timing. Why didn't He take Steve before we had to witness that harrowing ordeal?

What happened next was both disgraceful and appalling—not to mention illegal. The physician in charge made the merciless decision to release the patient and send him home...with us! "What? NO!" I contested, shouting through tears of disbelief and fury. "Are you crazy?" For minutes I pleaded with the apathetic jerk to consider our safety and the patient's wellbeing. "Please keep him overnight for observation," I begged. "Transfer him to the psych ward...or send him somewhere else for care." I was running out of suggestions. Gasping for air and using every ounce of energy I had, I exclaimed, "You can't just send him home with us! You just can't!"

He adamantly disagreed and obstinately refused to consider my desperate appeal. Even though there were plenty of hospital beds available and a national (MATALA) law prohibits the release of any patient from a hospital emergency room before their condition has stabilized, the physician unashamedly denied my pleas for help and ordered Steve to be discharged.

I was enraged and extremely concerned for our safety. *What were we going to do?* We just watched a scene from a real-life horror film...and it was becoming increasingly more dreadful. Like Robert Louis Stevenson's classic *Dr. Jekyll & Mr. Hyde*—the mild-mannered Dr. Jekyll was brought in to the ER and the head doctor wanted to send the girls and I home with the wildly out-of-control Mr. Hyde! Sure he was sedated now, but what was going to happen when the sedative wore off?

Deeply distraught, the three of us continued to solicit empathy and aid from every nurse within earshot as the release papers were being processed. "Please don't force us take him home. We don't feel safe." From what they observed, they knew our concerns were valid. Yet like the physician, they turned a deaf ear to our cries. Our relentless petitions followed the two male nurses who were wheeling Steve out to the car. We charged, "This is wrong! You know it is!"

"We're sorry. We're just following orders," they robotically repeated multiple times to quiet our insistent imploring. While putting Steve's sedated body in the backseat, they profusely apologized for the doctor's reckless decision. They fought to remain professional while knowing full well that what they were doing was not only illegal, but morally wrong. Even though they didn't agree with the orders that were issued, their job was to obey them, not to question them.

After buckling Steve in, one of the nurses pulled me aside. "You know," he paused, quickly scanning the area to make sure no one could overhear what he was about to say, "You could take him to the jail. They'd keep him overnight."

I was shocked! "Really? Jail?" I couldn't believe the nurse's recommendation. He was fully aware that they were putting our lives in danger by sending Steve home with us...but jail?

For a split second the thought crossed my mind. Even though he posed a possible threat, I couldn't warrant leaving the man I loved in a jail cell overnight where others might badger him or inflict harm. He didn't deserve that—he wasn't a criminal; he was ill. But in hindsight that would've been a much better choice than taking him home.

Shortly after leaving the hospital Steve regained consciousness and resumed his fury. It was unbelievably frightening. The girls and I remained quiet, ignoring his vocal outbursts and aggressive accusations. I hurriedly sped through the forest faster than I ever had before, bouncing up and down over the rough terrain. I couldn't get us home and out of the car fast enough.

As soon as we made our way up the driveway I ordered the girls to quickly jump out, go directly to their rooms, lock their doors, and stay put. The second I turned off the car, the three of us bolted into the house and locked ourselves inside the bedrooms. Holly went in her room and I went with Jenni into hers. We left Steve in the Blazer to find his own way in. None of us had any idea what to expect. We were hoping he'd head straight for bed...we would've been so lucky.

Jenni and I tried to be as still as statues when the back door opened and we heard Steve making his way down the hall toward the bedrooms. We held our breath as our hearts pounded ferociously against our chests. Trembling uncontrollably, we fixed our eyes on each other, anticipating what would happen next in this hellish nightmare.

Then the knob on Jenni's locked bedroom door started to turn. Our eyes grew wider and the stare between us intensified. Steve tried turning the knob again and again, pushing and pulling to try and open the door, each attempt became increasingly more ferocious.

"I know you're in there!" A loud, gruff voice accused. It didn't sound at all like Steve. Then he began pounding violently on the hollow door, threatening to take it down.

"Go away!" Jenni demanded.

"Come out here!" he ordered.

"What do you want?" Jenni yelled back, crying hysterically.

"I want your mother," he commanded. "I know she's in there."

We froze with fright as we waited for the reign of terror and the yelling to stop. It wasn't until four in the morning that Steve finally collapsed from exhaustion…and the girls and I could get some badly needed rest after such an emotionally charged escapade. Never before had we ever witnessed anything remotely close to that type of behavior from Steve. He's always been such a calm, gentle, patient man and loving father who never raised his voice or lifted a hand against us. But tonight something snapped—

The following morning Jenni, Holly, and I were over anxious to get out of the house and extremely grateful for a previously planned day trip to the river with Sylvia and her two kids. On the way out I quietly tiptoed into the master bedroom to grab my bathing suit—that was a monumental mistake! Steve sensed my presence and in one rapid-fire movement he sprang up from the bed and onto his feet, landing right in front of me and blocking my path. He rigidly stood inches from my face, glaring at me with wild eyes, before he resumed his hollering.

Consumed by unprovoked fear, he deliriously started accusing me of calling the sheriff or someone from the Silver City mental institution to come take him away and lock him up. He was visibly distraught, reliving the horror he'd experienced in Michigan when he was picked up and forced to spend a week in the psychiatric facility for threatening suicide. In self-defense, I once again denied the charges. The claims were untrue, yet he held onto the delusion that I had something to do with that impounding.

After breaking free from his barricade on my way out the door, I suddenly stopped, spun around, and bravely took a giant step toward him, got right up in his face and laid out his future. "Listen, I love you, but there is no way we can continue living like this. I wish there was some way to help you or get help for you. I have tried everything."

Overcome with exhaustion, immense sorrow, and utter frustration I sighed, then taking a deep, thoughtful breath I pointed my forefinger at him and delivered a stern warning. "If this madness continues, I'll have no other choice but to put you in a home—undoubtedly near a cell tower. We can't live like this anymore! You can't live like this anymore!" I turned and swiftly made my way out the back door.

I was further traumatized as the distressed man followed the girls and me out of the house to continue his accusatory rant. He was still shouting allegations as we drove down the driveway. I couldn't believe it! I really wanted to be empathic to his deteriorating mental condition and to his accelerating brain damage, but this threatening, irate behavior was the final straw. It was more than I could handle—more than I wanted to handle. I didn't know how to proceed...and I didn't want to.

When we met up with Sylvia I asked her kids to jump in the SUV with Jenni and Holly so she and I could ride solo. There was a lot I needed to unload on my dear friend. As we trailed the Chevy Blazer to the river, a ride taking over an hour, I filled her in on every detail that transpired since arriving at the hospital the night before. She was astounded and had a difficult time imagining that what I was telling her was true. I was having a hard time believing it myself.

The verbal recall of the horrific ordeal was excruciatingly painful. The emotional torment was insufferable, so much so that I asked God to make a decision. "Take either one of us today—him or me. I am s-o-o-o-o ready for this hell on earth to be over!" At that moment I truly didn't care which one of us He'd choose to take. One way or another the insanity had to end. I was done living the decade-long nightmare.

I was sincerely hoping the fifth of Bacardi rum I brought along would numb the pain. After hiking downhill to the slow-moving river, we set up our lawn chairs and looked forward to a relaxing, uneventful day. The girls and I desperately needed one. The three teenage girls and Sylvia's tween-age boy were excited to be at the swimming hole. From the water's edge they reported the temperature to be "a bit nippy," but that wasn't going to deter them from getting wet. As we reclined, basking in the warm sun, Sylvia and I continued chatting. I was so grateful to have her as a friend; she was truly a Godsend—so empathetic and easy to talk with.

Watching the kids frolicking, laughing, and splashing around in the water did little to elevate my anguished spirit. Slugging down one rum & Diet Pepsi after another didn't help much either. I was deeply grieved and confused. No matter how hard I tried to redirect our conversation and shift the focus away from our family's current hell to any other subject, it was impossible to shake off the happenings of the past fifteen hours.

The sun was setting and in the west beautiful tones of pink, purple, and orange decorated the sky. I vaguely remember stumbling back to the car and breaking my sandal strap along the way. Jenni drove Holly and me to Sonic, an old-fashioned drive-in restaurant, so we could get a non-alcoholic "special drink" and a bite to eat before heading home. We weren't ready to go home—we didn't want to go home.

After the ranting episodes of last night and earlier this morning we were extremely apprehensive. We had no idea what to expect. But it had been a long day, an even longer night before, and we were exhausted. All the way home we desperately prayed that Steve would be in bed asleep.

With headlights shining brightly we drove slowly and silently through the dark forest, taking our time, hoping to spot a woodland creature. We'd seen all kinds of critters driving home at night—wild pigs, long-eared hares, foxes, coyotes, and enormous snakes. Tonight we saw nothing.

As we drove out from the creek and started up the driveway nothing changed. We were still engulfed in blackness; there was no light coming through the trees from the house. We wanted to believe Steve was sleeping, but we instinctively shared an unnerving flashback to the last time we drove up to a dark house. After turning off the car we silently lingered for minutes just staring at one another, waiting to see if anything was going to happen—if Steve was going come out or if a light might turn on—we wanted some advance warning as to what we might be walking into.

Assuming he was probably asleep, but not quite sure, we quietly opened our doors and stepped out of the vehicle, closing them behind us without making a sound. We knew it was best if our presence went undetected. Warily, I slowly opened the back door and we entered the house without turning on any lights. It was incredibly eerie!

As our eyes adjusted to the dark we saw that the master bedroom door was slightly ajar, but we couldn't see inside. Together, we swiftly tiptoed into Holly's room and quietly closed the door, waiting to see if Steve was roused. Minutes passed before Jenni bravely left our hiding place to scope out the premises and check in on her dad.

She promptly returned with a torn piece of notebook paper in hand. It had her dad's handwriting on it. Her hands were shaking and her voice was quivering as she read these words aloud—"I love you all so very much. I can't continue living like this anymore. I'm sorry. Dad." Stunned by the discovery, the three of us intuitively huddled together, clinging onto one another for several minutes...hurting, grieving, and weeping.

The suicide note was found on the floor of the master bathroom, in front of the toilet en route to the shower, where the door was closed and Steve's dead body lay. Jenni reported seeing only a shadow through the frosted glass. In his thoughtfulness, our beloved strategically set the stage so that none of us would have to witness the sight of his grotesquely mutilated corpse with its self-inflicted rifle wound. For this, I am eternally grateful. Numb and trembling, I lifted the phone off its cradle and pressed 9-1-1, just as I had the night before. Mystified and speechless we sat in silence on Holly's bedroom floor with our two black dogs waiting for the response team to arrive.

Despite his failing memory, Steve had sporadic bouts of clarity when he was acutely aware of his fragile predicament. I was convinced he had one such moment earlier that day, giving him the opportunity to seriously contemplate his quandary. Reason being, is that while conversing with the sheriff who responded to my 9-1-1 call, I noticed the carpet shampooer leaning up against the dining room table with the cord neatly wrapped in place. Prior to taking his life, Steve cleaned the carpet where he had spilled a Coke a few days earlier.

Over the years I frequently asked Steve what he thought about while lying in bed all day, every day. He told me much of his time was spent devising the perfect escape from his progressively worsening, life-threatening disease—so the act wasn't entirely unexpected. With no known cure or remedy to ease his persistent pain; no drugs to effectively manage, control, or reverse his long litany of ailments; and with nothing to look forward to but the high probability of developing brain cancer or a brain tumor, Steve felt defeated.

As it was, he had no quality of life—his body was deteriorating; his mind was muddled; his physical limitations were great; his neurological, digestive, and cardiovascular systems were declining; he was suffering mental anguish; he wasn't eating; he was unable to communicate; he could no longer care for himself; and his memory was failing. I am sure he grappled with the grim reality of his future.

Without divine intervention, his despairing existence, accompanied by his drastic change of behavior, doling out $2,000 a month for useless prescription drugs (exceeding his finally-secured SSDI payments), the heartbreaking truth that one day he'd be unable to recognize or remember his loved ones, the likelihood he'd have to spend the remainder of his life in a nursing home *near a cell tower*, and the mounting medical bills that coincide with that lifestyle—Steve opted out of his miserable life at the young age of 48.

It was one in the morning when I woke my mom, then Steve's dad, with a phone call conveying the traumatic news. My mother and sister, bless their hearts, were on the next flight out of Grand Rapids, Michigan to El Paso, Texas. At 5:00 a.m., in a foggy state of shock, the girls and I jumped into our SUV and headed toward the airport to pick them up. The Christian radio station automatically resumed playing as soon as I turned the key. I paid little attention to the music until about an hour or so into the three-hour drive.

A song reciting the Lord's Prayer broke through my daze. I scarcely recall hearing any of the lyrics, except those that seemed particularly pronounced—"Forgive us our trespasses as we forgive those who trespass against us." At that moment the Lord filled me with an overwhelming sense of peace and reassurance—revealing that He had forgiven my best friend of all his sins, including the so-called unforgivable sin of suicide, because Steve had forgiven those who had sinned against him (and his brother) two weeks earlier.

Chapter 14

# Glimmers of Glory

*My soul finds rest in God alone;
my salvation comes from him.
He alone is my rock and my salvation;
he is my fortress, I will never be shaken.*[148]

Here it was Sunday again, but it wasn't just any Sunday, it was Father's Day. Just last week the girls and I were in church with Steve, rejoicing over his proclamation of faith. Now just three days after his passing, we remained in a fog-like state, still numb to the fact that he was gone.

Since the incident I avoided the master bedroom as if it were a den of demons. The space made me extremely uncomfortable. I could no longer sleep in the bed we once shared or use the master bathroom where the note was left; let alone shower in the same stall Steve used as a transport vessel to carry his spirit out from this world and into the presence of God.

"It was there that the angels came to escort Steve into heaven," my mother suggested, attempting to offer some consolation and encouragement.[149] Although I knew she was right, for some inexplicable reason I just couldn't shake off my disconcerting feelings. It would simply take time.

Every year the church holds its annual summer picnic the third Sunday in June. This year that just happened to fall on Father's Day. Jenni, Holly, and I attended every picnic for the last three years, but today we didn't feel like joining in the festivities. We were weary from grieving, lack of sleep, and making funeral arrangements. Even so, it was a glorious day; the sun was shining and a gentle breeze was blowing. There couldn't have been a more perfect day for a potluck in the park. Admitting that it might do us all some good to get out of the house, we readied ourselves and set out to the event.

Just a few miles away, at the base of Gomez Peak, a large gazebo was decorated with lime green balloons and salmon-colored streamers. Dozens of people were mingling around picnic tables with color-coordinated tablecloths. Assorted food dishes scattered the top of two head tables. There were plenty of familiar faces. Everyone was smiling and having a good time. Children were excitedly running around, shrieking and chasing after one another in a highly charged game of tag. The affair looked promising, but I wasn't quite prepared to jump into all the hoopla, so I strolled off to find a more peaceful place away from the crowd.

Sitting alone at one of the brown painted picnic tables adjacent to the gazebo, I gazed up into the beautiful blue sky musing over the week. Then reflecting on the past decade. I was so sorry for all the years of pain my dear, sweet Steve had suffered, when all he wanted was provide to for his family and have a happy life. I missed the joy of our young love and time spent with the girls in their early years. Deeply saddened that our fate had been sealed, tears slowly slid down my face.

Then, as if the Lord reached down and spun me around, I was instantly awakened to the incredible reality that Steve was finally free! Free from his chronic pain! Free from his mental distress! He was no longer in bondage. Today he was praising God with the angels and enjoying the afterlife with *his* Savior Jesus Christ! While daydreaming about what that might look like, a young woman approached.

"Hello," she greeted with a warm smile.

"Hello," I replied looking up at her, using my hand to block the sun. I didn't recognize her until she introduced herself as the pastor's niece who sang at last week's church service.

"You have a beautiful voice," I told her. "And you did a lovely job singing I Can Only Imagine. I really like that song."

"Me too." She hesitated, and then asked, "May I sit down?"

"Sure," I obliged.

"I heard about your husband," she started. "Sorry for your loss."

"Thanks." I replied trying to force a smile.

Inquisitively she asked, "Can I share something with you?"

"Alright," I consented.

"That wasn't the song I originally planned on singing Sunday morning. I had another selection picked out. One I was really looking forward to performing, but the Lord prompted me to sing *that* one." After a thoughtful pause she continued, "I debated with Him all week about the song choice. Telling Him I really wanted to sing the other song, but He firmly impressed upon me to sing I Can Only Imagine."

"Last week I had no idea why it was so important for me to sing *that* particular song…this week I do!" She exclaimed, ecstatically beaming. It was easy to see how much the experience had moved her. The outpouring of love from her gentle spirit was touching; her tear-filled eyes sparkled in the sun. "The Lord had me sing *that* song for Steve! Only He knew that Steve would be standing in His presence by week's end. Maybe it prepared his heart for what was to come."

"I wonder what it was like for him…" I said, marveling at the thought.

She smiled, gave me a hug, and said, "I can only imagine…"

Throughout the week people from church and women from my Bible study group called, visited, and brought meals out to the house. The girls and I genuinely felt loved as they demonstrated what it looks like to be the hands and feet of Jesus. During one of those visits Cindy, a Bible study friend, disclosed that God had blessed her with a very unique gift. She elaborated by saying, "I can ask God any question, thumb through the Bible, and with my eyes closed randomly stop and point to a word. The word on which my finger lands makes complete sense 99.9% of the time!"

"O-o-o-o-k-a-a-a-y," I replied, unconvinced of her declaration.

"I asked God about Steve," she enthusiastically reported. "Do you want to know what word my finger landed on?" She was smiling and eagerly nodding her head hoping to prompt an affirmative response.

Her passionate plea led me to believe it was a positive word, so I raised a brow of uncertainty and with a bit of hesitation I smiled and gave her the permission she was waiting for. "Go ahead."

Like a giddy little schoolgirl dying to share a juicy secret, Cindy blurted out the word—"Found!" And in case I wasn't able to hear her the first time, she shouted out again—"Found!" She paused, anxiously awaiting my reaction.

I was tickled by her fanatical passion. She hit the nail on the head, but she didn't know it. To the best of her knowledge Steve still hadn't been saved or *found* as predicted. As a matter of fact, she had prayed with me on a number of occasions for his salvation, yet she stood by her verdict unaware of what happened days before taking his life.

My face lit up with a broad smile as I proudly confirmed the accuracy of her verdict. "You are absolutely right!"

Cindy was ecstatic. Throwing her fist up in the air she exclaimed, "Yes!" Her zeal however, wasn't just for Steve who'd joined the body of believers; it was also for validating the fact that her peculiar gift once again proved to be spot on.

Prior to hearing from Cindy, I wanted assurance of my own that Steve's eternity was secure with God and not apart from Him. Although I was a bit reluctant to ask in case the answer wasn't one I wanted to hear, I had to trust God's Word that "everyone who calls on the name of the Lord will be saved."[150] Yet I truly didn't know Steve's heart or his level of conviction. Only God knows the driving force behind any person's thoughts, motives, or actions.

So out in the forest alone in my vehicle, free of distractions, I bravely asked the question I longed to have answered. "Lord," I managed to start; being extremely hopeful, "Is Steve with you?"

His instantaneous response was, "You *know* he is."

My heart leapt with joy. No more questions. *That* was our answer to prayer.

For ten years the girls and I prayed and petitioned for healing and restoration. With deep conviction we trusted God and believed for our miracle—our prayers were finally answered!

Although Steve didn't receive the physical *and* spiritual healing we all hoped for, God's perfect will was for his spiritual healing. His focus is always on the eternal, the infinite goal, not the temporary, earthly outcome. If given the choice, we would have made the same decision, spiritual over the physical, because now we *all* get to spend eternity together with God!

There is meaning and purpose in *everything* God allows to happen in our lives.[151] Even if we never understand His plan or His actions, God has proven Himself to be compassionate, faithful, and just.[152] Adversity, however, is a powerful and effective tool in the hands of an all-loving God. He uses it to get our attention, to bring awareness to our human limitations, to get us to yield, and to draw us closer to Him.[153] I'm not suggesting that's *why* Steve developed his progressive, degenerating disease, but it was instrumental in bringing him to his knees—right where God wanted him.

Living a self-reliant life, as Steve had done, does nothing to honor God. Autonomy nullifies the need to rely on anyone but yourself, broadening the chasm between you and your Maker. When life is favorable it's easy to be deceived into believing *you've* got everything under control, but if *you're* the one who's in control—where does that leave God?

The girls and I were sure we'd done everything spiritually possible to get our prayers answered *our* way, but they weren't. Trying to speculate why God doesn't answer certain prayers the way you expect Him to is mind-boggling. Sometimes it makes no human sense why things work out the way they do, instead of the way you think they should. Let's face it, we all have expectations in life and believers have expectations of God. From an early age we are taught if certain things are done certain ways we can expect certain results. But what happens when those expectations aren't realized? When A+B ≠ C?

The Bible is full of human disappointment and expunged expectations. For example, when Jesus came onto the scene the Israelites were expecting a king who would overthrow the Roman Empire, not a King who would be Savior of the world and reconcile people to God. John the Baptist expected Jesus to release him from prison prior to his beheading, but that didn't happen. The apostle Paul expected the Lord to remove a thorn from his flesh after repeatedly pleading with Him to do so, but it wasn't.[154] When Jesus predicted his own death, the disciple Peter was devastated and began rebuking Him because that wasn't what he expected.[155]

While God more often than not meets or exceeds the expectations of His people, there are times when He doesn't. Either way, we can trust that He always acts in accordance with His nature, His will, His purpose, and His promises. However in this life there are things we will never understand.

*'My thoughts are completely different from yours,'*
*says the LORD. 'And my ways are far beyond anything you could*
*imagine. For just as the heavens are higher than earth,*
*so are my ways higher than your ways*
*and my thoughts higher than your thoughts.'* [156]

Let's pull back the curtain on a scene in Habakkuk's life, the Old Testament prophet who dealt with shattered expectations and struggled to accept God's answer to his prayer. Acknowledging that God is just, Habakkuk was perplexed as to why He wasn't doing anything about the wickedness, violence, strife, oppression, and corruption in the nation of Israel. What was He waiting for? Frustrated by God's timing and His outward complacency, Habakkuk cried out. "How long, O LORD, must I call for help, but you do not listen?"[157]

God responded saying, "Look at the nations and watch - and be utterly amazed. For I am going to do something in your days that you would not believe, even if you were told."[158] He proposed to "raise up the Babylonians," a nation more vile than Israel; have their army invade and destroy Jerusalem; then enslave the Israelites! Babylon would later be punished, but the Israelites' faith would be restored and rewarded. Then "the earth will be filled with the knowledge of the glory of the LORD."[159]

The horrendous plot confused and infuriated Habakkuk. How was *that* supposed to get Israel to turn from their wicked ways? He did not understand; to him *that* made no sense. The prophet believed there had to be a better means to the same end, but despite how he felt, Habakkuk resolved if that's what God needed to do to bring His people to where He wanted them...so be it. And although it was extremely difficult for him to accept, Habakkuk surrendered his will and put his unwavering trust in God's inexplicable methodology.

> This was Habakkuk's response to the Lord:
> Though the fig tree does not blossom and there is no fruit on the vines, [though] the product of the olive fails and the fields yield no food, though the flock is cut off from the fold and there are no cattle in the stalls, yet I will rejoice in the LORD; I will exult in the [victorious] God of my salvation! The LORD God is my strength, my personal bravery, and my invincible army; He makes my feet like hinds' feet and will make me to walk [not to stand still in terror, but to walk] and make [spiritual] progress upon my high places [of trouble, suffering, or responsibility]![160]

"Lord, as I struggle with life's difficulties, fears, and uncertainties, bombarding You with questions and complaints, please align my heart with Habakkuk's. That even though I don't understand or agree with what You're allowing to happen, please grant me the grace, peace, and assurance I need to continue trusting You. Prepare my feet and give me strength to courageously walk whatever path You set before me. Remind me that You love me, You're with me, and You're always in control. Enable me to sense Your presence in my life and be comforted by it. Open my spiritual ears and to hear all that You have to say. Empower me to see through eyes of faith and give me an ongoing desire to praise You, even through times of great suffering, sorrow, and pain."

Before going to the cross, Jesus reassured His disciples, "I have told you these things, so that in me you may have [perfect] peace. In the world you have tribulation *and* distress *and* suffering, but be courageous [be confident, be undaunted, be filled with joy]; I have overcome the world [my conquest is accomplished, my victory abiding]."[161]

The apostle Paul offers these encouraging words. "For our light and momentary troubles are achieving for us an eternal glory that far outweighs anything we have to contend with here on this earth [surpassing all comparisons, a transcendent splendor and an endless blessedness]! So we fix our eyes not on things which are seen, but on things which are unseen; since that which is seen is temporary [brief and fleeting], but that which is unseen is eternal, everlasting and imperishable."[162]

The purpose for your storm and how it fits into God's plan may forever remain a mystery, but I can attest to the fact that without our decade-long ordeal, the girls and I would've never reached the level of faith and maturity we now share in Christ. I wouldn't have a testimony to inspire or help you grow in your faith. A million radio listeners would've never learned about cell phone industry deception or the proven adverse health effects resulting from exposure to wireless signals. I would've never written *Cell Phones and the Dark Deception: Find Out What You Aren't Being Told…and Why,*[163] one of the first and most comprehensive books ever transcribed on the subject—And most importantly, Steve may have never been "found!"

Never lose faith. You are a child of the King; you are loved; and you are invited to "boldly approach the throne of grace with confidence, so that you may receive mercy and find grace to help you in your time of need."[164] "For we do not have a high priest who is unable to sympathize with our weaknesses, but we have one who has been tempted in every way, just as we are—yet was without sin."[165]

"Blessed is the one who trusts (believes, relies on) in the Lord, whose confidence is in Him. He will be like a tree planted by the (life-sustaining) water that sends out its roots by the stream. It does not fear when heat comes; its leaves are always green. It has no worries (anxieties) in a year of drought and never fails to bear fruit."[166]

Chapter 15

# Hope of a Brighter Tomorrow

*You are God's special possession;
he has called you out of darkness into his wonderful light.*[167]

Days after Steve's passing, I was kneeling down in front of the living room sofa praying. It was early in the morning and the sun hadn't yet peaked over the mountain ridge. With my eyes tightly closed, a brilliant light pierced my prayer. It was the most magnificent illumination I had ever seen emerging out from the bleakest, blackest darkness. I asked, "Lord, what is *this*?"

He delivered a comforting promise of hope. "This is the light at the end of *your* tunnel."

While many people aim to be optimistic, inclined to believe there's always a light at the end of whatever tunnel they're going through, others aren't so confident—having lost their way in the dark channel of uncertainty doubt, and fear, wearied by countless twists and turns of diversion—they can become so consumed by their tribulation that the thought of *ever* seeing light again is unimaginable. But God can work wonders.

For years, the light at the end of my tunnel flickered. I fought to remain positive, clinging onto God's promises and every shred of hope I could find as the fabric of our lives was unraveling, but with each passing season my light's intensity waned. The Lord's response evoked so much emotion tears welled up in my eyes and splashed onto the couch. Steve was gone, but even so, God showed me the light at the end of my tunnel—*My* tunnel!

For the next few minutes I remained still, basking in His glorious presence, and soaking up His encouraging words. I was filled with an incredible sense of inner peace, wellbeing, excitement, strength, and confidence. He made it clear He was still sovereign—on the throne and in control, that He still loved me, and that everything was not only going to be alright from here on out, it was going to be better. My future was going to be brighter. I relished the thought. From that day forward I held tightly to that vision and its promise. God had something wonderful planned for me, just as He has for you, but I didn't yet know what that would be.

Since man's fall into sin, God's utmost desire has been to reconcile humanity to Himself. His effort to repair and restore the broken relationship resonates throughout Scripture. Even after the Israelites' rebellious nature, wicked behavior, and the hardening of their hearts, God longed to be reunited with His people.

After their homeland was destroyed and they had been taken captive into Babylon, there was a sense of utter despair. But God, in their darkest and most desperate hour, gave His prophet Ezekiel a prophetic revelation foretelling how He was going to revive His people and restore their hope. He was going to reignite the light at the end of their long, twisted tunnel so they could finally see it—What joy!

Although this divine insight into God's love, mercy, and amazing grace was given to Ezekiel sometime after 586

B.C., [168] God's promise of hope, restoration, and reconciliation still holds true for us today. The prophet writes:

> The hand of the LORD was on me and He brought me out by the Spirit of the LORD and set me in the middle of a valley; it was full of bones. He led me back and forth among them, and I saw a great many bones on the floor of the valley, bones that were very dry.
>
> He asked me, 'Son of man, can these bones live?'
>
> I said, 'Sovereign LORD, you alone know.'
>
> Then he said to me, 'Prophesy to these bones and say to them, Dry bones, hear the word of the LORD! This is what the Sovereign LORD says to these bones: I will make breath enter you, and you will come to life. I will attach tendons to you and make flesh come upon you and cover you with skin; I will put breath in you, and you will come to life. Then you will know that I am the LORD.'
>
> So I prophesied as I was commanded. And as I was prophesying, there was a noise, a rattling sound, and the bones came together, bone to bone. I looked, and tendons and flesh appeared on them and skin covered them, but there was no breath in them.
>
> Then he said to me, 'Prophesy to the breath;

prophesy, son of man, and say to it, This is what the Sovereign LORD says: Come, breath, from the four winds and breathe into these slain, that they may live.' So I prophesied as he commanded me, and breath entered them; they came to life and stood up on their feet—a vast army.

Then he said to me: 'Son of man, these bones are the people of Israel. They say, Our bones are dried up and our hope is gone; we are cut off.' Therefore prophesy and say to them: 'This is what the Sovereign LORD says: My people, I am going to open your graves and bring you up from them; I will bring you back to the land of Israel. Then you, my people, will know that I am the LORD, when I open your graves and bring you up from them. I will put my Spirit in you and you will live, and I will settle you in your own land. Then you will know that I the LORD have spoken, and I have done it, declares the LORD.'[169]

Ezekiel's vision paints another beautiful picture of a loving, compassionate God who wants you to know Him and be reconciled to Him. If you're in a dry, dead state in the middle of a desert valley where life seems hopeless and void of meaning, God longs to revive you—to raise you up out of your grave, to breathe new life into you, to fill you with His Spirit, and give you a renewed sense of hope—just as He did for the Israelites—just as He did for me.

It was more than a week after the tragedy that I felt comfortable enough to return to the bed Steve and I once shared. Lying there alone felt strange and awkward. Sleep eluded me for hours, but I was determined to stay put and accept the fact that this would be my new normal.

I must have fallen asleep because I was suddenly wakened in the middle of the night by a very life-like dream. Steve was holding me in a dance-dip position and was passionately kissing me on the lips. Lying there entranced, waves of emotion swept over me, flooding me with incredible sensations and an intense awareness of his deep, tender, exuberant affection. That single expression of love communicated so much, especially forgiveness and a genuine sense of gratitude. I smiled. The message was clear—"I am once again happy and full of life!"

Upon leaving the house the morning of his suicide, our final moments together, Steve was screaming and blaming me for his institutionalization. But God, in His goodness, allowed my beloved to return to me in a dream to mend my hurting heart, to help with healing, to infuse peace, and reinforce the hope all believers share.

Steve's cremains were ready to be picked up and his funeral arrangements were made. Instead of flying to Michigan for the occasion, the girls and I decided that a three-day road trip would be therapeutic. Before surrounding ourselves with family and friends, we wanted some uninterrupted alone time to reflect, to express our emotions, and to grieve our loss. We shared stories, we laughed, and of course, we cried. We pondered our futures and discussed what life would look like without a husband and without a father. One thing we knew for sure—wherever life was going to take us, it was going to be far away from the isolation of the Gila National Forest.

As soon we passed the "Welcome to Michigan" sign, I contemplated moving back near family. Grabbing my purse, I began fishing for my address book. Since I was driving, I had Jenni look up Keith's phone number, and then call him. The mortgage broker who taught me how to process loans while I was in real estate and the realtor who sold our house for us before moving out west, answered. I identified myself, briefly explained the situation, and asked about the greater Grand Rapids real estate market.

Then as a friendly gesture, I asked how he was doing. He informed me that his 13-year-old son had run away from home, he'd been missing for days, and no one knew where he was. The police had been notified and were also searching for him. Keith was deeply concerned. As he was sharing some of the details, I could tell the incident was weighing heavy on his heart, so I promised to keep he and his son in prayer.

At the close of our conversation he mentioned the possibility of getting together for coffee to discuss my real estate needs and I made an awkward attempt at social etiquette by inviting him to the funeral, but since we were merely acquaintances from the past, I really didn't expect him to show up.

The funeral was very nice and well attended. Considering we'd spent 16 years in California and another four in New Mexico, I was surprised at the number of people who came to pay their respects. There were plenty of well-known faces, new faces from Steve's high school, and unexpected faces. The outpouring of love for our family was heartwarming, sincere, and sincerely appreciated. The words spoken about Steve and the memories shared were moving. The girls and I were deeply touched. For the amount of time our beloved was involved in these people's lives, he made a remarkable impression with his friendly, easygoing, compassionate persona.

A surprising number of floral arrangements were received and strategically placed throughout the funeral parlor. They were all so beautiful, brightening up the place in an attempt to lighten the heavy atmosphere of a painfully tragic event. Yet there was one in particular that captured my attention and piqued my interest, perhaps because it dwarfed all the others.

Curiously, I walked over to the multi-colored display, reached in, and snatched the card hiding amongst ferns, daisies, and lilies. The card read "Sorry for your loss." It was signed, Keith. *How thoughtful.* Although he didn't attend the visitation or the funeral, sending flowers was a very sweet gesture.

During that whirlwind visit the two of us never did connect. But as soon as I snapped out of my daze, I called to thank him for the flowers and get an update on his son.

The boy's father regretfully informed me that his son was *still* missing. "It's been almost two weeks! I've combed the entire area. I don't know where else to look or what else to do." With a tinge of hope he added, "The police are still searching."

You could tell that the distressing circumstances, along with the passing of time without resolution, devastated him. It was apparent he truly loved his son and was genuinely concerned about his wellbeing. I too was empathetic to the situation, and since he wasn't married, I was willing to be a friend in his time of need.

Before leaving Michigan, Jenni flew out to California to visit a friend, and she would be returning to Tucson one week later. So two days after she left, Holly and I headed out on another cross-country excursion to pick her up and return home. On the long, indirect route to Silver City, I once again found myself pondering the future. There were so many questions and unknowns. *What was I going to do with my life? Where would life's journey take the girls at ages 17 and 21? Where were we going to live? Would we be together? Would they be on their own? Would I spend the rest of my days alone as a widow?* That one weighed heavily on my heart. *Would I?*

I was praying I wouldn't have to spend the rest of my life alone. I loved being married; I loved sharing life with Steve. Before he became ill, we were extremely happy and enjoyed a wonderful relationship. In time, I knew I'd be interested in remarrying another wonderful man, God willing.

From that moment on what I started doing might seem extremely premature for someone who just lost her mate, but ever since Steve's mind started slipping six years earlier, conversing had become a source of frustration for both of us. Because his long-term memory was limited and his short-term recollection was poor, our level of communication was reduced to that of a parent talking to a child, transitioning my role in the spousal relationship to one of caregiver.

Imagining that someday I could have a second chance at love was exhilarating. *What type of man would want someone like me? More importantly, what type of man would I want to spend my life with?* I began to contemplate the attributes of a perfect partner—his qualities, his beliefs, his character, his likes, and his dislikes. After being married 24 years I had a pretty good idea of what I would…and wouldn't want.

If you've been married for any length of time and were in my shoes, you'd probably have no problem coming up with a drawn-out list of your own. While there are certain things you absolutely love about your spouse and would definitely want in a future companion, there are also things that drive you absolutely bonkers and you'd do anything to avoid spending the rest of your life with someone who possesses those same quirks or habits. Am I right?

Over the next six weeks I whipped up a list of ingredients for the "man of my dreams"—the total sum was 100! These prerequisites would be a template to determine which men I'd date and would help me identify my ideal companion. I wasn't willing to step into the single world blind-folded. From what I was seeing, flipping through TV channels, the dating scene had dramatically changed—I wasn't sure what to expect.

The more I thought about the idea of dating, the less interested I became. I just wanted God to miraculously set me up with my husband-to-be so I could start living my "happily ever after" without having to jump through hoops or suffer heartache. But if that didn't happen, the list would help me aim for the type of man I was looking for, so I wouldn't be distracted by those who didn't share my beliefs, interests, etc. Either way, I put my fate in God's hands.

Everyone I shared my little secret with thought devising such a list was a nutty idea. "Who does that?" "There is no way you'll *ever* find anyone who will meet every condition on that list," were the resounding remarks.

One evening while Sylvia and I were out to dinner, I shared the list with our server. When he read it, he burst out laughing, then looked at me as if I had lost my mind. "You can't be serious! You'd be lucky to find a guy to match the first five!" He exclaimed, pushing the paper back into my hand. "Good luck!"

Weeks after the funeral Keith and I were still checking in on one another. Our calls had increased to two, sometimes three times, a week. Each one of us appreciated the support of the other. Having been nothing more than acquaintances, we knew very little about each other. As he shared aspects of his life, I shared aspects of mine. I learned that at the age of 41 he had one son, but had never been married.

He offered an authentic perception of single life and told me what I could expect. When I disclosed that I had devised a list of 100 things I wanted in a man, he chuckled, viewing it as a useless tactic that would ultimately result in nothing short of disappointment.

As time went on we found ourselves engaging in a diverse range of topics, but the ones that really captivated my attention were those centered on Christ. During the Great Recession of 2008/2009, when the real estate bubble burst, Keith landed a hospital job as a medical supply buyer. His co-workers, all professing to be Christians, started praying for him and his missing teenage son.

"They're unlike any Christ followers I've ever met." He'd say.

The stories he'd share about what they said and did just tickled me; they were contagious and always left me wanting more. It was obvious his fellow employees loved the Lord and that love overflowed into a selfless expression of compassion for my dear friend. He had never known anything like it.

He'd say things like, "I don't understand why these people care so much."

But it was clear as crystal to me. I knew exactly what was happening—God was working through his co-workers to draw Keith to Himself. "God loves you too much to leave you where you are," I'd tell him with reserved enthusiasm, so he wouldn't become apprehensive or shy away from what God was aiming to do in his life.

Our calls became more frequent and every time we talked the focus would come full circle and return to Jesus. Whenever the phone rang, I ran to pick it up, hoping my friend was on the other end. I looked forward to hearing how God was moving in his life. It was exciting and I was becoming increasingly attracted to Keith's growing hunger for the Lord. It gave me the opportunity to share what decades of being a believer had taught me.

During this time I commenced praying for direction and for my future husband—whoever he was, wherever he was. Since I was in the midst of researching and writing *Cell Phones and The Dark Deception: Find Out What You're Not Being Told...and Why,* I expressed my concerns to God and asked that my future husband not carry his cell phone on his body because of the potential damage it can cause.[170]

Days later while on the phone, Keith randomly asked, "You know what I like best about no longer being a realtor?"

"No. What?" I inquired.

"I don't have to carry my cell phone with me everywhere I go." Adding, "I now have much more freedom."

His comment blew me away! *Did he really say that? Why? How Bizarre!*

In my morning pray time, on bended knee in front of the living room sofa, I asked the Lord about Keith's random remark. "Please enlighten me. That was way too strange!"

He responded with a scenic vision. In the distance was a cluster of hills covered with a thick blanket of rich green grass amply scattered with daisies. Facing east, I watched as the sun crowned its topmost peak. Vivid tones of pink, orange, and purple filled the sky. The sight was glorious! "What is this?" I asked.

"*This* is a new beginning!" I cherished the thought and held onto His promise, but shared none of it.

By mid-September, three months after Steve's passing, Keith initiated the daily ritual of sending one thoughtful "good morning" email and phoning every night—the calls were anywhere between two and five hours! In the process of getting to know one another we chatted about everything— our lives, our children, our interests, our dreams, and our goals. Open-ended questions extended the conversation.

As we continued conversing over the next 30 days, racking up 100-plus phone hours and umpteen email exchanges, the dynamics of our relationship began to shift from being just friends into something more…*Was this my "new beginning?"* I wasn't sure. But when I started hearing the word "check" in my mind every time Keith said something favorable or responded positively to one of my generic questions, I was convinced I had my answer…

It wasn't as if I was quizzing him directly from the list, but without being consciously aware of what was happening, the inaudible voice would interject "check" every time something could be checked off. Whether it was me, or the Lord trying to make me cognizant of something I wasn't seeing, by the end of October I had made two unexpected discoveries—One, I had developed strong feelings for this man who lived over 1,800 miles away. And two, he had satisfied more than three-quarters of the stipulations on my "perfect mate" list!

I wasn't sure I was ready for this—No, I was certain I was not! The startling revelation made the next phone call a bit awkward. Up to this point the dialogue had flowed like warm honey, but tonight it had cooled to a thick, sticky mess. Through the phone Keith couldn't see the gigantic elephant in my room. I didn't know what to say, how to say it, or if I should say anything. I didn't know how he'd respond if I told him what was happening, so I contemplatively held back, but he sensed my apprehension.

"You seem withdrawn. Everything okay?" I hesitated.

"You know, you can talk to me about whatever's on your mind," he urged.

Trying to muster up the courage to share one of my discoveries I reluctantly asked, "Remember that list of 100 things I wanted in a perfect partner?"

"Yeah," he replied, curious to know where the question was leading.

"Well…since we've been talking…I uh, I mean you…" *Just spit it out.* I quickly blurted, "You've met close to 80% of the mandates on my list!" *There I said it.*

There was silence on the other end of the phone. Disbelief? Fear? I wasn't sure.

"Email me the list," he promptly instructed, "So I can see it." He had no idea what was on the list; its secret contents were never disclosed. He was eager to review it, certain I was exaggerating—there was no way he fit between the narrow parameters I had set for a perfect mate. We hung up and I nervously awaited his response after clicking "send."

*What was he going to think? Would the numerous similarities freak him out?* This would be the type of list one would create *after* getting to know someone to suggest compatibility, but Keith knew *this* list was compiled and completed before we ever started talking. That's what made it so intriguing.

Within minutes he replied with this urgent message— "WE HAVE TO TALK!" He was blown away! What was a gradual unveiling for me was a sudden eye-opener for him. And I couldn't help but laugh.

We got back on the phone and went through the entire list one by one, commenting on all 100 entries. At the end

Keith had to concede, agreeing that he did in fact match every prerequisite on the list, except one—he was five years younger than the "man of my dreams"—Not a problem!

The surprising realization prompted my friend to plan a trip to New Mexico for the long Thanksgiving weekend. During one of our phone conversations he proudly announced that he'd contacted the Silver City Chamber of Commerce to find out what there was to do and see in the area. After he enthusiastically proposed his detailed agenda, I just had to ask, "Are you coming to see a bunch of rocks and dirt or are you coming to see me?" He laughed, admitting he was looking forward to seeing me too!

Upon hearing the spicy news that the man I had feelings for was flying out to visit, my mother suddenly had something she needed delivered. Suggesting Keith meet her and my sister for lunch so he could pick up the package. Now I know my mother well enough to recognize her true intentions—she wanted to check out this mystery man who had stolen her daughter's heart, so she went out and bought something for him to bring me.

After telling her about Keith, she asked what he looked like. I stopped to think for a minute. I was stumped. I didn't remember. Although he attempted to email a picture, it was taken at a distance and was hard to see. The only recollection I had was from four years ago—he was tall, medium build, military-style flattop, and a mustache. That's all my memory could evoke!

Her next question threw me for a loop. "If you don't remember what he looks like, what if you don't like what you see?"

I hadn't given that any thought—*what if I didn't?* A large knot instantly formed in the pit of my stomach. *No!* I told myself it didn't matter. Keith was a wonderful man. "I love him for who he is, not for what he looks like."

As my mother's query continued to taunt me, what I found myself clinging to aside from God's promises of a new beginning and a light at the end of my tunnel, was Keith's cell phone comment, the matching of 99 out of 100 prerequisites for my "perfect" partner, the faint remembrances of our few business encounters, and most significantly, the thought I had while thanking him for teaching me how to process mortgages at the front door of our Michigan home—*If I wasn't married I'd go out with him*!

On the flip side, Keith knew exactly what I looked like. He'd seen recent photos. My appearance was going to be no surprise to him. But to satisfy the curiosity of two snoopy gatekeepers, he willingly met my mother and sister for lunch before flying across the country to see a woman he had fallen in love with over the phone and through emails.

For the next six hours the "man of my dreams" sat in a commercial aircraft staring aimlessly out the window, second-guessing his actions. *What am I doing? This is crazy!* As if watching a slideshow of his prospective future, each image portrayed a different scenario of how the next four days were going to play out and impact his life. He was nervous and had no idea what to expect.

With nervous excitement I anticipated Keith's arrival at the gate of the El Paso airport. As passengers paraded by, I vaguely recognized the man who made eye contact, shot me a big grin, raced over, and swept me up into his arms. The sensation was electrifying, like a teenybopper meeting her celebrity heartthrob. I was smitten.

Mesmerized by mutual feelings of affection, we stood there for minutes just drinking in each other's appearance, beaming at one another and hugging. He was an incredibly handsome man—six-foot tall, slender build, muscular, tan, and a great smile. The bouquet of red roses in his hand almost went unnoticed.

Gazing up I cheerfully noted, "You have blue eyes! I didn't remember that."

Holding hands, we proceeded to the baggage claim area. In that moment everything felt right. The light at the end of my tunnel was coming into view.

The two-and-a-half hour drive back to Silver City seemed like the right time to share another little well kept secret. One I'd been hanging onto for years. "You know that day you came over to the house to help me learn how to process mortgage applications?"

"Yeah," he answered with an inquisitive grin.

"When I walked you to the door and thanked you for helping me, I had a strange and unexpected thought."

"What was that?"

Prior to answering, I paused and momentarily looked away from the road to capture his "before" expression. "I thought—if I wasn't married I'd go out with him." I quickly turned to see his "after" expression. He was amused.

He threw a similar question back at me. "You know what I was thinking?"

"No, what?" I smiled, eager to hear what he had to say.

Affectionately looking over at me he replied, "I thought—if I could find a woman like Sue who is ambitious, fun, and attractive—I'd marry her!"

Overjoyed by our latent reciprocal interest, we simultaneously burst out laughing. Joking about God's sense of humor and how He set us up. That day while saying our good-byes, the great I AM must have been chuckling to Himself saying, "Just wait you two—you have no idea what I've got planned!"

## Chapter 16

# Rainbow After the Storm

*'Forget the former things; do not dwell on the past.*
*See, I am doing a new thing!*
*Now it springs up; do you not perceive it?*
*I am making a way in the desert*
*and streams in the wasteland.'* [171]

Needless to say, Holly was not a fan of Keith's visit. So instead of heading straight home, we took a pre-arranged detour to City of Rocks State Park. The "city," made up of extraordinary rock formations left after an immense volcanic eruption millions of years ago, is a magnificent sight I couldn't allow my friend to miss.

While hiking between and around the huge stone columns, climbing on the rocks, holding hands, and engaging in child-like play, we marveled in the simple beauty of the day and the joyful occasion of finally being together. Frequently I'd stop walking so he would turn to look at me and I could study his face—his smile was heartwarming, his mustache neatly-clipped, his medium brown hair closely shaved to his head, and there were those beautiful blue eyes that just took my breath away. After a hug I'd resume walking.

At sunset I spread out my Guatemalan blanket on a flat surface atop one of the towering rocks. The panoramic view across the desert's botanical garden was astounding. I opened the picnic basket I prepared earlier that morning, removed a bottle of champagne, and handed it to Keith. He popped the cork, filled our glasses, and made a toast to love and life. We sipped the bubbly and nibbled on crackers, cheese, sliced apples, and pears as the sun descended and filled the sky with color.

Darkness brought with it a stunning display of stars that shone brightly in the southwestern sky. Since the spectacle begged to be enjoyed and appreciated, we lay back on the blanket and watched. My friend put his arm underneath my head, and then gently drew me close to his chest. It felt as though the heavens were smiling down on us...

The following day we prepared a Thanksgiving feast, stuck the turkey in the oven, and left for a walk. Upon returning an hour-and-a-half later, we found the bird still sitting out on the counter where we had left it! We laughed, attributing the blunder to a possible bite from the "love" bug.

The remaining three days were spent touring downtown Silver City, exploring the fascinating Gila Cliff Dwellings National Monument, circling around Gomez Peak and climbing 1,035 feet to the top. Time together significantly dwarfed all our emailing efforts and phone hours. We enjoyed ourselves so much the time just flew by. But the best was yet to come—on Sunday morning before Keith's departure, he re-dedicated his life to Christ!

"As you know, we call those blessed [happy, spiritually prosperous, favored by God] who were steadfast and endured [difficult circumstances]. You have heard of the patient endurance of Job and you have seen the Lord's outcome [how he richly blessed Job]."[172] The Lord restored Job's fortune and gave him twice as much as he had before.[173]

After sharing pieces of my story with one of Keith's aunts, I flippantly made the comment, "I don't know why God has blessed me in so many ways."

"Yes you do!" She insistently shot back.

While reflecting on her powerful retort, I knew she was right. I did know why I was blessed. Throughout Scripture, more often than not miracles follow faith and obedience. God frequently promises—"If you do this…then I'll do that." In other words, our actions determine God's reaction.

To the faithful, God proves Himself faithful.[174] He does not show favoritism. [175] His favor rests on *all* who love Him. *All* who earnestly and diligently seek Him are showered with grace; rewarded with privilege, blessings, and eternal glory.[176]

When faced with indecision, do you look to God for answers or do you follow your own aspirations? Our natural tendency is to look within, weigh out the pros and cons, then select the best option. But it's wise counsel to invite God into your decision-making process. His desire is for you to seek His face and know His will, so you can follow the extraordinary path He's paved for you.

The Bible advises God's people to test everything.[177] And throughout history people of faith have done just that, pursuing God's will for their lives by virtue of prayer and testing alleged answers for authentication. Wanting irrevocable assurance that their actions were in accordance with the Lord's will instead of their own, they refused to leave anything to chance. Following their exemplary lead can help us identify God's will for our lives too.

*Through spiritual transformation and the renewing of your mind that takes place when Jesus comes into your heart, you will be able to test and approve (get confirmation) what God's good, pleasing, and perfect will is for you in your life.*[178]

Between 735-734 B.C. Israel was at war. King Ahaz of Judah was faced with a difficult political decision. So the Lord sent His prophet Isaiah to meet the king and advise him to, "Ask for yourself a sign (a token or proof) of the LORD your God [one that will convince you that God has spoken and will keep His word]."[179]

But Ahaz refused. "I will not ask, I will not put the LORD to the test."[180]

Then the prophet charged, "Hear now, you house of David! Is it not enough to try the patience of man? Will you try the patience of my God also?"[181]

Isaiah's harsh retort prompted the king to ask the Lord for a sign—and the Lord gave him one.

Abraham's chief servant also solicited a sign from God when he was sent out to find a wife for his master's son Isaac. He prayed, "LORD, God of my master Abraham, make me successful today, and show kindness to my master Abraham. See, I am standing beside this spring, and the daughters of the townspeople are coming out to draw water. May it be that when I say to a young woman, 'Please let down your jar that I may have a drink,' and she says, 'Drink, and I'll water your camels too'—let her be the one you have chosen for your servant Isaac. By this I will know that you have shown kindness to my master."[182]

Before finishing his prayer, a very beautiful young woman named Rebekah approached the well, carrying a jar on her shoulder. The servant hurried to meet her and asked for a little water. She handed him the jar saying, "Drink." Then using the same exact words indicative of the sign, she added, "And I'll water your camels too!"

Watering a herd of camels was no easy task, so making the offer to a complete stranger would have been highly unusual. Filling a trough with enough water to hydrate ten camels was not only strenuous, but also very time-consuming. Through her generosity, God not only revealed Rebekah's kind heart, He gave Abraham's servant a clear indication that she was the woman He had chosen for Isaac.[183]

On another occasion, the angel of the Lord appeared to a godly man named Gideon and extended this greeting, "The LORD is with you, mighty warrior."[184] Then the heavenly being informed the insecure man that he'd been chosen by God to save Israel. His mission was to strike down the Midianite people who had oppressed and impoverished the nation for seven years.[185]

Doubtful that the Lord had elected *him* for such a daunting task, Gideon asked for proof. "If now I have found favor in your eyes, give me a sign that it is really you talking to me."[186]

Gideon was a wise man who refused to risk his life or the lives of others without being 100% certain that God was the One asking him to take on the monumental task. If God was with him, Gideon knew he'd be victorious, but he had to validate the origin of the message, so Gideon made this appeal to the Lord. "If you will save Israel by my hand as you have promised—look, I will place a wool fleece on the threshing floor. If there is dew only on the fleece and the ground is dry, then I will know that you will save Israel by my hand, as you said." In the morning dew covered the fleece and the ground was dry.

Gideon boldly made a second appeal. "Do not be angry with me. Let me make just one more request. Allow me one more test with the fleece. This time make the fleece dry and the ground covered with dew." That night God re-confirmed his plan for Gideon. The fleece was dry and the ground was covered with dew. [187] God honored Gideon's petition because he was earnestly seeking to know and follow the Lord's will. He will most assuredly do the same for you!

Keith's trip out west reinforced our feelings for one another. According to the check marks on my list, he aced my test—99 out of 100! We appeared to be well matched and were looking for similar things in a partner. The fact that he was five years younger than stipulated was inconsequential. We truly enjoyed each other's company and wanted to see the relationship move forward, but having a long distance relationship was not going to make that easy.

Our daily *Good Morning I Love You* emails, which I began referring to them as, in addition to our nightly phone marathons, were in no way ample substitutes for being together. Six weeks after Keith left New Mexico, I flew to Michigan to spend a week with him, a month-and-a-half later he returned to visit me. The short stints together made it emotionally painful being apart.

Since Keith's initial visit at Thanksgiving, almost six months after Steve's passing, I'd been in constant prayer for wisdom and revelation concerning the relationship—was this all happening too fast or too soon? It certainly was for Holly, but it no longer was for me. For over six years I'd been without male companionship. I'm not just referring to sexual intimacy, but simply having someone to go out with, to talk to, to walk with, to play cards with, or to simply sit and watch television with at the end of the day. I really missed what Steve and I once shared. I wanted to enjoy living again. Keith made me feel special, loved, and most of all—Alive!

*Many are the plans in a person's heart,
but it is the Lord's purpose that prevails.*[188]

As the new year dawned, I no longer wanted to speculate whether Keith and I were meant to be together—forever. Although I'd been given plenty of signs that we were, I needed a definitive answer from God. I refused to step outside of His will by making my own decision and blindly following my heart—that, I knew, would be foolish. I needed to be sure that this was God's plan before becoming any more involved. The only way to know for sure was to *ask* for a sign. So following the examples of Abraham's servant, Gideon, and the Lord's directive to King Ahaz—that's exactly what I did!

I began with a prayer of praise and thanksgiving, confessing my need for Him and my readiness to surrender to His will. Whatever it was, I aspired to be obedient. After all, He's the only One with the key to unlock the door to what I was hoping would be my new beginning to a glorious future. To safeguard my request from Enemy influence or interference, I made my silent petition for a sign.

The requested sign of confirmation wasn't too farfetched, yet it seldom occurs outside the realm of romantic chick flicks. It's the climactic moment at the movie's end when the couple reveals their deep affection for one another and finally realizes they're destined to be together forever. Completely enraptured by love, they engage in a passionate kiss, one that seals the fate of their happily-ever-after. You can call it sappy, but I wanted the sign to be a true romantic kiss like that one—where the man holds the woman's face in his hands and deliberately gives her a very fervent and meaningful kiss, smack dab on the lips.

At the conclusion of my appeal I lingered in the moment, envisioning the episode, starry-eyed and mesmerized by its wonder. Then all of a sudden, as if reality slapped me across the face I snapped out of my fantasy, realizing I had made a dreadful mistake. *What have I done? How could I be so careless?* It became sorely apparent that I hadn't given the indicator for my test sufficient consideration. While it sounded like the makings of a fairytale, what were the odds of being kissed by a man 1,800 miles away?

I started beating myself up. Clearly, I proceeded too hastily. With so much at stake, the sign should have been something more feasible. I sabotaged the test; it was doomed for failure. The answer was already obvious—*No way, no how, wrong fella.* It was as if I burst my own bubble before it was even blown. Deflated by the unlikely chance I was going to get my desired confirmation, I left the lot in God's hands. If it's meant to be, it will be. Somehow, some way, He would make it happen.

Three nights later Keith and I were yapping on the phone and laughing about life. Two hours into the conversation I was comfortably lying in bed staring up at the ceiling when there was pause, followed by an extended sigh, coming from the other end of the phone. With a deep aching desire, words slightly louder than a whisper escaped his lips. "I really miss you. I wish you were here." Then he added, "I just want to touch you."

"Where would you touch me?" I playfully teased.

By the way I posed the question it was certain to elicit a sensual response. Any vigorous heterosexual man, like Keith, whose longing aspiration was to touch the woman he loved, would have triggered a suggestive comeback, but it didn't.

Without hesitation, these were his exact words—"I would take my hands, put them around your face, and just kiss you, right on your lips!!!"

I am *not* kidding! I was taken so off guard, his words literally took my breath away. I *never* saw *that* coming. I was speechless! The silence lingered a little too long as I scrambled to compose myself and gather my thoughts. *What on earth just happened?*

On the other end I heard, "Sue?" "Sue?" When there was no answer he raised his voice and his level of concern grew. Repeating the question, probing for a response. "Sue?" "Sue?"

I was choked up and on the verge of tears. I couldn't talk. My entire demeanor and thought process had drastically shifted. I was astonished and in utter disbelief.

"Are you okay?" he pressed.

I fought to contain myself; trying to stifle my feelings and curb my reaction to the wave of emotion that swept over me. Attempting to pull myself together, I softly replied, "Yeah."

For the next five minutes I tiptoed round the fact that I'd been secretly conducting a test to determine the Lord's will for our relationship. Great care would be required to unpack this revelation in a way that wouldn't freak out or scare off my seemingly "perfect partner." Informing Keith that God had chosen *him* as the man I would spend the rest of my life with could be frightening! But instead of being spooked or thinking it was too soon to bring up marriage, he embraced the idea that we'd been divinely ordained to be wed.

*Trust in the* Lord *with all your heart
and lean not on your own understanding;
in all your ways submit to him,
and he will make your paths straight.* [189]

God wants us to seek Him and know His will in every area of our lives. It doesn't have to be a mystery. He eagerly waits for the opportunity to be invited into our decision-making process and to be given an active, leading role. He is always willing to provide an answer when we ask. Sometimes we'll agree with His decision and other times we won't. Sometimes things will work out the way we want them to and other times they won't. Sometimes we'll have to wait and other times you won't. Regardless, as a beloved child of the Most High God, we are simply instructed to pray, seek, ask, listen, trust, and obey.

Chapter 17

# A New Beginning

*You turned my wailing into dancing;
you removed my sackcloth and clothed me with joy,
that my heart may sing your praises and not be silent.
L*ORD *my God, I will praise you forever!*[190]

Steam rose from the hot coffee, fogging my glasses every time I lifted the mug to my lips. My thoughts were equally blurred. The Lord had clearly laid out the path set before us. I was stunned like a doe in the headlights, still unable to fully grasp the reality of what had taken place the night before.

Sleep was anything but peaceful. I tossed and turned all night. The entire scenario was surreal. Now, sitting in the sunroom staring out at the snow-capped mountain, my mind whirled as I pondered my petition to God and my dialogue with Keith. *It wasn't a dream!* Everything happened exactly as described, yet without any physical contact! No other warm-blooded man with intense, intimate feelings for a woman would have ever responded the way Keith did following an open invitation to touch her anywhere he wanted to on her body—it had to be God!

Although I believed God was right alongside, guiding me in this direction for months—with the "new beginning" vision, the curious cell phone comment, the light at the end of my tunnel, the peculiar front-door feelings years earlier, and 99 out of 100 matches—asking Him for an actual sign was a daring move, yet I wanted to know with absolute certainty that our forthcoming plans were in sync. Putting on the brakes of our blossoming relationship at this point would be heart wrenching, but better to determine God's will sooner, than finding out it wasn't His will later.

The fact God provided absolute assurance that Keith and I were meant to spend the rest of our lives together, from a nearly impossible request, was truly incredible! And the way He put the exact words into Keith's mouth—the only words that could have sealed the deal—was astounding! Truth is I shouldn't have been shocked because there is nothing our God cannot do![191] With such unmistakable clarity it was time to take a leap of faith and follow the Lord's lead forward.

When Keith divulged how he wanted to touch me, I wasn't sure how to respond, and then questioned whether I should tell him about asking God for a sign. But after disclosing the secret and revealing its outcome, so he was fully aware of its implications, the prospect of spending the rest of his life with me didn't faze him one bit. He was either clearly (or crazy) in love!

At 41 years of age my dear friend had never met a woman he wanted to marry—until now! Other men might have freaked out, hung up, had their phone disconnected, or changed their number in order to avoid the Jesus fanatic who was trying to pin 'em down, but not Keith. Over the past six months he had heard the same amazing stories I've shared with you in this memoir, about the extraordinary ways God has shown up and intervened in my life. He had come to realize how much I trust and rely on God for everything. He was all in, fully accepting God's plan for our lives and agreeing to be joined together as one.

I reclined in my blue Adirondack chair soaking in the beauty of the mountainous woodland landscape. With the money we received from selling the adjacent mountainside, four eight-foot sliders were installed in the sunroom, giving me a spectacular panoramic view. I leisurely began to imagine what my new life would look like being married to the "man of my dreams." While savoring the succulent possibilities, my face beamed with joy. In my heart I was already packing and on my way out the door.

While the lengthy phone conversations enabled us to become increasingly familiar with each other's past, beliefs, likes, dislikes, dreams, goals, and character, the mini visits really broadened our scope of one another's true identity. Interacting and spending time together, doing things we mutually enjoyed, allowed us to see how we would function as a couple. It was also the only time we were able to have face-to-face encounters; although I considered myself lucky to have any Internet connection at all, dial-up didn't support live online interfaces like Skype. Nothing rivaled the proximity of being together, touching each other, sitting side by side, holding hands, wrapping our arms around each other…and kissing! The prospect of pursuing and growing our relationship was exciting! Yet the one lingering question was "How?"

Jenni, who had been working and taking classes at Western New Mexico University, made the decision to follow her lifelong dream of working with animals. She was accepted at an onsite zoo school in Florida near the state university where she was hoping to complete a master's degree. Months before her father's passing a lease was signed for student housing, shortly after she was scheduled to leave.

The time had arrived. A decision had to be made. Should

she stay or should she go? My firstborn was torn between following her ambitions and sticking around for mutual grief support. A few weeks was all she had to mourn the loss of her father...and those were busy weeks. Was she strong enough to cope on her own? Were we strong enough to manage without her?

Realizing our need for an immediate answer, Holly, Jenni, and I sat in a circle cross-legged on the living room floor. The full moon's light shone brightly through the large, bay window. Together we prayed, asking God for His wisdom regarding our quandary, then we did something we'd never done before—we cast lots!

Casting lots was a common practice in biblical times. Like rolling dice, priests used a pair of sacred objects (the Urim and Thummim) to determine God's will.[192] In the presence of the Lord, Joshua cast lots to establish division of the Promised Land for Israel's twelve tribes.[193] Sailors with Jonah cast lots to find out who was responsible for the violent storm that threatened their lives.[194] Lots were cast to decide who would replace Judas Iscariot as one of the twelve apostles.[195] Numerous examples concluded that if *they* received answers and direction from God by casting lots, then so could we.

Problem was we had no idea what we were doing, so we trusted the Lord to be our guide. After over an hour of prayer, inquiry, and dice rolling, the three of us accepted the recurring response as God's divine answer—Jenni would relocate to the Sunshine State. She was confident and thrilled; knowing she was obediently following the path God had set before her.

By now, Holly was not only missing her dad, she was missing her sister, and the fact that I was becoming preoccupied with Keith, didn't help. She was struggling to accept our growing affection and rejected the proposed direction of our lives. For her, it was way too soon. But unlike me, who'd been subconsciously mourning the loss of Steve for over six years as a means of self-preservation, she was just beginning to work through the process. Until the bitter end, she was either in denial or continuing to see through eyes of faith, steadfastly holding onto the hope that her dad would be miraculously healed—physically *and* spiritually. The fact that he wasn't devastated her.

In hindsight, I should have been far more mindful and sensitive, but being so love-struck and unbelievably ready to move on, the obvious eluded me. I had stars in my eyes and was happily engaged in my own little world. Even though we still spent a much of our time together, as soon as Keith called she was left alone, feeling rejected and abandoned.

We love birds longed to be together. There was no reason for Holly and me to stay in New Mexico after her high school graduation in the spring. With only a few exceptions, everyone we loved was back in Michigan. Keith and I agreed the decision to relocate from New Mexico to short-term housing in Michigan, with the escalating prospect that we'd be getting married, was senseless.

During one of our three-hour phone conversations Keith made a suggestion, "Why don't you and Holly just move in with me?"

*Yep, that would be nice.* The notion was tempting. Deep down that's really what I wanted, but I was unwilling to jeopardize my relationship with the Lord by living with a man who wasn't yet my husband. "You know I can't do that!"

"What if there was a commitment?"

"A commitment like what?" I innocently toyed.

With a hint of excitement in his voice he eagerly asked, "What if we were engaged?"

*Engaged.* The word rang sweetly in my ear. "You want to get engaged?"

"Yes, I want to be engaged." Then he optimistically concluded, "to be married!"

My head started whirling and my heart was screaming—*YES!* "But being engaged still doesn't give us license to live together."

"Then let's get married!" He proposed, leaping over the only obstacle standing in the way of the two of us being together.

I instantly recognized this as my promise for a new beginning. With exuberance, I blurted—"YES! Yes, I will marry you!"

Another six weeks dragged by ever so slowly and painfully, but today marked the end of our waiting. Keith was on a plane that was due to arrive in a just a couple hours. With the windows down and Christian music blaring, I sang at the top of my lungs, waving my right hand in the air worshipping God—Nothing beats praising the Lord with great music! The sun was shining brilliantly in the empty topaz-blue sky. *What a wonderful day! I couldn't be happier!* Although I was zipping along at top speed, I seemed to be making little headway. *Had the El Paso airport moved?* In anticipation of seeing my fiancé, the drive seemed farther than it ever had before.

*My fiancé...* Once again the thought graced my face with a generous grin and in my heart I was jumping for joy. I was anxious to see my beloved and spend time wrapped in his arms, but we had a great deal to accomplish in four short days. This trip's goal was to get the house ready to sell and on the market. Because of the property's unique location (far from town in the middle of nowhere), neither one of us had any idea how long it might take to find a buyer. But we agreed the sooner we listed it, the better off we'd be. Then as soon as Holly throws her cap in the air indicating that she's graduated, like a flag being waved at the racetrack signaling drivers to start their engines, we'd be tearing up the track, heading back to Michigan.

In the morning Keith and I were sitting with the top real estate agent in Grant County filling out paperwork and discussing price. To establish value, comparisons (or comps) had to be made with similar "recently-sold" properties in the area. For over 25 minutes the realtor searched for "comps" only to find one—and that *one* was set to expire in two weeks! The urgency to sell was clear—No lender provides financing for a property without "comps," not even to the most qualified buyer. It was that cut and dry! So pricing the house for a quick sale was imperative.

God's timing couldn't have been more perfect! Two days before that solitary "comp" expired, I accepted a full price offer from a buyer who'd already secured mortgage financing! And what's even more momentous is that sale transpired at the peak of the 2008 housing bubble—right before the real estate market collapsed! If the house hadn't sold exactly when it did, I could have been stuck out there in the wilderness for at least another four years…or longer. Owning the property free and clear didn't give me the option of just walking away.

"Can I offer you a beverage?" A female voice asked, interrupting my daydream.

I made eye contact with the flight attendant, smiled, and shook my head. Lost in thought, looking down at the world below, I continued crafting some of the most important words I would ever say…

It was late February, my turn to repeat the trip I made 12

weeks earlier. From the moment Keith proposed and I enthusiastically shouted, "YES!" we started planning our future. As our feelings intensified, we no longer wanted to wait for June to become husband and wife—that was still two trips and three months away. So being fully confident we were following the path God had paved, we set a date for the second night of my visit and planned a wedding celebration for our families in June, when we would finally, be together forever.

Keith and I agreed it would be more meaningful to add our own wedding vows to the traditional ones. So standing face to face in the glow of two individual candles, with the unity candle waiting to be lit, the man of my dreams reached down, took hold of my hands, looked deeply into my eyes, and delivered the most heartfelt words I have ever heard. The sincerity and depth of his love for me was apparent. As he spoke words of adoration and intent, silent tears slowly started sliding down my face.

Sniffles could be heard from the few family members invited to witness the event that was planned two weeks earlier. The intimate gathering took place at dusk in a luxury suite of the Amway Grand Plaza Hotel overlooking the Grand River and downtown Grand Rapids. Inside the small, cozy living room loved ones scooched together to squeeze onto two over-sized chairs and their ottomans, one sofa, and a loveseat. Outside the massive, ornately dressed windows, large fluffy snowflakes gently tumbled from the sky. When darkness fell, 22 stories up provided an impressive view of the city lights.

My groom was strikingly handsome in his new black suit, white button-up shirt, and wine-red tie. The aroma of his spicy, masculine cologne was intoxicating. Staring up into his baby blues before starting to read my vows reassured me that getting married to this wonderful man was the right decision.

I was in love and my heart was rejoicing. I was certain God would richly bless our union for seeking and following His plan. Smiling and bursting with exhilaration, I gently clasped hands with the "man of my dreams," looked into his eyes, and thoughtfully began reading the vows I'd spent days composing. Tears glistened in his eyes as he gazed into mine and heard me express my heartfelt feelings of affection.

The pastor was beaming as he handed us our wedding rings and started providing the words we were to say during the exchange. He knew something no one else did—our circular symbols of never-ending love were very distinctive. There were no other wedding rings like them. Since we were going to shop for our actual rings the following day, I bought fun, inexpensive rings from Claire's to swap at the ceremony. They were inscribed with the words "Best Friend."

When Keith met me at the airport I pulled the matching set out of my pocket, holding them up for him to see, he snickered. "How appropriate!"

Back in New Mexico, while reminiscing about our special affair, I recalled a vision God gave me months earlier. Kneeling on the floor, hands folded on the couch, I was shown two people standing erect, facing one another toe-to-toe. The dark silhouettes were unidentifiable, but as they stood stationary with sidelong curves exposed, rose petals, like snowflakes, slowly began to fall all around them. At the time the vision made little sense. *Could this have been another sign predicting and confirming our destiny? I wondered...*

Being married for three months without my spouse felt like an eternity. The last two scheduled visits never came soon enough or lasted long enough. During our time apart I focused on packing. Holly, who was still having a tough time coping with the changes, pleaded with me to control my excitement and eagerness to leave. Between her 18th birthday and her high school graduation she informed me that she would rather stay out west with the elder's family from church than move back to Michigan to live with Keith and me. That was a shattering blow! I wanted all of us to be happy together, but despite numerous attempts to get her to change her mind, she was firm on staying in New Mexico where she was plugged in to a loving church home and planned on taking advantage of their four-year, tuition-free college education program.

After Holly's graduation, she and I climbed aboard the loaded-down U-Haul and headed toward the Great Lakes State. She was going to attend our wedding "celebration" with Jenni, who we were flying in from Florida, and Andrew, Keith's son who had finally returned to his mother's.

Although my husband offered to fly down and drive up with us, I was really looking forward to spending some alone time with my youngest daughter. The two of us laughed and cried. We talked about the past and pondered the future. When Jenni joined us in Michigan, the three of us were thrilled to be reunited again after our ten-day Caribbean cruise at Christmas.

On a warm sunny afternoon in June, days shy of a full year from Steve's tragic death, our wedding celebration took place at the beautiful Frederik Meijer Gardens. Acres of scenic views, sculptures, and foliage made this the perfect place for guests to spend a Saturday afternoon. Everyone in attendance thoroughly enjoyed the occasion. At the catered sit-down luncheon Keith and I shared our story—how we met and how God brought us together.

What began as a mutual need for friendly, emotional support 12 months earlier, merged with divine intervention and steered us to the altar where God sealed His promises with a truly miraculous kiss!

Our God is the God of restoration. The God of all grace who has called you to His eternal glory in Christ Jesus promises that, "After you have suffered a little while, He will himself restore you and make you strong, firm and steadfast."[196]

Keith was instrumental in God's promise of restoration. Just as my visions portrayed—there was a light burning brightly at the end of *my* tunnel; there was a new beginning to look forward to; and the prophetic words spoken over me and my future at the conference years prior to Steve's passing, finally materialized—I *am* "soaring above the clouds." Glory to God!

# Conclusion

*Blessed is the one who perseveres under trial because, having stood the test, that person will receive the crown of life that the Lord has promised to those who love him.*[197]

Jesus' brother James writes, "Consider it pure joy, my brothers and sisters, whenever you face trials of many kinds *or* fall into various temptations. Be assured *and* understand that the trial *and* proving of your faith develops perseverance (endurance *and* steadfastness *and* patience). Perseverance must fully finish its work, so that you may be perfectly and fully developed [with no defects], mature and complete, lacking in nothing."[198]

During our decade of darkness I'd sarcastically spit out those words—"Consider it pure joy." *Pure joy? Really?* How could any of what we were going through be considered *pure joy?*

The Message Bible translates "pure joy" as "sheer gift." *A Gift?* Now let's be honest. If we could see adversity coming toward us, like a monster storm raging furiously across the horizon destroying everything in its path, we'd run and hide wouldn't we? Like seeking shelter from a hurricane, no one wants to suffer pain or endure hardship. But if God's intent is to have us go through trials so we can experience "pure joy" or receive the "sheer gift" of experiencing His glory, we should see the storms through. We shouldn't try to avoid them or get out of them prematurely, because if God's refining work isn't achieved in the first go 'round, we're sure to be given subsequent opportunities to become "perfectly and fully developed, mature, complete, entire, and lacking nothing."

God never promised to eliminate suffering until the restoration of all things, but to use it to spiritually transform believers into the likeness of His Son. The Refiner of our faith uses a purifying process similar to that of a goldsmith who values his treasure, closely monitors its progress, and exercises great care in perfecting its outcome. Due to its tremendous worth, the metal worker will never leave or turn away from what is to become his flawless masterpiece.

When asked how the artist could tell when the purifying process was complete, his response was, "It's only after the raw material has been exposed to the hottest part of the fire, its impurities have been burned off, and I can see my own reflection."

Jesus told His disciples to expect suffering, tribulation, and distress, but to take heart—to be confident, undaunted, and filled with joy. Why? Because *in all things* God works for the good of those who love Him, and *in all things* we are more than conquerors through Christ—overwhelming victory is ours![199]

Our present sufferings are only temporary. They are nothing "compared with the glory that is about to be revealed to us *and* in us *and* for us *and* conferred on us!"[200] So we can be "truly glad" even though we suffer and endure many trials, because wonderful joy lies ahead when our faith is proven genuine and strong. Much praise, glory, and honor will be our reward.[201]

Standing firm in faith during turbulent times isn't something we can accomplish on our own. Only through the power of God's Holy Spirit can we faithfully persevere without losing hope. When Paul pleaded with the Lord to remove his source of pain and suffering, His response was the same on three different occasions. "My grace is sufficient for you [My loving kindness and My mercy are more than enough—always available—regardless of the situation]; for [My] power is being perfected [and is completed and shows itself most effectively] in [your] weakness."[202]

El Shaddai—the All-Sufficient One—the God of abundance is all we need and more than enough for any circumstance or predicament we find ourselves in. He has the ability to turn our lives around. He can bring about resolution in more ways than we could ever imagine. He can alter nature, change minds, transform hearts, modify behavior, and motivate people into action. He can even fill us with a surpassing sense of peace and comfort as he carries us through our storms.

When Jesus received word that Lazarus, "the one you love is sick," He told His disciples, "This sickness will not end in death. No, it is for God's glory so that God's Son may be glorified through it."[203] Therefore, instead of abandoning their mission and rushing off to be with their friend, they stayed where they were another two days.

On the one-day journey to Bethany Jesus informed them that Lazarus had died, but "I am going there to wake him up."[204] "For your sake I am glad I was not there, so that you may believe."[205] Jesus knew an earlier arrival and healing of Lazarus' illness would never create the same height of exuberance or generate the same depth of faith as raising His friend from the dead.

Upon arrival Mary, Martha, and several others who were comforting the sisters, followed Jesus to the tomb where Lazarus' dead body had been lying for four days. They all held their breath as the stone was rolled away from the opening. Jesus looked to the sky, thanked His Father for always hearing His prayers, then shouted, "Lazarus, come out!" And the dead man walked out of his tomb! [206] Jesus posed a rhetorical question to the crowd. "Did I not tell you that *if you believed*, you would see the glory of God?"[207]

God wants us *all* to be witnesses of His glory.[208] But without faith, it's not only impossible to please God, it's unlikely you will ever see or experience His glory.[209] Even in His hometown, Jesus performed fewer miracles because those who lived there were blinded by their lack of faith. [210]

Faith is being sure of what we hope for and certain of what we do not see. [211] According to God, it is the single most important quality anyone can possess. Faith has greater worth than gold and brings glory to God. [212] Faith justifies us and makes us right with God.[213] Faith is the key that unlocks the door to God's divine favor and outpouring of blessing.[214] *If you believe*, your eyes will be opened to see and experience the presence, power, and glory of God.

There is meaning and purpose in *everything* God allows to happen in our lives.[215] Although we may never know what that is, every trial is an opportunity for God to open our eyes, to exponentially grow our faith, to conform us into the likeness of His Son, and to make the riches of His glory known to the objects of His mercy.

While deeply saddened by our loss and the course of events that led up to Steve's tragic death, there seems to be a

Conclusion | 229

parallel to Lazarus' story. If the Lord had answered our initial prayer request and Steve had received an immediate physical healing, chances are we could have all been blind to the miracle. Steve may have never been prompted to forgive others so God would forgive him; he may have never been reconciled to God by giving his life to Christ; and without being broken, he could have missed out on God's gift of eternal life.

Although we all would have preferred a speedy recovery, God graciously chose to wait—using this period of adversity to open our eyes, to grow our faith, to refine us, to prepare Steve's heart for his promotion to glory, and to produce a triumphant testimony that would not only impact our lives, but the lives of everyone who has ears to hear. Steve's life mattered to God...yet so does *yours*!

*Never once* during our decade of darkness could I have ever imagined being grateful for the experience. The girls and I truly loved Steve; watching him suffer and deteriorate the way he did was the most difficult and excruciatingly painful torment I hope we will ever have to endure. But years of contemplative reflection and prayer have led me to appreciate God's gift of "pure joy."

For faithfully persevering through our storm, the girls and I have been richly blessed. We are complete, full of joy, mature in faith, and lacking nothing. Left on our own with manageable strife, chances are we would have never been brought to our knees, we would have never gotten to know the Lord as intimately as we have, and our faith-fire would have never been fanned into fierce flames. Without being anchored in hope and totally dependent on God for our every need, we would have never expected Him to show up. And if He did, we could have been blind to the miracles, missing out on His glory and His best for our lives. Relying on ourselves would have only served to rob God of the opportunity to prove Himself genuine, faithful, and true.

Trials are inevitable, but instead of leaving us alone in our imploding circumstances, God chose to come alongside and journey with us. In times of emotional distress, He comforted. In times of danger, He protected. In times of uncertainty, He reassured. In times of financial hardship, He provided. In times of confusion, He clarified. Whenever we felt alone, He made His presence known. He upheld us with His righteous right hand, drew us close to His side and calmed our fears, filling us with His perfect peace. The Lord's loving kindness, tender mercy, and abundant grace *was* more than enough to carry us through. And His power *was* perfected in our weakness.

As Jesus and His disciples were leaving Jericho with a large crowd, a blind man named Bartimaeus was sitting at the roadside begging. When he heard Jesus of Nazareth was passing by he began to shout, "Jesus, Son of David, have mercy on me!"

Many rebuked him, telling him to be quiet and not to make a spectacle of himself, but he shouted all the more. Disregarding the onlookers and focusing entirely on Jesus, the beggar continued to yell, "Son of David, have mercy on me!"

As soon as Jesus heard Bartimaeus crying out for help, He stopped walking and instructed His disciples to, "Call him."

They hollered to the blind man, "Cheer up! On your feet! He's calling you."

Hastily throwing off his cloak, possibly his most valued possession, Bartimaeus jumped to his feet and with jubilant expectation ran to Jesus.

"Jesus asked, 'What do you want me to do for you?'"

"The blind man answered, 'Rabbi, I want to see.'"

"'Go,' Jesus said, 'your faith has healed you.'"²¹⁶ Instantly the man could see, and he followed Jesus, praising God. Everyone who witnessed the miracle also praised God.²¹⁷

Jesus hears your prayers and your cries for help. Today He is asking, "What can I do for *you*?"

Throw off your cloak of shame, guilt, hurts, habits, and hang-ups; disregard what others are saying; fix your eyes intently on Jesus; and with jubilant expectation—jump to your feet and race toward Him who is able to do superabundantly more than all we dare ask, could ever hope for, or imagine!²¹⁸

# Postscript

# God's Ultimate Gift

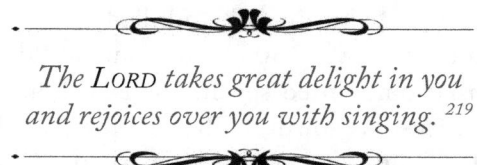

*The LORD takes great delight in you
and rejoices over you with singing.* [219]

"In the beginning was the Word (Christ), and the Word was with God, and the Word *was* God."[220] "All things," including the heavens and the earth, "were made *and* came into existence through Him."[221] "Life itself was in Him, and this life gives light to everyone" in the world.[222]

The Word became flesh and a prophet named John (the Baptist) was sent by God to prepare a way for Him and tell His people how to find salvation through the forgiveness of their sins.[223] John was bearing witness to the Light coming into the world to illuminate the life of every individual—so *all* would believe and put their trust in Him.[224]

John gave evidence to Jesus' true identity while baptizing Him in the Jordan River. "I have seen the Spirit descending as a dove out of heaven, and he remained upon him. I did not recognize him [as the Messiah], but he who sent me to baptize in water said to me, 'He upon whom you see the Spirit descend and remain, this one is he who baptizes with the Holy Spirit.' I myself have [actually] seen [that happen], and my testimony is that this is the Son of God!"[225]

Matthew, Mark, Luke, and Peter also recorded seeing the Spirit of God descend on Jesus like a dove and they too heard a voice from heaven saying, "This is my Son, whom I love; with Him I am well pleased."[226]

Throughout His ministry, Jesus referred to Himself as Son of the living God,[227] Son of Man,[228] Savior,[229] God,[230] Messiah,[231] and the only Way to eternal life.[232] He also publically proclaimed, "Everything which has been written about *me* in the Law of Moses and the [writings of the] Prophets and the Psalms must be fulfilled."[233]

Jesus fulfilled over 300 Messianic Old Testament prophecies that pinpointed specific details about the coming Messiah's ancestry, birth, life, ministry, death, and resurrection.[234] The odds of any one person satisfying even eight of the Messianic prophecies are 1-in-100-quadrillion or $10^{17}$. The likelihood of any one person fulfilling 48 of the Messianic prophecies is $10^{157}$![235] This gives compelling evidence that Jesus was who He claimed to be.[236]

As predicted in Scripture, after suffering brutal beatings, dying on a cross, being stabbed in the side, wrapped in a shroud, and securely sealed in a borrowed tomb for three days, Jesus rose from the dead—and God caused Him to be seen![237] Following His resurrection, Jesus spent 40-plus days with His apostles, providing sufficient evidence *and* irrefutable demonstrations that proved His identity.[238] Jesus also appeared publically to a crowd of more than 500 men—not including women and children.[239]

According to prophecy, Jesus (the Messiah) is the only One through whom salvation is possible; the only One able to forgive sins and reconcile the ungodly to God; the only One who can give new life to those already born; the only One who has ever conquered the grave, victoriously defeating sin and death, opening the door to eternal life; and the only One who has ever ascended into heaven to be seated at the right hand of God, head over every power and authority in heaven and on earth—still alive and active today![240]

When Jesus first appeared to His disciples, after rising from the dead, He proved His identity by showing them His nail-pierced hands and spear-impaled side. They were overjoyed to see Him![241] But when they shared the exciting news with Thomas, who was absent from the initial reveal, he was skeptical. "Unless I see the nail marks in his hands and put my finger where the nails were, and put my hand into his side, I will not believe."[242]

Although his comment dubbed him "Doubting Thomas," Jesus didn't scold him for his unbelief. Instead the first time they were together, Jesus addressed the disciple's concerns, showing the doubter His injuries and inviting him to touch them. "Put your finger here; see my hands. Reach out your hand and put it into my side. Stop doubting and believe."

"Thomas answered, 'My Lord and my God!'"

"Then Jesus told him, 'Because you have seen me, you have believed; blessed are those who have not seen and yet have believed.'"[243]

Where are you on your spiritual journey? Are you a skeptical seeker, blessed believer, or dubious doubter? To the seeker Jesus assures, "I will be found by you, when you seek me with all your heart."[244] To the believer, He promises to make Himself known.[245] To the non-believer, Satan has blinded your mind, preventing you from seeing the illuminating light of the gospel of the glory of Christ, who is God in flesh.[246] But take heart, you are being pursued and presented with an opportunity to have your spiritual eyes opened and be enlightened by Truth.

Irrespective of your current status, your Heavenly Father loves you.[247] He rejoices over you.[248] He knows everything about you.[249] And is familiar with all your ways.[250] You were created in His image.[251] In your mother's womb, He created your inmost being and knit you together.[252] You are His handiwork and His masterpiece.[253] You are not here by accident and you are not a mistake.[254] You were predestined *and* lovingly planned before the creation of the world to be adopted as God's child through Christ Jesus.[255]

"I have loved you with an everlasting love," says the LORD.[256] "My love for you will not be shaken..."[257] It doesn't matter where you're from or what you've done—your socio-economic status, your background, your ethnicity, your sexual orientation, your education, your religious upbringing, your self-applied labels, or societal tags—none of it has *any* influence on God's love for you. Christianity excludes no one—Jesus came down from heaven to give life to the world.[258] On the night of His birth, an angel of the Lord told the shepherds, "I bring you good news of great joy that will be for *all* people."[259] God richly blesses *all* who call on Him.[260] He does not discriminate or show favoritism, but accepts *all* who fear Him, seek Him, and do what is right.[261]

Even though past decisions and former actions are deserving of God's wrath, His desire is to bring about reconciliation and restoration. No matter how many times you've messed up, God will *never* give up on you.[262] "He is a forgiving God, gracious and compassionate, slow to anger and abounding in love."[263] He will not fail you.[264]

The Bible is full of imperfect people who loved the Lord, yet on occasion were led astray by their own selfish desires. Even so, God used these individuals along with their stories, to reveal His impeccable character, forgiving heart, and unconditional love. Inviting Jesus into your life doesn't make you perfect, but it does make you righteous—holy and flawless in the eyes of God—if you continue to have immovable faith.[265]

Did you know that when God showed up in the burning bush asking Moses to return to Egypt, to go before Pharaoh and deliver His people from bondage, Moses asked God to choose someone else?[266] Do you recall that the disciple Peter disowned Jesus three times before His crucifixion? Did you ever wonder how King David, an adulterer and a murderer, got the nickname "a man after God's own heart?" Were you aware that Rahab, an ancestress in the royal line from which Jesus came, was a prostitute? And that Paul, a top-ranking religious leader and murderer of Christians referred to himself as "the worst of sinners," yet was chosen by God to be His apostle and take the gospel message to the Gentiles (non-Jews), their kings, and the people of Israel?[267] Despite their shortcomings, God used each one of these imperfect people to accomplish His perfect plan for His glory.

"There is no one on earth who always does what's right and never sins."[268] We've all sinned and fall short of the glory of God.[269] This impurity makes it so none of us can ever become right with God through our own efforts.[270] Only through faith in Jesus Christ, the "Friend of sinners," can we become right in God's eyes.[271]

Let's take a glimpse at the heart of God and His incomprehensible love for imperfect people in two parables Jesus shared with the Pharisees. First, The Parable of the Lost Sheep:

> Suppose one of you has a hundred sheep and loses one of them. Doesn't he leave the

ninety-nine in the open country and go after the lost sheep until he finds it? And when he finds it, he joyfully puts it on his shoulders and goes home. Then he calls his friends and neighbors together and says, 'Rejoice with me; I have found my lost sheep.' I tell you that in the same way there will be more rejoicing in heaven over one sinner who repents than over ninety-nine righteous persons who do not (believe they) need to repent.[272]

Second, The Parable of the Lost Son, better known as The Prodigal Son:

There was a man who had two sons. The younger one said to his father, 'Father, give me my share of the estate.' So he divided his property between them. Not long after that, the younger son got together all he had, set off for a distant country and there squandered his wealth in wild living. After he had spent everything, there was a severe famine in that whole country, and he began to be in need. So he went and hired himself out to a citizen of that country, who sent him to his fields to feed pigs. He longed to fill his stomach with the pods that the pigs were eating, but no one gave him anything.

When he came to his senses, he said, 'How many of my father's hired servants have food to spare, and here I am starving to death!' I will set out and go back to my father and say to him: 'Father, I have sinned against heaven and against you. I am no longer worthy to be called your son; make me like one of your hired servants.' So he got up and went to his father.

But while he was still a long way off, his father saw him and was filled with compassion for him; he ran to his son, threw his arms around him and kissed him. The son said to him, 'Father, I have sinned against heaven and against you. I am no longer worthy to be called your son.'

But the father (absorbing all the shame his son put on the family) said to his servants, 'Quick! Bring the best robe and put it on him (the father covers the son's humiliation with his prominent social status). Put a ring on his finger (giving the son decision-making authority) and sandals on his feet (demonstrating restoration of sonship). Bring the fattened calf and kill it (meal of reconciliation between the son and the entire community he disgraced). Let's have a feast and celebrate. For this son of mine was dead and is alive again; he was lost and is found.' So they began to celebrate.[273]

Have you gone astray? Are you dead? Are you lost? If so,

it's time to be "found." Stop running and start living! Turn around and return home. You are unbelievably loved and treasured. God knows you better than you know yourself; He sees your full potential and how He can use you for His glory. You have an important role to play in the kingdom of God right here on earth. Even though you may still be a long way off, your Heavenly Father sees you and is filled with compassion, His arms are open wide in anticipation of you running into them.

While "the wages of sin is death, the gift of God is eternal life in Christ Jesus our Lord."[274] "God made him who had no sin to be sin for us, so that in him we might become the righteousness of God."[275] Christ died for sins once for all, the righteous for the unrighteous, to bring us closer to God.[276] "Salvation is found in no one else, for there is no other name under heaven given to mankind by which we must be saved."[277]

Jesus proclaimed, "I am the way and the truth and the life. No one comes to the Father except through me."[278] "The one who believes in me will live, even though they die; and whoever lives by believing in me will never die."[279] "My Father's will is that *everyone* who looks to the Son and believes in him shall have eternal life."[280]

However, it's not enough to simply acknowledge these facts—action is required. God commands *all* people everywhere to repent.[281] "Unless you repent, you will perish."[282] Jesus preached, "Repent [change your inner self - your attitude, your old way of thinking, regret past sins, live your life in a way that proves repentance; seek God's purpose for your life], for the kingdom of heaven is at hand."[283]

"If we confess our sins, he is faithful and just to forgive us our sins and purify us from all unrighteousness."[284] "As soon as you ask, your sins will be forgiven and remembered no more."²⁸⁵ God said, "I am he who blots out your transgressions, *for my own sake*, and remembers your sins no more."²⁸⁶ "I take no pleasure in the death of anyone, declares the Sovereign LORD. Repent and live!"²⁸⁷ "Repent and turn to God, so that your sins may be wiped out, that times of refreshing may come from the Lord."²⁸⁸

"The message of the cross is foolishness to those who are perishing, but to us who are being saved it is the power of God."²⁸⁹ Jesus promises new life, abundant life, and eternal life, but "the Devil prowls around like a roaring lion looking for someone to devour."²⁹⁰ Aspiring to steal, kill, and destroy all the goodness God has in store for you.²⁹¹ His aim is to convince you that a decision to follow Christ is irrational and unnecessary—a crutch for the weak. Manipulating God's truth with lies—you'll *never* be good enough; you'll *never* be accepted; things will *never* change; *more* religious mandates are required; or Jesus' "once for all" sacrifice falls short of eradicating your sin, making you holy and blameless in the eyes of God, and freeing you from the condemnation of His wrath. Don't yield to the malicious conspiracy devised to destroy your life.

On your own you are unworthy and undeserving of such a magnificent "gift," but God's gift is *not* dependent on *you* earning it—it's *fully* reliant on Jesus' sacrifice that paid your debt in full. ²⁹² "For it is by grace [God's remarkable compassion and favor drawing you to Christ] that you have been saved [actually delivered from judgment and given eternal life] through faith. And this [salvation] is not of yourselves [not through your own effort], but it is the [undeserved, gracious] gift of God."²⁹³

"God has called you out of darkness into his wonderful

light."²⁹⁴ You no longer have to be a slave to sin—whatever struggles, hurts, habits, hang-ups, regrets, insecurities, fears, shame, guilt, addictions, weaknesses, or temptations you're afflicted with or encumbered by, cast them all onto Jesus because He cares for you and wants to free you from the heavy burdens that weigh you down.²⁹⁵ Whatever controlling influences have you ensnared—whether words of condescension, abuse, neglect, resentment, anger, offense, jealousy, or anything else that's adversely affecting your life— God wants to snap off every one of those destructive strongholds, to fill your life with peace, and bring about restoration, hope, healing…and joy.

"For God so loved the world that he gave his one and only Son, that whoever believes in him shall not perish but have eternal life. God did not send his Son into the world to condemn it, but to save the world through him."²⁹⁶

There is no hope in the world without God.²⁹⁷ That is why "He reconciled you to Himself by giving you new birth into a living hope through the resurrection of Jesus Christ from the dead."²⁹⁸

When Nicodemus, a religious ruler, secretly asked Jesus how to get right with God, He answered—"I assure you *and* most solemnly say to you, unless a person is born again [reborn from above—spiritually transformed, renewed, sanctified], he cannot [ever] see *and* experience the kingdom of God."²⁹⁹ Because, "Flesh gives birth to flesh, but the Spirit gives birth to spirit."³⁰⁰ To "see *and* experience" the kingdom of God in your life today and throughout eternity, Jesus says, "You must be born again."³⁰¹ "Everyone who believes that Jesus is the Christ is a born-again child of God."³⁰²

To be reconciled with God and free from condemnation, a decision has to be made. No one can make that decision for you. Being raised in a Christian home or regular church attendance doesn't make you a Christian any more than swimming in the ocean makes you a fish.

Jesus said, "You have not chosen me, but I have chosen you."[303] "Look! I stand at the door and knock. If you hear my voice and open the door, I will come in."[304]

"Today, if you hear His voice, do not harden your hearts."[305] Your precious, priceless gift of new life, abundant life, and eternal life is waiting to be accepted, unwrapped, and enjoyed.

You can invite Jesus into your life right now with a simple prayer like this—

"Dear Heavenly Father,

Thank You for loving me and choosing me to be Your child. I recognize that I am a sinner in need of a Savior. I repent of all my wrongdoing (sin) and ask for Your forgiveness. I believe Jesus is Lord and that He paid the penalty for my sins in full when He died on the cross. I also believe You raised Him from the dead. I want to be reconciled with You and have our relationship restored, so I am opening the door and inviting Jesus in to be Lord of my life. Your Word says if I confess with my mouth 'Jesus is Lord' and believe in my heart that You raised Him from the dead, I will be saved! Born again into new life![306] I pray these things in the powerful name of your Son, Jesus Christ. Amen!"

If you just prayed that prayer with sincerity, all of heaven is celebrating—rejoicing over *you*![307] **By faith**—your sins have been forgiven;[308] you are now a child of God;[309] filled with His Holy Spirit;[310] a new creation and heir to all God's blessings.[311] Your life won't be perfect, but I assure you, it will *never* be the same again![312]

# Growing in Godliness

*Whatever you do, do it all for the glory of God.*[313]

Christians aren't just people who believe Jesus is (the Son of) God crucified for the forgiveness of sins and resurrected to secure eternal life, they are people who aspire to model their lives after His—choosing to live beyond belief. If you've repented and have been reconciled to God through Jesus Christ, the Bible says you are a new creation—your old moral and spiritual condition is gone.[314] It has been crucified with Christ and you are no longer under the controlling power of sin.[315]

"You are made new in the attitude of your mind and created to be like God in true righteousness and holiness."[316] "Reborn from above, spiritually transformed, renewed, and ready to be used to do the good things he planned for you long ago."[317] The decision to live for God instead of yourself is where your amazing adventure begins!

As soon as His gift of mercy, love, and eternal life is accepted, "God establishes *and* confirms our relationship with Christ by putting his seal on us [that is, he has appropriated us and certified us as his] and has given us the [Holy] Spirit in our hearts as a pledge [like a security deposit to guarantee the fulfillment of his promise of eternal life]."[318] "The Spirit himself testifies *and* confirms that we are children of God."[319]

The indwelling of God's Holy Spirit fills us with "power from heaven," enabling us to do all that Jesus did throughout His ministry—and more! [320] The Holy Spirit guides us into all truth, revealing unknown mysteries, and telling us "what is yet to come."[321] He "comes to our aid *and* bears us up in our weakness."[322]

When we pray, the Holy Spirit "intercedes *and* pleads on our behalf according to *and* in harmony with God's will."[323] He empowers believers with spiritual gifts to benefit the Christian community. [324] And through His power, God progressively works to transform us into the likeness of His Son.[325] Once God's transformational process of sanctification commences, it never stops.

Trying to explain this spiritual metamorphosis to anyone who's never experienced it is like trying to get a toddler to understand how an ugly caterpillar turns into a beautiful butterfly. Until you witness or experience the conversion yourself you can't fully grasp the totality of its effect, because nothing on earth compares with being a new creation in Christ and having God's Holy Spirit living inside you.

Living a holy life pleasing to God is not something that can be accomplished apart from Him. It's a daily discipline like physical training, but "godliness has value for all things; holding promise for both the present life and the life to come."[326]

There are numerous ways to grow in godliness, but above all is to honor God's greatest commandments—"Love the Lord your God with all your heart and with all your soul and with all your strength and with all your mind." AND "Love your neighbor as yourself."[327]

As children of God, we are to imitate Him. Always walking in love, practicing empathy and compassion.[328] Being kind to everyone.[329] Treating others as we'd like to be treated.[330] Demonstrating hospitality and mercy.[331] Being unselfish and humbling ourselves to lift others up.[332] Love should be evident in the life of every Christian. There is nothing greater than love![333] Love covers a multitude of sins.[334] And "Love never fails."[335]

Instead of engaging in godless chatter, believers should focus on praying together and for one another.[336] Frequently meeting to encourage and build each other up, prompting one another to pursue love and good deeds.[337]

Many claiming to be followers of Christ argue that regular church attendance isn't necessary, but for those wanting to remain strong in their faith, being connected to a body of believers is vital. A lone ember taken off the charcoal grill can only burn so long on its own before growing cold. The same is true for our Christian walk—our flame will burn hotter and brighter for longer by routinely congregating with other believers.

Prayer, conversing with God, is an integral part of every Christian's life. Jesus devoted early morning to daily prayer. Giving God the first part of our day exemplifies His priority and sovereignty over our life. Starting each day with prayer instills focus, brings joy, and imparts a sense of unity, peace, and strength.

If mornings don't work for you, set aside another part of the day to be alone with God. Whether it's for an hour or ten minutes, shut the door on the world and bask in His presence. There is no right or wrong way to pray as long as a pure heart, godly motives, and reverence drive your prayer.[338] You don't have to assume any particular posture. Kneeling, folding your hands, or closing your eyes are all optional. Simply open your heart and talk to the Lord as you would a dearly beloved friend.

The Bible tells us to be faithful in prayer.[339] Always pray and never give up.[340] "The prayer of a righteous person is powerful and effective."[341] God's ears are attentive to their prayers.[342] Whoever you are, whatever you're going through, God invites you to approach His throne with confidence, so you may receive mercy and find grace to help you in your time of need.[343]

Jesus told His disciples, "Pray, then, in this way: 'Our Father who is in heaven, Hallowed be your name. Your kingdom come, your will be done on earth as it is in heaven. Give us this day our daily bread. And forgive us our debts, as we forgive our debtors [letting go of both the wrong and the resentment]. And do not lead us into temptation, but deliver us from evil. [For yours is the kingdom and the power and the glory forever. Amen.]'"[344]

Based on Jesus' example, Evangelist Billy Graham devised the ACTS model, a powerful 4-step prayer guide to aid believers. ACTS stands for Adoration, Confession, Thanksgiving, and Supplication.

1) **Adoration.** Begin prayer by worshipping, adoring, and praising God for who He is and for all He's done for you. God delights in the praises of His people!

2) **Confession**. As saints of God we don't deliberately continue to sin, but "if we know the good we ought to do and don't do it, we sin."[345] "If we [freely] admit that we have sinned *and* confess our sins, He is faithful and just, and will forgive our sins and cleanse us *continually* from all unrighteousness [our wrongdoing]."[346] Invite the Lord to expose any repressed or hidden sins so you can ask for and receive forgiveness.

3) **Thanksgiving**. Having an attitude of gratitude is glorifying to God. "Always be joyful and thankful."[347] "Give thanks in all circumstances."[348] "Always give thanks to God the Father for everything in the name of our Lord Jesus Christ."[349] What are you thankful for?

4) **Supplication**. At all times, in every situation, and on every occasion confidently present your requests to God. He hears when you ask anything according to His will.[350] Seek His guidance and wisdom in every area of your life. Pray not only for yourself, but for the needs of others.[351] Jesus told His followers, "Up to this time you have not asked a [single] thing in my name; but now ask, using my name, and you will receive, so that your joy may be full *and* complete."[352]

Immerse yourself daily in God's Word and you'll soon discover that studying Scripture is like opening a treasure chest brimming with valuable coins and precious gems that promise to enhance your life. A life that reflects true reverence for God is deeply rooted in His Word.

"The Bible is too complex," I'm told. "It's difficult to understand—the messages are confusing and there are multiple interpretations." While its sheer size can be intimidating, the Enemy uses these excuses to keep you from diving in. The King James Bible, written in the early 1600s with its Thees and Thous, is challenging to comprehend, but modern-day versions like the New International Version (NIV) and the Amplified Bible (AMP), used throughout this manuscript, are user-friendly. Even easier, are the New Living Translation (NLT) and the Message Bible (MSG).

To find a Bible that you like, visit a Christian bookstore or go online to BibleGateway.com and view the different variations. I highly recommend a study Bible because it offers greater insight into the text. The best place to begin reading is in the New Testament book of John.

"The Bible is the infallible and authoritative word of God."[353] "All Scripture is God-breathed."[354] While it's true that men wrote the Bible, these weren't just any men, they were men of God, directed by God, and carried along by the Holy Spirit to record His words and prophetic messages. No prophecy in Scripture ever came true because the prophet spoke it; prophecies materialized because God spoke His words through them.

"The gospel is the power of God that brings salvation to everyone who believes."[355] All Scripture points to Jesus.[356] His teachings and miracles were recorded so you would believe that He is who He said He was—the Messiah, the Son of God, and the only way to God—and by believing receive the incredible gift of eternal life.[357]

"The word of God is living and active *and* full of power [making it operative, energizing, and effective]. It is sharper than any two-edged sword, penetrating as far as the division of the soul and spirit [the completeness of a person], and of both joints and marrow [the deepest parts of our nature], exposing *and* judging the very thoughts and intentions of the heart."³⁵⁸

"God's word provides guidance useful for teaching, rebuking, correcting and training in righteousness, so that the servant of God may be thoroughly equipped for every good work."³⁵⁹ Therefore, "Do not merely read or listen to the word, and so deceive yourselves. Do what it says."³⁶⁰

Everyone who accepts God's gift of salvation ought to be baptized. The underwater immersion of a believer in the name of the Father, Son, and Holy Spirit, is an act of obedience that follows Jesus' example. It is a sign of allegiance and a public declaration of one's faith in Christ, "the pledge of good conscience toward God."³⁶¹

The backward plunge into the water symbolizes the believer's repentance, death to sin, and burial of the old life. Rising up out of the water represents the believer's resurrection into new life in Christ and his commitment to actively pursue God's kingdom.³⁶² This Christian tradition unifies believers.

"A person is considered righteous not by faith alone, but also by what he does."³⁶³ Part of living a godly, purpose-driven life is putting your faith into action—utilizing whatever spiritual gift(s) God has entrusted you with to serve others. ³⁶⁴

"Since we have gifts that differ according to the grace given to us, each of us is to use them accordingly: if [someone has the gift of] prophecy, [let him speak a new message from God to His people] in proportion to the faith possessed; if service, in the act of serving; or he who teaches, in the act of teaching; or he who encourages, in the act of encouragement;

he who gives, with generosity; he who leads, with diligence; he who shows mercy [in caring for others], with cheerfulness."[365]

Although works don't get you into heaven, just "as the body without the Spirit is dead, so faith without deeds is dead."[366] Therefore, "let us not love with words or speech but with actions and in truth."[367] Being rich in good deeds and generous with all we have.[368] "God loves a cheerful giver."[369]

Serving others in love is an expression of faith in action. "Let your light (godly influence) shine before men in such a way that they may see your good deeds *and* moral excellence, and [recognize and honor and] glorify your Father who is in heaven."[370]

There are countless opportunities and capacities in which to serve—What are you passionate about? What brings you joy and fulfillment? God has wired each one of us differently. Your particular character and gifts are unique to you, so serve others in a way that fits your personality, matches your gifting, brings you gratification, and glorifies God.

Invite the Holy Spirit to guide you where He wants you to volunteer your time. Start by exploring the needs of your church, and then if necessary, expand your search to openings in your community. Whatever you choose to do, "serve wholeheartedly, as if serving the Lord instead of people, and you will be rewarded."[371]

Five years ago Keith and I began attending a church closer to our new home. I wanted to serve, but wasn't sure where to get plugged in. Since I've always enjoyed working with children, ministering to them seemed like a no-brainer. My comfort zone was elementary school and there just happened to be an opening for a second grade Sunday school teacher coming available at the month's end. *Perfect!* I thought, accepting the role.

The following Sunday the middle school pastor stood in front of the congregation and made a plea for leaders. I listened, but had no interest. Yet the moment he stepped off stage, tears began streaming down my face. I could say I was crying, but that would be a lie, because there was absolutely no emotion tied to the tears. *Very bizarre!* A little freaked out, I gently elbowed my husband to get his attention. When he looked at me I raised my eyebrows and lifted open hands to my face. My puzzled expression begged to know—*what's happening?*

The inexplicable eruption of tears stopped after about 30 seconds. Crying in church isn't unusual for me, but I definitely took notice of the unprovoked tears. Turning to God I asked, "What am I supposed to make of this?" For the remainder of the service I prayed for clarity.

When we were dismissed I located the youth pastor in the lobby, and after sharing the peculiar incident, I bravely divulged, "I strongly feel that God wants to pluck me out of my comfort zone and plop me into middle school!" An assignment I would have never chosen for myself.

Now after four years of serving and moving up with my small group from junior high to high school, I am grateful God has given me the opportunity to pour into their young, impressionable lives. Sharing His love with them and watching them blossom spiritually has been a real joy and privilege. God chose for me what I would have never chosen for myself and I couldn't be more grateful. Trust Him to direct your path—His way is always best!

A tithe is one tenth of earnings or produce. It was formerly taken as a tax to support the church and its clergy. Storehouses were built in the temples to receive the tithe. Since tithing was a significant part of Jewish religious worship, and has biblical references, Christians have adopted this monetary form of worship.

Tithing carries with it a promise of blessing. "'Bring the whole tithe into the storehouse, that there may be food in my house. Test me in this,' says the LORD Almighty, 'and see if I will not throw open the floodgates of heaven and pour out so much blessing that there will not be room enough to store it.'"[372]

Jesus told His followers, "You do *not* belong to the world [you no longer belong to it], but I have chosen you *out* of the world."[373] We are aliens and strangers [in this world].[374] "Our citizenship is in heaven."[375]

Therefore, "Do not be conformed to this world."[376] Come out from it and be separate.[377] Keep yourself from being contaminated by it.[378] "Whoever chooses to be a friend of the world [that is, loving the things of the world] makes himself an enemy of God."[379] So flee from the evil desires that governed you in your former ignorance and pursue righteousness, godliness, faith, love, endurance, peace, and gentleness with those who call on the Lord out of a pure heart.[380]

"The whole world [around us] lies in the power of the evil one [opposing God and His precepts]."[381] "Resist the Devil and he will flee from you. Come near to God and he will come near to you."[382]

Maintaining godly focus in an ungodly world isn't easy. Therefore, "Protect yourselves from idols—[false teachings, moral compromises, or anything that would take God's place in your heart]."[383] Jesus warned His disciples, "Be on your guard against the yeast of the Pharisees and Sadducees."[384] Yeast represented poison religion, man-made traditions, self-righteousness, pompous arrogance, evil disposition, and false teachings that cause believers to stumble and be lured away from God's truth. "A little yeast works through the whole batch of dough."[385]

Don't be misled or caught up with people who are not living to glorify God. Avoid temptations and situations that could cause you to compromise your integrity. "Bad company corrupts good character."[386] Choose your friends wisely and remain strong in your faith, "For the time will come when people will no longer put up with sound doctrine. Instead, to suit their own desires, they will gather around a great number of teachers who say what their itching ears want to hear."[387]

"Mark this: There will be terrible times in the last days. People will be lovers of themselves, lovers of money, boastful, proud, abusive, disobedient to their parents, ungrateful, unholy, without love, unforgiving, slanderous, without self-control, brutal, not lovers of the good, treacherous, rash, conceited, lovers of pleasure rather than lovers of God - having a form of godliness but denying its power. Have nothing to do with such people!"[388]

The activities you engage in, the TV programs and movies you watch, the internet sites you visit, the social media platforms you participate in, the music you listen to, as well as the company you keep, all influence your thinking, your attitude, your behavior, and your witness. Be intentional about guarding yourself and your children from the corrupt things of this world that do not glorify God—things that cause spiritual and moral separation.

As believers, we are to live fruitful lives. That is to say our lives should mirror our faith; our actions should affirm our beliefs. We are called to be salt and light in the world. The best way to live into that is by being fruitful, producing good fruit.[389] The theme of "fruit" is woven throughout the New Testament.

Fruit is the outward expression of an individual's true character. Providing accurate insight into the purity or wickedness of a one's heart, thoughts, motives, and conduct. According to Jesus, you either produce good fruit or bad fruit. Good fruit is a reflection of godly living. Bad fruit is evidence of an immoral, ungodly, self-centered lifestyle.

Jesus metaphorically explained that every individual is a tree. "Every good tree bears good fruit, but a bad tree bears bad fruit. A good tree cannot bear bad fruit, and a bad tree cannot bear good fruit."[390] He warned His followers, "Watch out for false prophets. They come to you in sheep's clothing, but inwardly they are ferocious wolves. By their fruit you will recognize them."[391] In the same way you will be able to identify true saints.

The only means by which you can produce good fruit is through the power of the [Holy] Spirit; hence the term "fruit of the Spirit." The external manifestation of good fruit is "love, joy (gladness), peace, patience, kindness, goodness (benevolence), faithfulness, gentleness (meekness, humility), and self-control."[392]

Jesus told His disciples, "I am the Vine; you are the branches. Whoever lives in me and I in him bears much fruit. However, apart from me [cut off from vital union with me] you can do nothing. If you live in me [abide vitally united to me] and my words remain in you *and* continue to live in your hearts, ask whatever you will, and it shall be done for you.

When you bear much fruit, my Father is honored *and* glorified, and you show *and* prove yourselves to be true followers of mine."[393] "I have told you these things so that my joy *and* delight may be in you, and that your joy may be made full *and* complete *and* overflowing."[394]

Examine your life through God's eyes. If there's something you're struggling with or if anything is hindering your spiritual growth, ask God for help. He is the Gardener who's eager to lift you up so you can bear good fruit, pruning away, and delivering you from whatever hindrances are causing you to stumble.

While the Deceiver tries to bring you down, doing whatever it takes to trip you up and get your focus off God, luring and trapping you in the areas you are weakest, "God is faithful; he will not let you be tempted beyond what you can bear. When you are tempted, he will provide a way out so you can endure the temptation."[395] Lean on God for your exit strategy and for your deliverance.

Christ followers are to live wisely among non-believers and make the most of every opportunity to share their faith, bringing the "good news" to the ends of the earth.[396] Some of Jesus' last words before ascending into heaven were—"Go and make disciples of all nations, baptizing them in the name of the Father and of the Son and of the Holy Spirit, and teaching them to obey everything I have commanded you."[397] Christians call that the Great Commission—spreading the gospel message of salvation, forgiveness, love, hope, and eternal life through Christ Jesus with everyone, everywhere.

My prayer for you today reflects the heart of Paul and Timothy in their letter to the Colossians—I ask:

> God to fill you with the knowledge of his will through all the wisdom and understanding that the Spirit gives, so that you may live a life worthy of the Lord and please him in every way: bearing fruit in every good work, growing in the knowledge of God, being strengthened with all power according to his glorious might so that you may have great endurance and patience, and giving joyful thanks to the Father, who has qualified you to share in the inheritance of his holy people in the kingdom of light. For he has rescued us from the dominion of darkness and brought us into the kingdom of the Son he loves, in whom we have redemption, the forgiveness of sins.[398]

"Finally, brothers and sisters, whatever is true, whatever is noble, whatever is right, whatever is pure, whatever is lovely, whatever is admirable—if anything is excellent or praiseworthy—think about such things."[399]

# Eternal Hope of Glory

*At the name of Jesus EVERY KNEE SHALL BOW [in submission], of those who are in heaven and on earth and under the earth, and that every tongue will confess and openly acknowledge that Jesus Christ is Lord (sovereign God), to the glory of God the Father."*[400]

After being baptized Jesus emerged from the water, heaven opened, and the Spirit of God was seen descending and lighting on Him like a dove. A voice from heaven was heard saying, "This is my Son, whom I love; with him I am well pleased." [401] This embodiment of God's Spirit is what empowered Jesus to launch His ministry.

Jesus admitted to doing nothing on His own.[402] All of His power was derived from the presence of God's Holy Spirit dwelling inside His physical body. For this reason, when alerted of future events, Jesus' disciples became genuinely concerned about how they were going to continue ministering without the power and guidance the Son was receiving from the Father.

Cognizant of their apprehension, Jesus promised not to leave them on their own, but to equip and empower them to pursue their appointed task. "I will ask the Father, and He will give you another Helper (Comforter, Advocate, Intercessor - Counselor, Strengthener, Standby), to be with you forever - the Spirit of Truth, whom the world cannot receive [and take to its heart] because it does not see Him or know Him, *but* you know Him because He (the Holy Spirit) remains with you *continually* and will be in you. I will not leave you as orphans [comfortless, bereaved, and helpless]; I will come [back] to you. After a little while the world will no longer see me, but you will see me; because I live, you will live also. On that day [when that time comes] you will know for yourselves that I am in My Father, and you *are* in me, and I *am* in you."[403]

Following His resurrection and 40-day appearance on earth, Jesus told His disciples, "Do not leave Jerusalem, but wait for the gift my Father promised, which you have heard me speak about. For John baptized with water, but in a few days you will be baptized with the Holy Spirit."[404] "You will receive power when the Holy Spirit comes on you; and you will be my witnesses in Jerusalem, and in all Judea and Samaria, and to the ends of the earth."[405] With those final words Jesus ascended into heaven right before their very eyes.

While intently watching their Teacher and Friend being lifted high and out of sight, two men dressed in white suddenly appeared. "Men of Galilee," they said, "why do you stand here looking into the sky? This same Jesus, who has been taken from you into heaven, will come back in the same way you have seen him go into heaven."[406]

Aside from salvation, Jesus' second coming is the most important doctrine in the Bible—referenced eight times more often than His first coming and cited by all nine New Testament authors a total of 318 times![407] "Christ will appear a second time, not to bear sin, but to bring salvation to those who are waiting for him."[408] Prior to the crucifixion, Jesus assured His disciples that He was going to prepare a place for them in His Father's house, and when everything was ready, He would return to take them where He was—so they could spend eternity together.[409]

Paul tells believers not to be ignorant or to grieve over Christians who have died, or have fallen asleep in death, because they're not really dead—their souls and spirits are "absent from the body, but present with the Lord" in paradise.[410] Jesus said, "My Father's will is that everyone who looks to the Son and believes in him shall have eternal life, and I will raise him up on the last day."[411]

Jesus' second coming is the "blessed hope" of the Christian faith:

> We believe that Jesus died and rose again [as in fact He did], even so God [in this same way - by raising them from the dead] will bring with Him those [believers] who have fallen asleep in Jesus [in death]. For we say this to you by the Lord's [own] word, that we who are still alive and remain until the coming of the Lord, will in no way precede [into His presence] those [believers] who have fallen asleep. For the Lord Himself will come down from heaven with a shout of command, with the voice of the archangel and with the [blast of the] trumpet of God, and the dead in Christ will rise first. Then we who are alive and remain [on the earth] will *simultaneously* be caught up (raptured) together with them [the resurrected ones] in

the clouds to meet the Lord in the air, and so we will always be with the Lord! Therefore, comfort *and* encourage one another with these words [concerning our reunion with believers who have died].[412]

When Christ returns to rapture believers, we will all appear with Him in glory and will become like Him, with a new, resurrected, immortal body.[413] Paul enlightens us with this revelation:

> I declare to you, brothers and sisters, that flesh and blood cannot inherit the kingdom of God, nor does the perishable inherit the imperishable. Listen, I tell you a mystery: We will not all sleep, but we will all be changed— in a flash, in the twinkling of an eye, at the last trumpet. For the trumpet will sound, the dead will be raised imperishable, and we will be changed (wonderfully transformed). For the perishable must clothe itself with the imperishable, and the mortal with immortality. When the perishable has been clothed with the imperishable, and the mortal with immortality, then the saying that is written will come true: 'Death has been swallowed up in victory.'[414]

After Jesus was asked when this event would take place, He replied:

> The day or hour no one knows, not even the angels in heaven, nor the Son, but only the Father. As it was in the days of Noah, so it will be at the coming of the Son of Man. For in the days before the flood, people were eating and drinking, marrying and giving in marriage, up to the day Noah entered the ark; and they knew nothing about what would happen until the flood came and took them all away. That is how it will be at the coming of the Son of Man. Two men will be in the field; one will be taken and the other left. Two women will be grinding with a hand mill; one will be taken and the other left.[415]

Jesus gave His followers this warning—"Be on guard! Be alert!"[416] "Be ready, because the Son of Man will come at an hour when you do not expect him."[417] "Be patient and stand firm, because the Lord's coming is near."[418]

Since our citizenship is in heaven, we eagerly await the return of our Savior and look forward to an incredible homecoming with believers who have gone before us.[419] For Christians, also known as "the church" and "the Lord's Bride", this will be a time of jubilation—a grand reunion in the air and a wedding feast like no other after being escorted home to the Father's House. Fire-refined faith proved genuine will result in praise, glory, and honor.[420]

Once a decision is made to follow Christ and salvation is secure, the Lord expects us to use our time, talent, and treasures wisely—maturing in faith, expressing love to others, sharing the gospel, and taking advantage of every opportunity to advance His kingdom here on earth. Following the rapture, Christians will be judged on how well they served and administered those resources.[421] God will determine each believer's reward "according to what he has done."[422] And crowns will be distributed.

But woe to the unsaved at the time of the Lord's return, because of their unbelief they will have to endure the "coming wrath"—seven years of intolerable anguish and peril that will test the inhabitants of earth.[423] A time of "great distress, unequaled from the beginning of the world until now."[424]

The Bible says those who repent and give their lives to Christ *after* the rapture will be heavily persecuted and most will be put to death. "They will be hated by all nations because of my name. At that time many will be offended and repelled [by their association with me] and will fall away [from the one whom they should trust] and will betray one another [handing over believers to their persecutors] and will hate one another. Many false prophets will appear and mislead many. Because lawlessness is increased, the love of most people will grow cold. But the one who endures and bears up [under suffering] to the end will be saved."[425]

Jesus' disciples asked for signs leading up to His second coming and the end of the age. He told them, "When you hear of wars and rumors of war."[426] "There will be great earthquakes, famines and pestilences."[427] "Nation will rise against nation."[428] "This gospel of the kingdom will be preached in the whole world as a testimony to all nations."[429] Christians will be hated by all nations; they will be persecuted and even put to death.[430] And those doing the killing will think *and* claim they are doing God a service.[431] But the final sign of the end times is "when you see the 'abomination that causes desolation' standing [in the Holy Place] where it does not belong."⁴³²

To date, the majority of end-time prophecies in the Bible have been fulfilled. Paul elaborates on this final prophetic marker:

> Let no one in any way deceive *or* entrap you, for that day will not come unless the apostasy comes first [that is, the great rebellion, the abandonment of the faith by professed Christians], and the man of lawlessness is revealed, the son of destruction [the Antichrist, the one who is destined to be destroyed], who opposes and exalts himself [so proudly and so insolently] above every so-called god or object of worship, so that he [actually enters and] takes his seat in the temple of God, publicly proclaiming that he himself *is* God.⁴³³
>
> The coming of the [Antichrist, the lawless] one is through the activity of Satan, with great power [all kinds of counterfeit miracles] and [deceptive] signs and false wonders, and by unlimited seduction to evil *and* with all the deception of wickedness for those who are perishing, because they did not welcome the love of the truth [of the gospel] so as to be saved [they were spiritually blind, and rejected the truth that would have saved them]. Because of this, God will send upon them a misleading influence, [an activity of

error and deception] so they will believe the lie, in order that all may be judged *and* condemned who did not believe the truth [about their sin, and the need for salvation through Christ].[434]

The Antichrist, who scholars believe will hold a key government position or will be the one-world government leader, will initiate the start of the seven-year Tribulation by promising world peace and entering into a seven-year covenant with Israel. Three-and-a-half-years later, the Antichrist will break his covenant with Israel; he will stand in the temple "publicly proclaiming that he himself *is* God;" and will order everyone to bow down and worship him.[435]

Jesus says, "Immediately after the distress of those days (the seven-year tribulation trailing the rapture), the sun will be darkened, and the moon will not give its light; the stars will fall from the sky, and the heavenly bodies will be shaken."[436] But then, "As lightning that comes from the east is visible even in the west, so will be the coming of the Son of Man."[437]

"The Son of Man [coming in His glory] will appear in the sky, and all the peoples of the earth [and especially Israel] will mourn [regretting their rebellion and rejection of the Messiah]. They will see the Son of Man coming on the clouds of heaven with power and great glory [in brilliance and splendor]. And He will send His angels with a loud trumpet and they will gather His elect (God's chosen ones) from the four winds, from one end of the heavens to the other."[438] This Glorious Appearing will take place when the Lord makes His grand entrance and descends upon the earth with His Bride—"countless thousands of His holy ones to execute judgment on the people of the world."[439]

Led by the Antichrist, all who despise God will gather together for war with the largest armies of the world. But there will be no fighting at the Battle of Armageddon, because by word of the Lord's mouth, all the armies and all the people who accepted the mark of the beast (666) during the Tribulation, will be consumed. Satan will be bound in chains and thrown into the abyss. And the souls of those beheaded for proclaiming God's Word, rejecting the mark, and refusing to worship the beast or his statue, will return to life. This will end the horrific Tribulation period and will usher in God's ideal 1,000-year kingdom here on earth. This will be more glorious than anything the world has ever seen since the Garden of Eden.

At the millennium's end, Satan will be released to go out and deceive the nations, gathering them for battle. The number of non-believing descendants from those who endured the Tribulation will be "like the sand of the seashore." They will swarm the earth, surrounding God's people and the beloved city [Jerusalem], but fire will fall from heaven and consume them. The Deceiver will be hurled into the fiery lake of burning sulfur, where he—the beast (Antichrist) and the false prophet will be tormented day and night, forever and ever.[440]

Since God is just, the salvation of each individual soul will be determined by the measure of Light (knowledge and truth of Jesus Christ) they received.[441] Those who chose to believe and trust in Jesus as their Lord and Savior will be free from condemnation.[442] And can look forward to spending eternity in Paradise—forever with God![443] But those who have chosen to reject the Son stand condemned already; they will not see life, for God's wrath remains on them.[444]

The non-believing dead will be resurrected to the Great White Throne Judgment where books will be opened and they will be judged according to their deeds. If their name is not listed in the Book of Life, where all believers' names are recorded, they will be flung into the lake of fire to endure the punishment of everlasting destruction, banished forever from the presence of the Lord and the glory of His power.[445]

The Revelation (Apocalypse) of Jesus Christ was given to the apostle John by an angel of the Lord to enlighten and encourage believers of events following the imminent and final showdown between God and Satan—where God wins!

> Then I saw a new heaven and a new earth, for the first heaven and the first earth had passed away, and there was no longer any sea. I saw the Holy City, the new Jerusalem, (the temple and the Garden of Eden)[446] coming down out of heaven from God, prepared as a bride beautifully dressed for her husband. It shone with the glory of God [filled with his radiant light], and its brilliance resembled that of a rare and very precious jewel, like jasper, shining and clear as crystal.[447]

> And I heard a loud voice from the throne saying, 'Look! God's dwelling place is now among the people, and he will dwell with them. They will be his people, and God himself will be with them and be their God. He will wipe every tear from their eyes. There

will be no more death or mourning or crying or pain, for the old order of things has passed away.'

He who was seated on the throne said, 'I am making everything new!' Then he said, 'Write this down, for these words are trustworthy and true.'

He said to me, 'It is done. I am the Alpha and the Omega, the Beginning and the End. To the thirsty I will give water without cost from the spring of the water of life. Those who are victorious will inherit all this, and I will be their God and they will be my children.'"[448]

One day soon we will meet the Lord face to face.[449] "Anything that is accursed (detestable, foul, offensive, impure, hateful, or horrible) will no longer exist."[450] There will be no more night, and no need for the sun or moon to shine, for the glory of God will shine brightly.[451] And we will reign with the Lord forever and ever.[452]

Jesus says, "I am coming quickly, and my reward is with me, to give to each one according to the merit of his deeds (earthly works, faithfulness)."[453] "Whoever is thirsty come; and whoever wishes, let him take and drink the free gift of the water of life."[454]

"Yes, I am coming quickly!" says the Lord Jesus.[455]

Are *you* ready?

# ACKNOWLEDGMENTS

I want to sincerely thank my husband Keith, my mother Susan, and my two wonderful daughters Jennifer and Holly for all of their love, support, and patience. I want to express gratitude to my mother-in-law Jeanette, sister-in-law Arlene, dear friend Sylvia, sister Jane, and stepsister Kathy for reading and re-reading the book in its early stages, encouraging me to proceed.

Also a very special thanks to pastor Craig Rees and former teaching pastor Brad Gray of Central Wesleyan Church in Holland, Michigan; your insightful and challenging messages were an ongoing source of inspiration and encouragement over the past three years while working on this memoir.

I'd also like to express sincere appreciation to James L. Young and Susan Vlug for their feedback, insight, reassurance, and editing expertise.

# Endnotes

Unless otherwise referenced, all Scripture was derived from the New International Version® (NIV®) of the Holy Bible. Verses from The Amplified® Bible (AMP) and New Living Translation Bible (NLT) are noted.

---

[1] 1 Peter 3:15
[2] Revelation 12:11
[3] Psalm 46:10
[4] Romans 2:11, 10:12
[5] Acts 10:34 NIV, AMP
[6] Jeremiah 24:7
[7] Matthew 5:44; Luke 6:27
[8] Isaiah 65:1; Romans 10:20
[9] Exodus 12:38
[10] Exodus 12:31
[11] Exodus 12:31
[12] Deuteronomy 4:32-35 Author emphasis in italics
[13] Jeremiah 9:24 Author emphasis in italics
[14] Ephesians 1:17-19
[15] Hosea 13:6
[16] Psalm 139:14
[17] Ephesians 1:12
[18] John 15:13-14
[19] Deuteronomy 8:10-18
[20] Psalm 106:8
[21] Psalm 106:12-14
[22] Deuteronomy 4:9 Author emphasis in italics
[23] Exodus 32:1-8
[24] Hebrews 9:4
[25] Joshua 4:2-3 Author added comment in brackets
[26] Joshua 4:6-7 Author added comment in brackets
[27] Mark 6:30-44
[28] Mark 8:1-13
[29] Mark 8:17-18 Author emphasis in italics
[30] Isaiah 12:4-5
[31] Malachi 3:6; Hebrews 13:8; James 1:17
[32] Isaiah 26:3 AMP
[33] 2 Corinthians 5:17
[34] Psalm 91:14-16

[35] 1 Peter 4:12
[36] Matthew 6:25-27; Luke 12:22-26
[37] Luke 12:22 NIV, AMP; Matthew 6:25
[38] Luke 12:32
[39] Luke 12:30 AMP; Matthew 6:8
[40] 1 Peter 5:7
[41] Mathew 6:33; Luke 12:31
[42] *Cell Phones and the Dark Deception: Find Out What You're Not Being Told... and Why* written under Sue Rosendahl's pen name Carleigh Cooper. To view or purchase go to Amazon.com and search "Cell Phones and the Dark Deception." (4.5 star rating)
[43] Psalm 31:9-10
[44] 1 Peter 4:12
[45] John 16:33
[46] Romans 8:37
[47] Romans 8:31
[48] 2 Chronicles 20:12
[49] 2 Chronicles 20:17
[50] 2 Chronicles 20:20
[51] 2 Chronicles 20:24
[52] 2 Corinthians 5:7
[53] Isaiah 55:9
[54] Isaiah 41:3-10 NIV, AMP
[55] Isaiah 41:13
[56] Lamentations 3:19-26
[57] John 10:10 Author added comment in brackets
[58] Psalm 34:18
[59] Psalm 91:15; Isaiah 40:11
[60] Philippians 4:6-7 AMP
[61] Psalm 29:11
[62] Hebrews 12:1-3
[63] Isaiah 30:18-19 NIV, NLT
[64] Psalm 40:1-3
[65] Daniel 2:28
[66] Acts 1:8
[67] Ephesians 1:13-14
[68] John 14:12
[69] John 14:16-17 AMP
[70] 1 Corinthians 12:1
[71] 1 Corinthians 12:7-11 Author added emphasis
[72] Acts 2:1-4 NIV, AMP
[73] Acts 10:1-46
[74] 1 Corinthians 14:3-4

[75] 1 Corinthians 14:2, 14:14
[76] Romans 8:26-27 AMP
[77] 1 Corinthians 14:2 AMP
[78] Jude 20 AMP; Ephesians 6:18
[79] 1 Corinthians 14:3-4 Author added comment in parenthesis
[80] 1 Corinthians 14:5
[81] 1 Corinthians 14:39
[82] 1 Corinthians 2:9 NIV & AMP; Isaiah 64:4
[83] 1 Thessalonians 5:19-21 AMP
[84] Psalm 30:8-10
[85] Luke 4:21
[86] Isaiah 61:1-3 The Year of the Lord's Favor
[87] Philippians 4:19
[88] Mark 11:24
[89] Matthew 6:8
[90] Matthew 7:9-11 AMP
[91] James 5:16 AMP
[92] James 1:17
[93] Romans 10:12
[94] Psalm 37:4
[95] Joshua 1:5-6 Author added note in parenthesis
[96] Joshua 3:5
[97] Joshua 3:5 NLT
[98] Joshua 3:15-17
[99] Exodus 19:10-11 NIV Study Bible notes
[100] Colossians 3:13
[101] Jeremiah 31:3
[102] Lamentations 3:22-23
[103] 1 John 5:17
[104] Romans 3:23
[105] 1 John 1:9
[106] Hebrews 12:1
[107] Jeremiah 31:34
[108] Isaiah 55:11
[109] Luke 15:10
[110] Numbers 14:18
[111] Ezekiel 18:32
[112] Acts 3:19
[113] 1 Peter 1:3-4
[114] Romans 8:1; Hebrews 9:14
[115] Ezekiel 18:21-22
[116] Ephesians 4:32
[117] Mark 11:21

[118] Mark 11:22-24
[119] Matthew 9:21
[120] Matthew 9:20-22
[121] Matthew 8:9
[122] John 4:49-53
[123] Mark 11:24-25 Author emphasis in italics
[124] Matthew 6:12
[125] Matthew 6:14-15
[126] Ephesians 6:12
[127] Jeremiah 29:13
[128] Psalm 33:20-22
[129] 1 John 5:14
[130] Jeremiah 33:2-3
[131] Genesis 13:16
[132] Genesis 12:3; 18:18
[133] Genesis 12:4
[134] Genesis 16:3-4
[135] Genesis 21:5
[136] Romans 4:13
[137] Hebrews 11:1
[138] 2 Corinthians 4:16-18
[139] 2 Chronicles 16:9
[140] Hebrews 11:6
[141] Luke 17:5
[142] Romans 10:17
[143] Jeremiah 29:11-14
[144] Isaiah 40:31 AMP
[145] Lamentations 3:24-25 NLT & AMP; Isaiah 30:18
[146] Isaiah 49:23
[147] John 14:27
[148] Psalm 62:1-2
[149] Luke 16:22
[150] Acts 16:31; Romans 10:13
[151] Ezekiel 14:23; Isaiah 43:7; Romans 5:3-4
[152] Job 42:12-16 NIV Study Bible notes
[153] Job 36:10, 13-15 NIV Study Bible notes
[154] 2 Corinthians 12:7-8
[155] Matthew 16:22; Mark 8:32
[156] Isaiah 55:8-9 NLT
[157] Habakkuk 1:2
[158] Habakkuk 1:5
[159] Habakkuk 2:14
[160] Habakkuk 3:17-19

[161] John 16:33 AMP
[162] 2 Corinthians 4:16-18 NIV, AMP
[163] Search Amazon.com for the book *Cell Phones and the Dark Deception*. Written under Sue Rosendahl's pen name Carleigh Cooper.
[164] Hebrews 4:16
[165] Hebrews 4:15
[166] Jeremiah 17:7-8 AMP
[167] 1 Peter 2:9
[168] Zondervan NIV Study Bible Note 1985 - Ezekiel 37:1-28
[169] Ezekiel 37:1-14 italics added by author
[170] Bodily System Disorders—*Neurological:* headaches, fatigue, Tinnitus, concentration difficulties, depression, memory loss, sleep disorders, neurotransmitter function impairments, brain damage, and neurodegenerative diseases. Other Bodily Systems Adversely Affected: *Cardiovascular, Reproductive, Respiratory, Gastrointestinal, Immune, Hormonal* and *Urinary*. Genotoxic (Chromosome/DNA) Damage & Cancer. Buy the book at Amazon.com Search *Cell Phones and the Dark Deception* under the author's pen name Carleigh Cooper.
[171] Isaiah 43:18-19
[172] James 5:10-11
[173] Job 42:10
[174] 2 Samuel 22:26
[175] Acts 10:34; Romans 2:11; Galatians 2:6; Ephesians 6:9; Colossians 3:25
[176] 1 Samuel 26:23; Psalm 37:4; Matthew 6:33; Romans 8:17 NLT, 10:12; Hebrews 11:6
[177] 1 Thessalonians 5:21
[178] Romans 12:2 Author added words in parentheses
[179] Isaiah 7:11a AMP
[180] Isaiah 7:12; Deuteronomy 6:16
[181] Isaiah 7:10-13 AMP
[182] Genesis 24:12-14
[183] Genesis 24:17-20
[184] Judges 6:12
[185] Judges 6:1-6
[186] Judges 6:17-18
[187] Judges 6:36-40
[188] Proverbs 19:21
[189] Proverbs 3:5-6 AMP
[190] Psalm 30:11-12
[191] Matthew 19:26; Mark 10:27; Luke 18:27
[192] Exodus 28:30 NIV Study Bible notes
[193] Joshua 18:10
[194] Jonah 1:7

[195] Acts 1:24
[196] 1 Peter 5:10
[197] James 1:12
[198] James 1:2-4 NIV, AMP
[199] Romans 8:28, 37 NIV, NLT
[200] Romans 8:18
[201] 1 Peter 1:6-7 NLT; Hebrews 10:35
[202] 2 Corinthians 12:9 AMP
[203] John 11:4
[204] John 11:11
[205] John 11:15
[206] John 11:43-44
[207] John 11:40 author added emphasis
[208] John 17:24
[209] Hebrews 11:6
[210] Matthew 13:58
[211] Hebrews 11:1
[212] 1 Peter 1:7; Romans 4:20-21
[213] Romans 4:3, 5, 9
[214] Hebrews 11:6
[215] Ezekiel 14:23; Isaiah 43:7
[216] Mark 10:46-52; Matthew 20:29-34; Luke 18:35-42
[217] Luke 18:43 NLT
[218] Ephesians 3:20
[219] Zephaniah 3:17
[220] John 1:1 AMP; Isaiah 9:6 Author added bold italics
[221] John 1:2-3 AMP
[222] John 1:4 NLT
[223] Luke 1:76-77
[224] John 1:6-9 AMP; Malachi 3:1
[225] John 1:32-34
[226] Matthew 3:16; Mark 1:11; 2 Peter 1:17
[227] Matthew 16:16-17; Luke 1:35, 22:70
[228] Mark 8:31
[229] John 10:9, 12:47
[230] John 8:58, 10:30
[231] John 4:25-27; Matthew 26:63-64; Mark 14:61-62
[232] John 3:16, 5:24; John 11:25-26 Author added bold emphasis
[233] Matthew 5:17; Luke 24:44 AMP Author added emphasis
[234] John 1:45
[235] http://m.christianity.com/bible/prophecy/what-the-old-testament-prophesied-about-the-messiah-11541169.html

[236] Do Old Testament Prophecies Prove That Jesus is the Messiah? Andy Rau Blog April 7, 2012 https://www.biblegateway.com/blog/2012/04/do-old-testament-prophecies-prove-that-jesus-is-the-messiah/
[237] Acts 10:40; Matthew 28:17; Luke 24:15; Luke 24:36; John 20:19; John 20:26
[238] Acts 1:3
[239] 1 Corinthians 15:6
[240] Hebrews 8:1; Colossians 2:9-10, 3:1; Luke 22:69
[241] John 20:20
[242] John 20:25
[243] John 20:27-29 AMP
[244] Jeremiah 29:13-14
[245] John 14:21
[246] 2 Corinthians 4:4
[247] John 15:9
[248] Isaiah 62:5
[249] Psalm 139:1
[250] Psalm 139:2
[251] Genesis 1:37
[252] Psalm 139:13
[253] Ephesians 2:10 AMP
[254] Psalm 139:15
[255] Ephesians 1:4-5 AMP, 1:11; Galatians 3:26
[256] Jeremiah 31:2-4
[257] Isaiah 54:10
[258] John 6:33; Titus 2:11
[259] Luke 2:10 Author added italics
[260] Hebrews 10:12
[261] Romans 2:11; Deuteronomy 10:17; Acts 10:34-35 NIV, AMP Author added italics
[262] Hebrews 13:5 Author emphasis in italics
[263] Nehemiah 9:17
[264] Deuteronomy 4:31
[265] Colossians 1:21-23
[266] Exodus 4:1-13
[267] Acts 9:15
[268] Ecclesiastes 7:20
[269] Romans 3:23
[270] 1 Corinthians 1:10
[271] Romans 3:22, 3:24 AMP
[272] Luke 15:4-7 Author's words in parenthesis
[273] Luke 15:11-32 Author's notes in parenthesis
[274] Romans 6:23

[275] 2 Corinthians 5:21
[276] 1 Peter 3:18
[277] Acts 4:12
[278] John 14:6
[279] John 11:25-26
[280] John 6:40 with author emphasis
[281] Acts 17:30 AMP with author emphasis
[282] Luke 13:3
[283] Matthew 4:17 AMP
[284] 1 John 1:9
[285] Hebrews 10:17
[286] Isaiah 43:25 with author emphasis
[287] Ezekiel 18:32
[288] Acts 3:19
[289] 1 Corinthians 1:18
[290] 1 Peter 5:8
[291] John 10:10
[292] 1 Corinthians 1:10
[293] Ephesians 2:8 AMP
[294] 1 Peter 2:9; Colossians 1:12-13
[295] 1 Peter 5:7
[296] John 3:16
[297] Ephesians 2:12
[298] 1 Peter 1:3
[299] John 3:3
[300] John 3:6
[301] John 3:7
[302] John 1:12-13; 1 John 5:1
[303] John 15:16
[304] Revelation 3:20 NLT
[305] Hebrews 3:7-8
[306] Romans 10:9 personalized
[307] Luke 15:4-7
[308] Colossians 1:14
[309] John 1:12
[310] Ephesians 1:13
[311] 2 Corinthians 5:17; Romans 8:16, 17
[312] John 10:10; 1 John 5:12,13
[313] 1 Corinthians 10:31
[314] 2 Corinthians 5:17 AMP
[315] Romans 6:6
[316] Ephesians 4:23-24
[317] Ephesians 2:10 AMP, NLT

[318] 2 Corinthians 1:21-22 AMP; Ephesians 1:13
[319] Romans 8:16 AMP
[320] Luke 24:49 NLT; John 14:12
[321] John 16:13
[322] Romans 8:26 AMP
[323] Romans 8:27 AMP
[324] 1 Corinthians 12:7; 1 Peter 4:10-11
[325] 2 Corinthians 3:18 AMP
[326] 1 Timothy 4:7-8
[327] Matthew 22:36; Luke 10:27; Deuteronomy 6:5; Leviticus 19:18
[328] Ephesians 5:1-2 AMP
[329] 1 Thessalonians 5:15
[330] Luke 6:31 AMP
[331] Luke 6:36 AMP; 1 Peter 4:9
[332] Romans 12:3 AMP; Philippians 2:3
[333] 1 Corinthians 13:13
[334] 1 Peter 4:8
[335] 1 Corinthians 13:8
[336] 2 Timothy 2:16
[337] Hebrews 10:24-25; 1 Thessalonians 5:11
[338] James 4:2
[339] Romans 12:12; Colossians 4:2
[340] Luke 18:1; 1 Thessalonians 5:17
[341] James 5:16
[342] 1 Peter 3:12
[343] Hebrews 4:16
[344] Matthew 6:9-13 KJV
[345] James 4:17
[346] 1 John 1:9 AMP
[347] Colossians 3:15, 4:2; 1 Thessalonians 5:16; Hebrews 12:28
[348] 1 Thessalonians 5:18
[349] Ephesians 5:20
[350] Ephesians 3:12 AMP; 1 John 5:14-15; Philippians 4:6 personalized
[351] Galatians 6:2; Ephesians 6:18 NLT, AMP; I Timothy 2:1
[352] John 16:24 AMP, NLT
[353] NIV Study Bible notes: 2 Timothy 3:16 pg#1846; 2 Peter 1:20-21 pg#1900
[354] 2 Timothy 3:16
[355] Romans 1:16
[356] John 5:39
[357] John 20:31
[358] Hebrews 4:12
[359] 2 Timothy 3:16-17
[360] James 1:22

[361] Hebrews 3:21
[362] Luke 3:8
[363] James 2:24
[364] 1 Peter 4:10
[365] Romans 12:6-8 AMP
[366] James 2:17, 2:26
[367] 1 John 3:18
[368] 1 Timothy 6:18
[369] 2 Corinthians 9:7
[370] Matthew 5:16
[371] Ephesians 6:7-8
[372] Malachi 3:10
[373] John 15:19
[374] 1 Peter 1:1, 2:11
[375] Philippians 3:20
[376] Romans 12:2
[377] 2 Corinthians 6:17
[378] James 1:27
[379] James 4:4 AMP; 1 John 2:15-17 AMP
[380] 1 Peter 1:14-15 AMP; 1 Timothy 6:11; 2 Timothy 2:22
[381] 1 John 5:19 AMP
[382] James 4:7-8
[383] 1 John 5:21 AMP
[384] Matthew 16:6
[385] Galatians 5:9
[386] 1 Corinthians 15:33
[387] 2 Timothy 4:3
[388] 2 Timothy 3:1-5
[389] Matthew 3:8
[390] Matthew 7:17-18
[391] Matthew 7:15-16
[392] Galatians 5:22-23 AMP
[393] John 15: 5; 7-8 AMP
[394] John 15:11 AMP
[395] 1 Corinthians 10:13
[396] Colossians 4:5; Acts 1:8, 13:47
[397] Matthew 28:19-20
[398] Colossians 1:9-14
[399] Philippians 4:8
[400] Philippians 2:10-11 AMP
[401] Matthew 3:16
[402] John 8:28
[403] John 14:16-20 AMP

[404] Acts 1:3-5
[405] Acts 1:8
[406] Acts 1:11
[407] LaHaye, Tim. (2001). *Understanding Bible Prophecy for Yourself.* Eugene, OR: Harvest House Publishers pp. 23
[408] Hebrews 9:28
[409] John 14:1-3 NLT
[410] 2 Corinthians 5:8, 12:4
[411] John 6:40
[412] 1 Thessalonians 4:14-18 AMP
[413] Colossians 3:4; 1 John 3:2
[414] I Corinthians 15:50-54 AMP
[415] Matthew 24:36-41; Mark 13:32; Luke 17:34-35
[416] Mark 13:33
[417] Matthew 24:44
[418] James 5:7-8
[419] Philippians 3:20
[420] 1 Peter 1:7
[421] 1 Corinthians 3:11-15, 4:5
[422] 2 Corinthians 5:10
[423] Revelation 3:10; 1 Thessalonians 1:10, 5:9; Luke 21:35
[424] Matthew 24:21
[425] Matthew 24:9-14
[426] Mark 13:7; Luke 21:9; Matthew 24:6
[427] Luke 21:11; Matthew 24:24:7; Mark 13:8
[428] Matthew 24:7; Mark 13:8; Luke 21:10
[429] Matthew 24:14; Mark 13:10
[430] Matthew 24:9
[431] John 16:2
[432] Matthew 24:25 AMP; Mark 13:14
[433] 2 Thessalonians 2:3-4 AMP Author emphasis added
[434] 2 Thessalonians 2:9-12 AMP
[435] LaHaye, Tim. (2001). *Understanding Bible Prophecy for Yourself.* Eugene, OR: Harvest House Publishers pp. 73; 2 Thessalonians 2:3-4 AMP Author emphasis added [Note: The rebuilding of the Jewish Temple is an ongoing controversy, but must happen to fulfill this final end-time prophecy.]
[436] Isaiah 13:10; 34:4; Ezekiel 32:7; Joel 2:10, 2:31; Luke 21:25-26 Author added note in parenthesis; Revelation 6:12, 6:13; 8:12;
[437] Matthew 24:27; Luke 17:24
[438] Matthew 24:30-31 AMP, NIV; Mark 13:24
[439] Jude 14, 15
[440] Revelation 20:7-10 NLT

[441] NIV Study Bible notes Romans 2:12
[442] John 3:18; Romans 8:1-2
[443] John 3:36, 14:6
[444] John 3:18, 3:36
[445] 2 Thessalonians 1:8-9 AMP; Revelation 20:15
[446] Revelation 21:1-22:5 Author added comment in parenthesis taken from NIV Study Bible notes for corresponding verses
[447] Revelation 21:11 NIV, AMP
[448] Revelation 21:1-7
[449] Revelation 22:4
[450] Revelation 22:3
[451] Revelation 21:23
[452] Revelation 22:4-5
[453] Revelation 22:12 AMP Author added comment in parenthesis
[454] Revelation 22:17 AMP Author added definition in parenthesis
[455] Revelation 22:20 AMP

## About the Author

Sue Rosendahl is an inspirational speaker, evangelist, and founder of Beyond Belief Ministries. She has been a devout follower of Christ for over three decades, one being the darkest, most difficult of her life. And although her faith was greatly challenged, God not only validated His existence, He repeatedly showed up in extraordinary ways to prove He and His Word could be trusted.

As a result of God's lavish outpouring of love and grace, Sue's faith has flourished, planting within her a fervent desire to reach the lost, enliven seekers, and reinvigorate the faith of fellow believers. Her distinctive testimony offers a truly compelling message of hope and promise that gives convincing evidence that the all-knowing, all-loving, all-powerful, ever-present God of the universe *is* real! He's on your side and sincerely wants what's *best* for you. His greatest aspiration is for you to open your heart and invite Him into your life.

Sue is a graduate of Aquinas College in Grand Rapids, MI and Chapman College in Placerville, CA. She holds a bachelor's degree in both Psychology and Elementary Education with a minor in Communication Arts. Her schooling and extensive background in sales, marketing, and public speaking, were instrumental in equipping her to become a successful small business entrepreneur.

Long before her late husband of 24 years was diagnosed with toxic encephalopathy and progressive brain damage, Sue was determined to identify the cause of his bizarre, seemingly unrelated symptoms, pinpoint his peculiar malady, and get him the medical attention he so desperately needed. Since Steve had been building and testing high-powered microwave amplifiers for cell tower base stations under a microscope for over ten years, she began to question the safety of his long-term, close-range exposure to non-ionizing radiofrequency microwave radiation—the energy used to transmit wireless signals.

Outraged by what she had learned after years of research, Sue authored her first book *Cell Phones and the Dark Deception: Find Out What You're Not Being Told…and Why*. Published in 2009 under her pen name Carleigh Cooper, it was the most comprehensive compilation of investigative data ever written on the subject, uncovering industry deception and proving numerous adverse cause-effect relationships between wireless signals and the human body. An estimated 1,000,000 people have heard Sue (aka Carleigh) speak on air and in person.

Upon completion of her memoir Sue launched Beyond Belief Ministries, a Christ-centered outreach that extends a hand of hope, love, encouragement, and support to women struggling through difficult seasons of adversity. But unlike other ministries fueled solely by donations, book sales drive the majority of this uplifting, potentially life-transforming endeavor.

For every four *Anchored in Hope* books sold, a complimentary copy is gifted to a woman in a rescue mission, homeless shelter, domestic violence shelter, safe house, halfway house, recovery, or prisoner re-entry program. Distribution typically follows an evangelistic message of hope and prayer for those choosing to accept Jesus as their Lord and Savior.

If you were moved by Sue's story and would like to help support her ministry, recommend *Anchored in Hope* to a friend; share the BeyondBeliefMinistries.org link on your social network; purchase additional copies as gifts or witnessing tools; advocate for *Anchored in Hope* to be read in your small group, book club, discussion group, or Bible study; you could even host a fundraiser. Learn more at BeyondBeliefMinistries.org.

Contact SueRosendahl@BeyondBeliefMinistries.org to send a message or to inquire about her being a guest speaker at your church, club, or Christian organization.

www.ingramcontent.com/pod-product-compliance
Lightning Source LLC
LaVergne TN
LVHW051544070426
835507LV00021B/2399